The North Georgia Mountains

The North Georgia Mountains

A Comprehensive Guide to Sightseeing,
Shopping, Activities, Restaurants,
and Accommodations

11 Maps
42 Illustrations

Harry Milt
Karen S. Bentley
David C. Jowers

Cherokee Publishing Company
Atlanta, Georgia
1992

Library of Congress Cataloging-in-Publication Data

Milt, Harry.
    The north Georgia mountains : a comprehensive guide to sightseeing, shopping,
activities, restaurants, and accommodations / Harry Milt, Karen S. Bentley, David C.
Jowers. – 1st ed.
    p.   cm.
    Includes index.
    ISBN 0-87797-236-2 (acid-free : $13.95 est.)
    1. Georgia–Guidebooks. 2. Blue Ridge Mountains–Guidebooks.
I. Bentley, Karen S. II. Jowers, David C., 1948-1991. III. Title.
F284.3.M55   1992
917.58'10443–dc20   92-19437
                                             CIP

Copyright © 1992 by Harry Milt, Karen S. Bentley and David C. Jowers

This book is printed on acid-free paper which conforms to the American National
Standard Z39.48-1984 *Permanence of Paper for Printed Library Materials*. Paper that conforms to this standard's requirements for pH, alkaline reserve and freedom from ground-
wood is anticipated to last several hundred years without significant deterioration under
normal library use and storage conditions.

Manufactured in the United States of America

First Edition

ISBN: 0-87797-236-2

98   97   96   95   94   93   92   10   9   8   7   6   5   4   3   2   1

Edited by Alexa Selph

Index and Design by Pamela H. Naliwajka

Cover Photography by Scot Roberge,
Photographic Services, Clayton, Ga

Maps prepared by Rick Waterhouse,
Gap Graphics and Printing
Mountain City, Ga

Cover design by Jeanine Merrigan

 **Cherokee Publishing Company**
P O Box 1730, Marietta, Ga 30061

This book is dedicated to the memory
of our friend and co-author
David C. Jowers,
whose love for the nature and beauty
of these mountains shaped his life
and permeated with a spiritual touch
the pages he wrote for this book.

Contents

Maps

Acknowledgements

Books of this geographic scope reflect the contributions and cooperation of many people. We thank all the individuals who took time to tell us about their businesses, activities and events; the writers and historians whose words we've quoted; the Chamber of Commerce and Welcome Center personnel throughout the region; and our families and friends who supported the project from the beginning.

Special thanks to Randy Dilliott of the Rabun County Chamber of Commerce and Jo Ann Jarrio of the Rabun County Welcome Center. Thanks also to Janie P. Taylor for her "Tiger Tales" and Rick Story for the history of his family's home.

We especially thank Thomas O. Rusert for filling in so capably on David's behalf during the final stages of manuscript production.

Welcome To Our Mountains

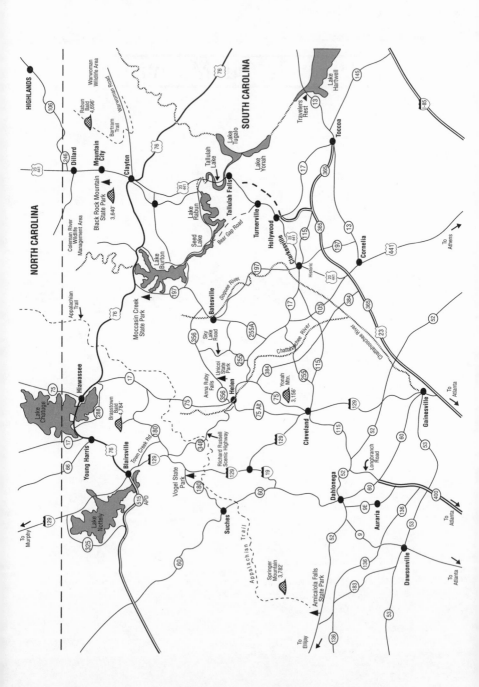

Welcome to Our Mountains

The north Georgia mountains are among the most beautiful and enchant-ing in the East. They start as rolling foothills along an irregular line from Toccoa in the east to Rome in the west. Then, looking northward, they mount gradually but consistently until they become a series of long, lofty, undulating ridges, attaining a height in many places of between 4,000 and 5,000 feet.

Viewed from a mountaintop or scenic overlook, they extend north, east, south, and west in breathtaking vistas, as far as the eye can see, tier upon tier, one range rising up behind the other, all bathed in a bluish haze, the feature that gives the Blue Ridge Mountains their name. North of Georgia, our mountains merge into the Great Smoky Mountains and the rest of the Blue Ridge and Appalachian chains.

What strikes you about the north Georgia mountains as you view them from a distance is their majesty and grandeur. But as you come nearer and begin to travel among them, something strange happens. You are there, but where have the mountains gone? What you see in front of you and all around you are not mountains, but rolling hills, sloping away separately from their rounded tops and folding softly and gently into each other. And you sense a quality about them that led Andrew J. Ritchie, a local histori-an, to call them "the most inviting, friendly and hospitable in the world," and inspired a regional artist, John Kollock, to write about them in a book to which he gave the name *These Gentle Hills*, illustrating the text with his own paintings of mountain homes and farms, countryside scenes, and the mountain people who still live here.

These are wonderful people, friendly, kind, gentle people, but indepen-dent and self-reliant, never asking for help but every ready to give it. You will meet them and mingle with them in the stores and shops. You will find them at roadside stands selling you boiled peanuts or fresh apple cider or fruits and vegetables that come from their small farms, or wood for your fireplace or campfire. They will greet you in their craft shops, displaying and selling their own handiwork or that of some of their neighbors.

The folkways and lore of the Appalachian mountain people are still very much a part of life in these hills. There are "singin's" where gospel singing groups come to perform at revivals or at functions to raise funds for a victim of illness or other misfortune. You turn on the local radio stations and you hear hour after hour of old-time mountain music and gospel singing. Wherever there is entertainment, you will find cloggers, children and adults, dancing to the music of mountain fiddlers and "pickers" who never took a lesson in their lives but "just larned."

There are folks throughout these hills living in cabins built by their grandfathers or great-grandfathers, families who can tell you about "quiltin's" and "house raisin's" and "pea thrashin's" and "log rollin's" and "corn shuckin's" of not too long ago. Some, even today, plant by the signs, and predict weather by the signs, medicate themselves with homemade remedies, birth children with the help of "grannies." And a few who still do a little moonshining, if they know you well, will tell you how and where they do it.

And, if you give yourself over to exploration and discovery, following some old trail that seems to lead nowhere, you are likely to find, in the words of John Kollock: "traces of the past ... on a mountain ridge, a wagon trail that led the pioneers west; a streak of red on a mountainside, marking the end of a vein of gold, pinched off, ... a covered bridge, ... a forgotten summerhouse in a dense thicket of forest and pines."

Spring comes early in these mountains, heralded in mid-April by a fresh green wash of color on the mountainsides, erasing the grays and browns and rusts of the winter. Then from late April on, the mountains are covered with a dense lush foliage–maples, oak, hickory, gum, poplar, intermingling with the pine and hemlock. Throughout the spring and much of the summer the woods and hillsides are bedecked with an intermittent array of native flowering trees and shrubs–redbud, dogwood, mountain laurel, azalea, and rhododendron–growing everywhere in profusion. In September, with the first touch of cool weather, the leaves begin to turn, continuing to change day by day, until at leaf-viewing peak in late October, they produce a spectacular display of color that lasts into November, attracting people from everywhere to come view this miracle of nature.

The entire region is laced with countless streams and creeks, erupting in many places in cascades and waterfalls, merging below in streams that wind through the valleys, and gathering in sparkling, hill-rimmed lakes.

Little creeks and rivulets that arise out of these hills merge to form the headwaters of three major rivers: the Little Tennessee, which flows north from the Blue Ridge Divide at Mountain City; the Chattahoochee, which flows south from the other side of the divide near Blairsville, coursing through Georgia, Alabama, and Florida and into the Gulf of Mexico; and the Savannah River (via the Chattooga), flowing into the sea.

Between the mountain ridges, are broad expanses of farmland with peaceful scenes of silos, barns, and farmhouses, cows and horses grazing in the meadows and along the slopes.

One need not make any special trips to seek out these scenes of natural beauty. They are everywhere, everywhere the automobile roads and mountain trails take you, throughout the breadth and length of these mountains–along twisting S-turn curves skirting the ridges and mountaintops, through the fields and farmland, into dense forests, along the shores of the lakes.

Just listen to the description of one typical scenic setting written by Marie Mellinger, a local naturalist:

> Panther Creek descends steeply through its rock-filled gorge, bursting with cascades and waterfalls. Rimmed by hardwood and hemlock forest, lined with thickets of rhododendrons, it is shaded by trees of tremendous size and age. Away from highways and habitation, much of it is still untouched country. There are several very rich coves filled with rare plants. Autumn is a beautiful time to walk Panther Creek Trail. Then, glorious masses of foliage line the trail, the brilliant reds and scarlets of the scarlet oak intermingling with the bright gold of the hickory.

It is not just these alone–these scenes of natural beauty, the peace and quiet, the endearing mountain people, and the enchanting Appalachian lore–that these mountains offer to the tourist, traveler, and vacationer. They offer in addition such a richness of recreation, entertainment, and discovery–so many things to do, sights to see, places to visit–that one could start in early spring and continue to late fall and still not have experienced them all.

And, as for the weather, you will see on the front license plate holders, in the eastern part of these mountains, a picture of the hills with the slogan: "Rabun County: Where Spring Spends the Summer." This is a promotional slogan adopted by the county's Chamber of Commerce, but what it says is true. The spring weather, not only in Rabun County but throughout the north Georgia mountains, is moderate, lovely, and pleasant and it stays that way for most of the summer, except for a few intermittent hot spells. But even in those hot spells the temperature is an average of ten degrees cooler than it is in the cities, and much less humid. There is also a regional boast that even during the hot spells, you always need light cover during the night. And that, too, is by and large true.

The summers are pleasant and cool, but blessed with abundant sunshine. The winters–December through February–are, most of the time, cold enough to let you know that we have a true change of seasons. Yet there are days when it is balmy and you think winter has gone, but it hasn't. The temperature frequently drops below freezing, and occasionally near zero, but it does not stay that way long. Most winters there will be some snow, and on occasion there will be snowfall as much as a foot and a half in depth. But that does not happen often. When it does, people living on a steep hill may be snowbound for two or three days, having to depend on neighbors with four-wheel-drive vehicles to get them where they want to go.

Swimming, Fishing, Boating

When nature formed these mountains millions of years ago, no lakes were created, only a number of rivers coursing through deep, winding valleys. So, when engineers came here shortly after the turn of the nineteenth century seeking a source of water power to generate electricity, they decided on the Tallulah River and erected a dam and power station at Tallulah Falls.

That was in 1913. Subsequently five additional dams were built–the last one in 1926–resulting in a chain of beautiful lakes as the water backed up into the valleys and coves: Lake Burton, the northernmost, then Lake Seed, Lake Rabun, Lake Tallulah, Lake Tugaloo, and Lake Yonah.

It was all still wilderness then, except for the little town of Burton and a few scattered houses in other localities. As the waters rose, these were inundated, leaving a scene of primeval beauty undisturbed except for the bear, deer, bobcats, raccoons, and other animal life that came down to the water to drink and hunt, and some mountain folk who came there to fish.

Then, in the early thirties, homes and boathouses began to appear along the shoreline, and as the years went by, more and more of them—but so constructed and situated as to blend in with the natural beauty of the lakes and the hills.

Although most of the shorefront is privately owned or leased, the Georgia Power Company, which owns and controls the remainder, has made sure that these lakes are also accessible to the public. There are several public beaches for swimming and fishing, and several launching ramps where canoes, rowboats, sailboats, and motorboats may be put into the water.

There are also several privately owned marinas on the lakes. These come in quite handy for part-time and full-time residents who may own or rent

homes or cottages that are not right on the lake, and who therefore do not have direct access to the lake. A boat docked at a marina solves that problem.

Fishermen report good catches of bass, trout, bream, and catfish in the lakes. In addition, there are several state-stocked streams favored by fishermen in pursuit of trout.

Hiking and Camping

The term "national forest" evokes images of deep, dense woods, free of human habitation; towering trees; ancient narrow trails worn there by Indians, trappers, and hunters; streams, cataracts, and waterfalls; bear, deer, and other wildlife; enveloping silence, broken only by the sounds of birds and the snapping of a twig underfoot.

If this is what you envision, then this is what you will find, since a great deal of the land in the north Georgia mountains falls within the Chattahoochee National Forest and the nationally managed Cohutta Wilderness. Additional thousands of acres of similar character are within the boundaries of eight state parks in these mountains.

For day hikers, tenters and backpackers these woods and forests provide endless opportunities. There are hundreds of miles of trails, ranging in difficulty from "very easy" to "very strenuous," and in length from a fraction of a mile to 79 miles.

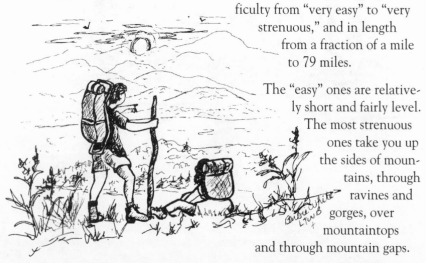

The "easy" ones are relatively short and fairly level. The most strenuous ones take you up the sides of mountains, through ravines and gorges, over mountaintops and through mountain gaps.

The world-famous Appalachian Trail actually originates (or terminates, depending on your direction) in the north Georgia mountains. It begins on Springer Mountain west of Dahlonega and winds about in a northeasterly direction, exiting Georgia into North Carolina, some 79 miles later, at Bly Gap, northeast of Hiawassee.

Not as famous, but of greater historical significance, is the Bartram Trail. This trail (38 miles in length) is located in the northeastern corner of Georgia. It is named for William Bartram, one of the first white men to penetrate this Indian country. The trail follows the original route explored and documented by Bartram in 1773–76.

Mountain Wildlife and Wildflowers

Part of the charm of the Georgia mountains lies in its abundant wildlife and wildflowers.

Elk and woodland buffalo once roamed here, as did wolves and panthers. They're gone now, of course, but there are black bears, bobcats, deer, turkeys, ruffed grouse, and foxes. Golden eagles are making a comeback and have been sighted around the Chattooga River corridor. There are also falcons, hawks, vultures (the black and the turkey), owls, and ravens. Canadian geese fly through here on their migration, and many different water foul swim in the mountain lakes and ponds.

Butterflies–countless species of them–have made the mountains their home. During the first or second week of September the monarchs, skippers, and sulphurs migrate to their winter homes in south Florida, Mexico, and even Central America. Those that survive the winter will mate on their way back here in the spring and summer.

Naturalists attribute the abundance of butterflies here to the spectacular mountain wildflowers. Most people know about our dogwoods and thick stands of mountain laurel and rhododendron, but many do not realize that during April and May alone, some one hundred different flowers and ferns make an appearance. Shy spring flowers, such as bloodroot, trillium, foamflower, and showy orchid, inhabit the deep woods, but wave after wave of later season blossoms–daisy, lily, butterfly weed, Queen Anne's lace, aster, ironweed, and more–explode into color along roadsides and in open fields. There's always a display of wildflowers in bloom on the roadsides and in the meadows and forests–from March until the killing frosts in late October.

White-Water Rafting and Canoeing

The Chattooga River, say old-time residents here, was known to very few on the outside before 1973, the year the film *Deliverance*, starring Burt Reynolds, was shown on movie screens across the country. Even then, it took some time for word to get around that the fierce, wild, white-water canoeing scenes in the movie were filmed on the Chattooga, a river flowing as a natural border between the northeast corner of Georgia and adjacent South Carolina.

Since then, hundreds of thousands of white-water canoeing and rafting enthusiasts have come here to experience the excitement and thrill of a ride down the Chattooga.

It is not only for the white-water excitement that visitors come to the Chattooga, but also for its primitive beauty. In 1974, this river was designated by an act of Congress as a Wild and Scenic River. This designation preserves and protects the river itself, and a quarter-mile corridor along both sides, in their natural state, free of residential and commercial intrusion.

Native Crafts

If these mountains were known for nothing else, they would be known for their native crafts–the handiwork of men and women whose families have been here for generations and who create now, for pleasure and for sale, articles of the kind their forbears created by hand, of necessity. Of course, some of the craft items now offered for sale are made by newcomers to the area, but the methods used, for the most part, are the ones that have been handed down.

Here are the kinds of articles you may expect to find: pottery, in the form of bowls, vases, urns, trays, candlesticks, lamps, sculpture; hand-cut and hand-sewn quilts in traditional designs such as Double Wedding Ring, Attic Window, Four Doves, Dutch Doll, Nine Diamonds, Lonely Star, Gate Latch, Basket, and others; hand-woven items of clothing, scarves, sweaters, rugs, mats, napkins, tablecloths; handmade furniture, cradles, wall decorations, shelves, etagères, and toys; hand-carved animals and figurines; baskets; stuffed dolls, pillows, and animals artistically and ingeniously decorated; decorative items woven from vines and fashioned from bark; stained-glass birds, flowers, designs, and windows; handmade jewelry; forged iron lamps, hinges, locks, utensils, sconces, gates; and handmade dulcimers and other folk instruments.

A number of craftsmen who own and operate their own studios and workshops invite the public to visit and see them at work–at their pottery wheels and kilns, spinning wheels, looms, forges, carpenter shops, woodworking benches and so forth.

The craft shops, in which a variety of these different types of items are displayed and sold, abound—in the towns, along the road, down country lanes. Among these are several "cooperative craft shops," owned and operated commercially by the crafters themselves.

Antiques, Galleries, Gift Shops, Etc.

An abundance of antique shops and auctions makes these mountains a rich hunting ground for antique shoppers. It is still possible to find authentic regional antiques that have come out of the attics, homes, and barns of mountain folk—furniture, farm and kitchen implements, glassware, china, clothing, jewelry, trinkets, pictures, etc. A fair amount of the items have been brought in from elsewhere. Some shops specialize in imports from abroad. There are a few where the finest antique furniture, china, and paintings are sold.

There are also a number of picture galleries and studios displaying and selling watercolors, oils, and various types of engravings by some well-known local artists and artists from other regions, together with other attractive works.

Gift shops—dozens of them—sell a wide variety of craft items made in the vicinity as well as imported items. Several shops carry fine items of clothing imported from Ireland, Scotland, and the Scandinavian countries.

For "discount shoppers," there is a manufacturer's outlet mall in Helen, representing national brands of kitchenware; men's, women's and children's clothing; shoes, and other items.

There are also jewelry stores, stores selling made-on-the-premises candy, Christmas shops, glass shops, leather shops, shops selling perfumes, country stores and more.

Fairs, Festivals, and Country Music

This being "the country," you'd expect to find country fairs and festivals and there are–no end of them. These are not all the kinds of fairs where 4-H clubs exhibit their prize heifers or sows and where farmers compete to see who grew the largest tomato or pumpkin. Mostly, these are mountain fairs where people come from all around to feast on country cooking, to sell their crafts and home-cooked foods, to give demonstrations of soap-making, hominy making, spinning, weaving, log splitting, and basket weaving, to listen to and dance to old-time mountain music played by mountain musicians, to watch groups of young cloggers go through their intricate, rhythmic dance formations.

These fairs–also called festivals–begin in April and keep coming along until the late fall, and there are even one or two during the winter. Throughout the year, up to early November, there's a fair or festival going on somewhere. Here are some of the festivals that took place during an average season: The Wildflower Festival of the Arts in Dahlonega; the Spring Country Music Festival in Clarkesville; the Sorghum Festival in Blairsville; the Mountain Maffick in Wiley; the Blue Ridge Divide Arts & Crafts Festival in Mountain City; the Great Cabbage Festival in Dillard; the Georgia Mountain Fair in Hiawassee; the Old-timers Day–Traditional Music Festival in Vogel State Park; the Harvest Festival in Dillard; the Chattahoochee Mountain Fair in Clarkesville; the Clogging and Square Dancing Festival in Helen; the Trout Festival in Helen; and the Oktoberfest in Helen.

The fairs and festivals are not the only place where you'll find country music. There are country music concerts and bluegrass concerts going on at different times and locations throughout the summer, and wherever there's music, you are likely to find clogging. And if you're lucky, you just may come into a town square some Saturday and happen on an impromptu, al fresco country music concert, being given by a couple of local mountain folks, sitting in front of a store, "pickin' away" on some old mountain tune. Then, just as likely as not, another "picker" might saunter along and join the two with his own banjo or guitar, catching up the tune without missing a beat. Then, while this is going on, you might just see one or two folks step out from the little crowd of onlookers and start clogging, right there, on the sidewalk; and then another and another might join them until you have half a dozen or more clogging away out there in the open.

Helen

And then there's Helen. Helen is a phenomenon, a happening all unto itself. Imagine an Alpine village with a storybook Swiss-Bavarian-Austrian motif, the stores and inns and restaurants constructed in Alpine design with turrets, gables, chalet decks and roofs, painted in pinks, yellows, blues and greens, many of the shops and streets bearing German names, some storekeepers in lederhosen and dirndls, German music wafted overhead by a sound system, a carillon sounding out the hour, several restaurants serving all sorts of wurst, braten, schnitzl, ripchen, and schinken together with imported beers; charming quaint shops and stores–dozens of them–offering a variety of arts, crafts, collectibles, and gift items; a year-round series of festivals including the month-long Oktoberfest with its authentic German bands, vocalists, and dances and the Fasching Karnival marking Lent in February.

True, Helen is synthetic, and the product of a deliberate effort by a group of businessmen to revive a dying town. But it surely took a great deal of enterprise and imagination to do this, and while the objective was to revive business and profits, for the traveler, it is a delightful, colorful experience, with hours of browsing, shopping, sightseeing and dining. There are numerous lodging accommodations in and around Helen (inns, lodges, motels, cabins) for those who might care to make this a stopover point.

The State Parks

There are eight state parks in the Georgia mountains, five in the east and three in the west. Only thumbnail sketches are given here. More detailed descriptions with other essential information will be given later in the guide, each state park being taken up separately within the context of the area in which it is located.

The eastern state parks:

Unicoi State Park within a few miles of Helen. A 100-room lodge and conference center and a restaurant open to the public. Swimming, fishing, and boating in a lake. Rental cottages and tenting and trailer sites. Tennis courts. Scenically beautiful but "modern" in concept and design.

Black Rock Mountain State Park, atop Black Rock Mountain, north of Clayton. Named for a sheer cliff of dark granite. Elevation of 3,640 feet provides spectacular views. A lake (part of a flood control program) offers fishing only. No swimming or boating. Rental cottages, tent and trailer sites, picnic shelters, a playground.

Moccasin Creek State Park, on Lake Burton in the Clayton area. Designed mainly as a site for trailers and tenting. A boat dock and ramp is nearby. No accommodations for swimming, but fishing is allowed.

Vogel State Park, south of Blairsville. Rustic and woodsy in character with cottages of different design nestling in groves of trees. A lake offers fishing, swimming and pedal boats. In addition to the rental cottages, there are tent and trailer sites and a family group shelter. Near Neel's Gap, a scenic mountain pass, also near Brasstown Bald, the highest point in Georgia.

Amicalola Falls State Park, in the Dawsonville area, named after its 729-foot falls, the highest in Georgia. Combines the rustic and the modern. A 60-room lodge and conference center, rental cottages, trailer and tent sites, picnic shelters and playgrounds.

The western state parks:

Cloudland Canyon State Park, northwest of Lafayette. Regarded as the most scenic and rugged (in terrain) of all the state parks. Rental cottages, tent and trailer sites, a 40-bed group camp, winterized group shelter and walk-in campsites. Tennis courts and a swimming pool.

Fort Mountain State Park, in the area of Chatsworth. Derives its name from a mysterious, ancient rock wall that snakes its way across the top of the mountain, thought to have been erected by Indians for ceremonial purposes about 1,000 years ago. Rental cottages, tent and trailer sites, swimming, fishing and pedal boating in a lake. A 50' stone observation tower.

James H. (Sloppy) Floyd State Park, south of Summerville, near the Alabama border. Named for James H. "Sloppy" Floyd, a Georgia state representative, a strong advocate of the outdoors and preservation. Originally created by the Department of Game and Fishing, it was turned over to the State Parks Department, which claims that the fishing in the park's two lakes is "outstanding." There is a fishing dock and a boat ramp (canoes, rowboats, or electric motor boats only) on each lake. There are 25 tent and trailer sites, also pioneer camping, a playground, and picnic shelters.

All state parks have hiking trails, and in Amicalola State Park, an access trail eight miles in length leads to Springer Mountain, the southern terminus of the Appalachian Trail.

Other Things to See and Do

There are still in existence, throughout the area, reminders of the past in their original state or partially restored–covered bridges; water-driven mills still grinding grain; historic churches and cemeteries; old trading posts; Indian mounds; relics of the gold-mining days around Helen and Dahlonega; old country stores.

Theatre goers will find a highly professional summer-stock theatre company in nearby Highlands, North Carolina, with top-notch performances of popular plays throughout the summer. *The Reach of Song*, an Appalachian drama celebrating the song, dance and heritage of the north Georgia mountains, is presented for several weeks during the summer in Hiawassee. Classical-music lovers will find frequent concerts–instrumental and vocal, orchestral and chamber music groups–being performed in the auditoriums of schools and churches. There is also, in Gainesville, about 55 miles to the south of Clayton, a series of fine concerts and recitals by orchestras, ensembles, soloists and dance groups of national caliber. These are given at Pearce Hall, Brenau College, under the auspices of the Arts Council, a group of local sponsors of the arts.

Golfers need not leave their clubs behind for there are any number of fine courses located throughout the region. And horseback riders will find numerous stables and hundreds of miles of forest and mountain trails.

In winter, there is also skiing at Sky Valley Resort, and Scaly Mountain (North Carolina), a few miles east of Dillard.

There are enough things to do and see in the north Georgia mountains for as many days or weeks or months you may spend there. But while you are there, it would be a shame to miss some other interesting and exciting places not too far away. To the northeast in Asheville, North Carolina, a distance of about 80 miles from Clayton, there is the Biltmore Estate, the fabulous Vanderbilt mansion, preserved in its original state with magnificent furnishings and paintings, vast gardens, and a vineyard. To the northeast, about 70 miles from Clayton is Brevard, North Carolina, the site of the Brevard Music Center, where throughout the summer, advanced students, faculty members and invited artists present concerts and operas. To the north, 50 miles from Clayton, is the city of Cherokee, North Carolina, the center of a Cherokee Indian reservation, with a number of truly worthwhile attractions–the Museum of the Cherokee Indian, the Cherokee Indian Cyclorama and Wax Museum, an authentic recreated Indian village of 225 years ago, and the outdoor Mountainside Theatre where the moving drama of the Cherokee–*Unto These Hills*–is performed during the summer. Once there, it is a relatively short drive to the awesome Great Smoky Mountains, an experience never to be forgotten, and from there to the picturesque town of Gatlinburg, Tennessee, with its boisterous but interesting shops, boutiques, and other attractions.

Where to Stay

Folks who want to experience the atmosphere of bygone days will find any number of gracious, old homes with wraparound porches that have been converted into inns or bed-and-breakfast places. Some still contain the antique furniture left there by their former owners. Others have been furnished with antiques purchased by the new owners. Every one of these that we have been into has a lovely feel of the Victorian or pre-Victorian eras. Some are located near town; others are "out in the country."

Then, of course, there are any number of the conventional motor inns, most of them relatively new, comfortable, nicely equipped and furnished, and at reasonable rates. Some have special features such as fireplaces. One or two are in the deluxe category.

There are also quite a few groups of housekeeping cabins to rent by the day, week or month, and any number of trailer camps for recreational vehicles.

What's Cookin' in the Mountains?

When it comes to dining, then it is authentic southern country cooking for which these mountains are noted, and it would be a shame to come here and not have your share of it. Fact is, you would have a hard time avoiding it, even if you wanted to. It is everywhere–and not the kind you might get in the big cities, but what you'd expect to find in a country home–barbecued pork, beef, ribs, and chicken; fried chicken, country-fried steak, country ham, and biscuits; catfish, trout, and hushpuppies; roast beef and baked ham and country ham–all generously served with three, four, and five vegetables, including such specialties as corn pudding, cabbage casserole, squash casserole, fried okra, plus turnip greens, corn on the cob, green beans swimming in butter, plus relishes and pickles. And for dessert, home-baked cherry cobbler, apple cobbler, peach cobbler, and a variety of homemade pies and puddings.

Breakfasts are just as "country" and just as plentiful–eggs, country ham, sausage, bacon, pancakes, or waffles, and of course biscuits and grits, plus jams, honey, sorghum, and all the rest.

There are numerous restaurants that serve the conventional fare of steaks, chops, seafood, salads; as well as sandwich shops serving the customary sandwich shop fare, but with some special regional touches (several with a foreign touch); and even a number of the fast-food-chain variety.

Before leaving the subject of dining, we should mention that there are a small number of "gourmet" type restaurants in the region, particularly in Highlands, North Carolina. Some live up to the name, others do not, but all charge gourmet-type prices.

As for the cost of dining on the whole, it is very reasonable, inexpensive, indeed, by city standards. You can get a good, substantial, nicely cooked and served country meal, including beverage and dessert for between $10 and $15. Restaurants serving conventional "city-type" meals charge, on the average, between $9 and $15 for the main course with appetizers running between $3 and $5, and desserts between $1.50 and $2.50.

Homemade Food Products

A specialty of the region are the homemade food products put up and sold at roadside stands, in craft shops, and in country stores: jams and jellies and preserves of every kind of berry and fruit; pickles of all kinds and chowchows and chutneys; country soup mixes; honeys and candies and syrups; sausage and country hams; home-baked breads and cakes; pit-cooked barbecued pork, beef, chicken, and ribs; boiled peanuts, and much more.

In season, the local farmers and fruit growers bring their produce to the roadside on stands and in trucks: tomatoes, cucumbers, bell peppers, squashes, melons, grapes, blueberries, strawberries, apples and apple cider (this is apple country), cabbages (this is also cabbage country), green beans and pumpkins. At several farms, the

buyer is invited to pick the fruit or berries or vegetables and pay for what
he picks.

The First Summer Resorts

The history of this region as a summer resort area goes back more than
150 years.

It started in the 1830s in Clarkesville. The records vary as to who got here
first, exactly when, and how. But we do know that by the middle 1830s
hundreds of families were making their way here during the summers to
escape from the unbearable summer heat, humidity, mosquitoes, and fever
outbreaks in Charleston, Savannah, and Augusta.

These were no log cabins to which these travelers came. They were,
according to the standards of the time, fine summer homes and elegant
hotels. Travel from the coast was by wagon, of course, but this did not
seem to impose any hardship, and the vacationers came in large numbers,
many to stay several weeks, many for the entire summer.

With the discovery, somewhat later, of even better resort possibilities in
the area of Tallulah Falls, with its magnificent falls and picturesque gorge,
the Tallulah Falls area began to rival and outdistance Clarkesville in its
attraction to summer vacationers and residents, with sumptuous hotels
and fine homes.

This trend continued apace into the 1860s, and then came to a halt with
the Civil War.

It was revived again with the introduction of a new mode of travel–the
railroad–in the 1870s. As the railroad line pushed northwest from Athens
to Toccoa, Lula, Demorest, Clarkesville, and Tallulah Falls, new resort
centers sprang up around each of these locations, spreading by the end of
the century to Cornelia and Cleveland and the Nacoochee Valley. Then,
in the early 1900s the railroad extended northward, first to Wiley, then to
Clayton, and finally to Franklin, North Carolina. And where the railroad
went, new hotels sprang up.

But then, between 1910 and 1913, the trend came to an end. One immediate cause for the cessation was the damming up of the Tallulah River in

1913 and the installation of a power plant at Tallulah Falls. This altered considerably the scenic character of the surrounding area. But there were much deeper and more widespread causes–namely social and economic changes that dried up the flow of summer visitors to the foothills and mountains.

One after another the hotels disappeared–victims of fire or demolition crews, or just abandoned to rain, sun, and decay. Here and there, there is an old hotel or summer home still standing, reminiscent of the grandeur of the past. Otherwise, the Belle Epoque of the Georgia foothills and mountains is just a vague memory.

The "Trail of Tears"

When you look at the maps in this guide, you will see some unusual names–Nacoochee, Sautee, Tallulah, Tugaloo, Soque, Unicoi, Chattahoochee, Chattooga, Dahlonega, Hiawassee, Yonah, Stekoa–all Indian names. And the reason is that this is, or rather was, Indian country, Cherokee Indian country.

Up until about 150 years ago, the Cherokee nation lived in, and ruled over, a vast territory embracing western South Carolina, eastern North Carolina, Virginia, West Virginia, the eastern half of Kentucky and Tennessee, and all of the northern half of Georgia. Its center and capital was at the old Chota town on the Tennessee River, just a few miles south of where Knoxville, Tennessee, stands today.

That is all gone, except for the Indian reservation at Cherokee, North Carolina.

In north Georgia today, there are no Indians, only traces of their former presence: the Indian names, an Indian mound or two, a few collections of Indian arrowheads and axes.

How this noble and powerful Indian nation came to an ignominious end is mentioned only briefly in American history books of today. The tragic details, however, are related in full, in history books of that time, some of which are available today. We give you a synopsis.

The first significant encounters between the Cherokee Indians and the white men from Europe took place in the course of the so-called French and Indian Wars of 1764–73. These wars, you will remember, were fought between colonists from France and colonists from Britain, the British seeking to oust the French from their possessions in Canada and in the Ohio and Mississippi river valleys. Allied with the French were Indians who came, mainly, from west of the Mississippi. Allied with the British were warriors of the Cherokee tribes from the Southeast.

As the wars progressed, with the British winning one victory after another, the Indians who had been allied with the French, made peace with the British and were welcomed by them as "brothers." The Cherokee, on the other hand, having fought on the side of the British, suddenly found themselves defending their own land against the invasion of British colonists who wanted this land and British troops who were not unhappy to help them seize it. In 1761–62, there was a massive uprising of the Cherokee against the British colonists and troops, with some of the battles taking place in nearby South and North Carolina. After several battles the Indians were defeated, and the British troops, avenging a massacre perpetrated by the Indians, burned out dozens of Indian villages and drove the survivors into the woods to starve.

With that defeat of the Indians, the way was opened for migration of colonists from Pennsylvania, North Carolina, South Carolina, Virginia, and West Virginia into the mountains of north Georgia.

Barely a trickle in the 1780s, the migration increased substantially in the 1790s and early 1800s. As the white population in this region increased, the Cherokee were forced into signing one treaty after another ceding more and more of their land.

In 1817, under threat of total extermination, the Cherokee were forced to accept a treaty agreeing to "voluntary removal" to an "Indian Territory," so designated by the U.S. government, first in Arkansas then in Oklahoma. This was part of the government's plan to remove five eastern Indian nations–the Choctaw, Creek, Chickasaw, Siminole and Cherokee–and to turn over their land to white colonists.

While a few thousand Cherokee did agree to removal from Georgia to the Indian Territory, the majority chose to remain and continue the struggle for their ancestral land.

Then an event occurred that made their plight impossible and their total removal inevitable.

In 1828, some gold nuggets were found in Duke's Creek in the vicinity of what is today the town of Dahlonega. Word of this find spread like wildfire and the first gold rush of the United States was on–21 years before the 1849 gold rush in California.

Thousands of prospectors from every part of the eastern seaboard flooded into the area, overrunning, usurping and ravaging the land that belonged to the Indians. As the gold craze spread, engulfing the land around Helen and Dahlonega, mining companies sprang up one after another and thousands of acres of primeval land was devastated by ruthless mining measures.

The Indians appealed to Congress, to the U.S. Supreme Court, to President Andrew Jackson, all to no avail. Emboldened by the federal government's hostility to the Indians, the state of Georgia acted peremptorily to seize their land. In 1832 all the Indian land was divided into parcels, and the white settlers were authorized to draw for it by lot in a giant lottery.

Still, the Indians held on. To settle the matter, General Winfield Scott of the United States Army was dispatched to Georgia to remove the Cherokee, by force if necessary, and dispatch them to the "Indian Territory" in the West.

The removal took place in 1838. The Indians, 17,000 in all, were herded into stockades in the Sautee Valley, divided into 13 detachments and sent off by wagon, on horse, and on foot, one detachment at a time.

There is a tablet on Route 17 in the Sautee Valley that reads: "On this site, the white settlers gathered the

Indians from surrounding valleys and highlands to begin the tragic Trail of Tears."

The first detachment left in October 1838, the last in December 1838. The 800-mile march took an average of five to six months. Every detachment was on the march during the severest months of winter. The preparations that had been made proved entirely inadequate for these rigors, and the suffering was indescribable. More than 5,000 died along the way, mostly women, children, and old people.

Thus, with the Trail of Tears ended the history of the Cherokee Indians in Georgia.

As a sad footnote to the above, we add the following. Far from being savages, these Cherokee were quite civilized, having developed farming to the level of plantations and commercial enterprise. Many intermarried with the white settlers, and some of their chieftains bore English names, the best known being Chief John Ross and Chief James Vann. Many gave up the primitive wigwams and built houses for themselves, some of them being of the finest architecture of the time. In fact, there still stands today, in the western part of the state near Chatsworth, a two-story Federal-style home, built by Chief Vann in 1804. It is now a state historic site.

The Cherokee had also moved away from tribal laws, adopting written laws of the type used by the white settlers, even going so far as to establish a legislature in 1825, with its capital at New Echota in what is now Calhoun. With all that, it seems almost anticlimactic to note that the Cherokee of that time had a written language. One Cherokee, Sequoyah, had invented a written "alphabet" consisting of spoken syllables, each represented by a different symbol. The alphabet enabled the Cherokee to have written communications and even, in 1828, to publish a newspaper, the *Cherokee Phoenix*.

In Calhoun, there is now a New Echota State Historic Site, including a museum, the reconstructed Supreme Courthouse of the Cherokee Nation, and the print shop in which the *Cherokee Phoenix* was printed.

The People Who Live in These Mountains

It is possible that the world outside these mountains would, today, have no intimate knowledge of the people who live here, were it not for the creativity and insight of a teacher by the name of Eliot Wigginton, the originator of the Foxfire concept and publications, now known throughout the United States and many other parts of the world.

Raised in Georgia, Wigginton went north for his academic training in education. When he came back to undertake his assignment as a high school teacher, he found, in a matter of days, that the teaching methods he had learned just did not work in this rural mountain region. The students were uninterested, bored, even hostile. Born out of desperation and inspiration, the idea emerged that the students would produce a magazine, some of the material of which was to come from interviews with the elders here, in many cases their own grandparents.

Out of these stories came the magazine *Foxfire*, and eventually nine *Foxfire* volumes plus several additional books all published by Doubleday.

Along the way Wigginton and the scores of *Foxfire* students have preserved for posterity a written record of the people of southern Appalachia. All this would have been lost as the older generation dies. Instead, as Wigginton himself notes, "the magnificent hunting tales, the ghost stories that kept a thousand children sleepless, the intricate self-sufficiency acquired through years of trial and error: spinning, weaving, soapmaking, planting by the signs of the moon, hog-slaughtering, cabin-building, beekeeping, native medicines, making wagons and wheels ..." and the vivid portraits of the mountain people will remain with us forever.

Some of the people written up in the early issues of *Foxfire* still live here. Many have descendants who live in the cabins and work the homesteads built by their great-grandfathers. Others have moved closer to town, and many of their children have become townspeople. Some are storekeepers, innkeepers, mechanics, plumbers, electricians, painters, builders. Many are working in the stores, inns, restaurants, and the few small manufacturing plants that are here. Many of the names you will read on the storefronts, billboards, street signs, and newspapers go back more than 150 years, a few to the time of the American Revolution.

There are "newcomers" here, too, people whose families have come here in the past 50 years or so, from other parts of Georgia, from Florida, from North Carolina and South Carolina, from the Northeast, and from the north central states.

This area has also become a magnet for professional people, artists and writers, musicians, college professors and others, many of whom had come here just for the summer months and then decided to stay.

It is truly a rich and interesting mix of people, and visitors to these mountains will find in meeting them still another rewarding experience.

We hope that we have been able to give you in this introduction more than general information about these mountains, their beauty, their history, their people, the things to do and see, the places to stay and to dine. We hope that we have been able to convey to you the same feeling of affection that we, the authors, have for "these gentle hills."

Now we will take you through the north Georgia mountains, location by location, and we hope that the information you will find here will make your visit to these mountains one of the most pleasurable, enjoyable, and rewarding of your life.

Region One

Tallulah Falls and Gorge
Lakemont, Wiley, and Tiger
Clayton
Mountain City and Rabun Gap
Dillard
Sky Valley
The Lakes

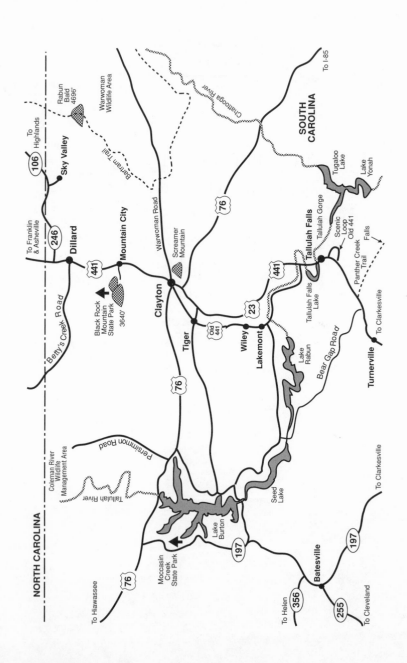

NORTH CAROLINA

SOUTH CAROLINA

To I-85

To Highlands

Rabun Bald 4696'

Warwoman Wildlife Area

Bartram Trail

Chattooga River

106 Sky Valley

246 Dillard

To Franklin & Asheville

441 Mountain City

Warwoman Road

Screamer Mountain

76

Tugaloo Lake

Lake Yonah

Tallulah Falls

Tallulah Gorge

Scenic Loop Old 441

Falls

Panther Creek Trail

Berty's Creek Road

Black Rock Mountain State Park 3640'

Clayton

Tiger

Old 441

Wiley

441

23

Lakemont

Tallulah Falls Lake

Lake Rabun

Bear Gap Road

To Clarkesville

Turnerville

76

Coleman River Wildlife Management Area

Tallulah River

Persimmon Road

Seed Lake

To Clarkesville

To Hiawassee

76

Moccasin Creek State Park

Lake Burton

197

Batesville

356

255

197

To Helen

To Cleveland

Tallulah Falls and Gorge

For anyone driving through the quiet town of Tallulah Falls today, it is difficult to believe this was once a bustling resort. But at the height of its popularity–between 1882 and 1913–Tallulah Falls had four grand hotels and more than a dozen smaller establishments. The Tallulah Falls Railroad scheduled one round trip daily from Cornelia to the little mountain town. At the depot, brass bands welcomed guests with a flourish, and horses and carriages carried them off to their hotels. There they passed the time playing billiards, tennis, tenpins, or sitting in hammocks and comfortable chairs on porches, enjoying the fresh mountain air. In the evening, they attended dances in the ballrooms of the grand hotels.

What prompted this early tourism was the famous **Tallulah Gorge**– a 2-mile-long canyon measuring 1,000 feet across and nearly 1,200 feet deep–and the falls tumbling in stages through this gorge.

The gorge was cut through quartzite rock tens of thousands of years ago by the Tallulah River, whose water plunged more than 650 feet in less than a mile over a series of six steplike falls, ranging in height from 16 to 96 feet. As it crashed through falls, pools, and rapids, the water made a thunderous sound that echoed along the rocky canyon walls and could even be heard a mile away. In his book *The Life and Times of Tallulah ... The Falls, The Gorge, The Town*, John Saye adds these descriptions:

> Mist rose from the falling water to partially obscure the moss and lichen-covered rock and the twisted evergreens. Visitors were entranced, awed and inspired by this monumental spectacle ... Local men blazed trails to the floor of the gorge, kept them clear, and hired themselves out as guides. Stairways and walks took tourists to all points of interest, both in the gorge and on the rim. An eighty foot observation tower was built at the foot of Tempesta Falls which could be climbed to the top of the waterfall.

On July 24, 1886, high-wire artist Professor Leon attempted to cross the gorge on a tightrope. According to reports, a guy wire snapped, forcing him to stay suspended over the gorge for 20 hair-raising minutes, while some 6,000 spectators watched in horror. The Professor finally made it to the other side, but did not attempt the return trip. (Nearly a century later, on July 18, 1970, Karl Wallenda successfully duplicated Professor Leon's walk across the gorge.)

Tallulah Gorge

Despite all this, Tallulah Falls' glory days were destined to end. By 1910, the company that would later become Georgia Power Company had taken steps to harness the great power of the Tallulah River. Citizens mounted several campaigns to block the development and to turn Tallulah Gorge into a national park, but their efforts failed. The company built a series of dams and powerhouses and a 6,666-foot-long tunnel (an unpresidented engineering feat) through which the Tallulah River was diverted. And in September of 1913, 18,000 horsepower of electricity–generated in a little mountain town–ran the trolley cars in Atlanta.

Gone forever were the thunder and mist rising from the gorge; gone forever the untamed beauty of what was one of Georgia's mightiest rivers. One by one the hotels closed. Then, on a windy night in December 1921, a fire ignited, flared out of control, and burned for several days, razing the town. Little that was destroyed was ever rebuilt.

But the gorge is still there, deep and awesome, and the falls and river, while not as wild, still course and plunge through the chasm, presenting dramatic and beautiful scenes. That, and numerous other points of interest nearby, bring travelers and tourists by the thousands to this area as one of the major centers of attraction in the mountains.

Driving "The Loop"

The main four-lane highway that cuts through the Tallulah Falls area was put in just a few years ago to bypass a serpentine drive through the mountain, considered hazardous at night in fog and rain. But this also cut out a scenic drive and access to the gorge, and to several interesting shops. However, the old road was left untouched and there are signs leading to it marked "15 Loop–Scenic Drive."

The thing to do then is to take this road, which is a right turn if driving north on Highway 441. These are the places you come to, in succession:

Tallulah Point Public Recreation Area, built and owned by the Georgia Power Company, is equipped with sheltered picnic areas and public restrooms. This provides another perspective on the gorge, and you can see the Tallulah Generating Station as well as the Tugaloo Dam and Generating Station. To get there, turn right (if driving north) at the signs.

Tallulah Gallery was established as an educational project for the Tallulah Falls School in 1973. It houses paintings, pottery, weavings, quilts, baskets, wood carvings, jewelry, books. Both the quality and selection here are impressive. Some of the Georgia and regional artists and craftspeople represented are well known, others are up-and-coming, but all the work is excellent and reasonably priced. All profits go toward scholarships for students. Open daily, 10 a.m.-5 p.m. 706-754-6020.

Indian Springs Trading Post is the oldest tourist stop along the gorge. It sells some snacks, beverages, and standard souvenir items, but is also an "authorized trading post for genuine Cherokee articles." A bewildering assortment of items is housed here, obviously reflecting the interests and heritage of the owners whose family built the place before the turn of the century. You'll find Indian artifacts and memorabilia, tumbled and rough semiprecious gems and minerals, antique dolls, stuffed and mounted wildlife, jewelry, baskets, baseball cards and Asian collectibles and antique Asian furniture. (A special tip: look overhead at what's hanging from the ceiling!) Open only May through October. 706-754-6611.

Tallulah Village, a shop adjacent to the Indian Springs Trading Post, has T-shirts and other typical gift-shop items, pottery, antiques, and some refreshments. Open May through October.

Tallulah Point is the location of the gorge overlook. There is ample parking, and no admission charge. Walk out on the open deck and use the coin-operated viewfinders to study the landscape of "America's Second Grand Canyon." You can also see down into the gorge from the railing at the roadside and from inside the building, where there are souvenir and gift items for sale and public restrooms. But be sure also to visit Tallulah Gorge Park, which we describe later on, for even better views of the gorge and falls.

Other Places to Visit

If you are driving "the loop" north, it will end at the intersection with the new Highway 441. Driving on, you'll come to a cluster of additional points of interest. (You will come to these, also, if you have not taken the "loop" and are driving through on Highway 441.)

The first of these are two buildings (on the left if driving north), one located on a rise above the road, the other on road level. The first is Pine Terrace and the second is the Co-op Craft Store.

Pine Terrace is a lovely, two-story frame Victorian mansion, complete with shuttered windows and wraparound porches. Once the family home of R. L. Moss, one of the first townspeople, it now belongs to the Tallulah Falls School and is used for adult education classes and special events.

Should it be open for a special event while you are in town, stop in and admire its interior workmanship and turn-of-the-century charm. To inquire about special events and classes held there, contact the school: Tallulah Falls School, Tallulah Falls, Ga 30573; 706-754-3181.

Co-op Craft Store. The building housing this craft store was the town's railroad depot, built in 1914 as a "showcase station." This is the original building. Note its distinctive "depot" shape and original orange tile roof. The craft store now occupying the building features hundreds of well-made, reasonably priced handicrafts: quilts, pillows, wooden toys, pottery, soft sculpture, jewelry, and so forth. All are made locally by members of the Georgia Mountain Arts Products Association, a cooperative that was formed in 1969 for the preservation and promotion of mountain crafts. Many of its members have been featured in the *Foxfire* books and magazine. This craft co-op also runs two other shops, one in downtown Clarkesville, and the other in Rabun Gap. It is open daily, 10 a.m.-5 p.m. Mail orders accepted: Box 67, Tallulah Falls, Ga 30573; 706-754-6810.

Old Town General Store. When the town of Tallulah Falls burned in 1921, one of the few buildings that remained was the general store. That building (erected in the early 1900s), with several interior and exterior alterations but with the original timbers and some sections of the walls, today houses the Old Town General Store. Of course, it no longer serves as a functioning general store, but rather as an interesting tourist attraction. The ownership is, however, still in the family. The original owner was J. E. Harvey; the present owner is his grandson James Turpin, Methodist minister for the Rabun County area.

The store currently carries local crafts, gift items, decorative items, a variety of oak rocking chairs for children and adults, as well as snack items. There are also a number of memorabilia and antiques, several from the original store, others gathered from the surrounding area.

Maumee Meehan, who reopened the store in 1989, decided to place her for-sale rocking chairs on the porch, and found that they soon became a favorite resting place for locals. That gave her the idea to sell "time shares" to the rockers for a nominal charge. Buyers receive a personalized, numbered certificate of ownership entitling them to come any time and rock on the porch. A list of the "time-share" owners is posted at the entrance. It bears the names of visitors from as far away as Australia.

To get to the store, look for the sign directing you to the town post office and city hall. This is Main Street, running beside the Hickory Mountain Restaurant. The Old Town General Store is closed Tuesdays. 706-754-6363.

Tallulah Gorge Park. Diagonally across from the Co-op Craft Store, you will see a white frame building with the sign "Tallulah Gorge Park." This is the entrance to the park from which you get a better view of the gorge and the falls below, from a well-maintained, 2,200-foot-long trail along the rim of the gorge. The walk, which takes about 30 minutes, has seven observation points and affords views of L'Eau d'Or, Tempesta, and Hurricane falls. In winter and during flooding, the fourth falls, Oceana, is visible. The dirt path is easily negotiated except in very wet weather, when it may be slippery in places. Throughout the park, many native trees and flowers have been tagged for identification.

Inside the park building are cold drinks and snacks, locally produced pickles, relishes, jams, jellies, and honey, and an assortment of pottery and books with a local focus. Plans are underway to open a museum here which will house artifacts and present the history of Tallulah Falls and the gorge. This enterprise is owned by the Tallulah Falls School, and all profits go toward student scholarships. Nominal admission fees; open daily 10 a.m. to 5 p.m.

Incidentally, adjacent to the Gorge Park building is another white frame structure bearing the sign "Cliff House." Actually, the Cliff House was a grand, turn-of-the-century hotel built up on the hill, which burned many years ago. The sign was removed to this building, which has served many different purposes over the years.

Tallulah Falls School. Driving the loop or the main route, you will notice signs pointing to the Tallulah Falls School. While the school isn't open to the public, it sponsors several programs that are, and it is also a local, historical landmark. The school was founded in 1909 by Mary Ann Lipscomb with funds raised by the Georgia Federation of Women's Clubs—the group that owns it to this day.

This preparatory school for grades 6-12 has a green, rolling campus with several little stone houses for the faculty, the Willet Building, which contains the administrative offices plus a large, fully equipped dining hall, and just beyond that, the most beautiful and modern Young Matrons' Circle Building, with its excellent Gertrude Long Harris Auditorium, plus a gymnasium and Olympic-sized heated pool. Farther up the hill are the classroom building, dormitories, and the Norwood Key Taylor Chapel. The Mary Ann Lipscomb Cottage, where the founder lived and the first female students boarded, now houses a small museum of the school's history, complete with early school artifacts, photos, and scrapbooks. This is open to the public from 9 a.m. to 5 p.m., Monday through Friday.

As a community service, and to promote the arts, music, history, and fellowship, the school conducts several public programs. Their Adult Education Center sponsors classes that are free of charge (unless a nominal materials cost is involved) on a reservation-only basis, and cover such varied topics as computer literacy, estate planning, basket making, painting, writing, etc. Sometimes day trips are offered (at nominal bus fare) to botanical gardens or historic sites several hours' drive away; evening trips to special entertainment in other cities are another feature. Each summer an Adult Retreat is conducted in four one-week sessions, and is open to individuals and couples. Their annual Monday Night Concert Series, scheduled during the summer months, brings professional soloists, chamber ensembles and orchestras to the music hall of the school for several engagements (individual and season tickets available). Buffet-style dinners, served in the school's dining hall, precede each concert; reservations are required. For specific information on the concerts, adult education classes and adult retreat, contact the school. Tallulah Falls School, Tallulah Falls, Ga 30573; 706-754-3181.

Terorra Park Visitors Center and Campground, owned and operated by Georgia Power Company, is a 300-acre complex (on the north side of the Highway 441 bridge) that includes a Visitor Center, park, and campground. Since the park is on Tallulah Lake, it is described in our Lakes chapter. However, we will include the Visitors Center and Campground here.

The center is the first structure on the left, after you cross the bridge. It is open year-round, and serves as a welcome center (with wheelchair access) offering public restrooms and racks of brochures about the area. Friendly and knowledgeable staff can answer questions or help with directions. There are permanent, hands-on displays of mountain culture, as well as rotating exhibits and videos that feature various aspects of the area's natural attributes, such as wildflowers, and craftspeople. A permanent, elaborate multimedia exhibit explains the hydroelectric system established in the region at the turn of the century, and the subsequent role electricity has played in the development of northeast Georgia. The center is open Monday through Saturday, 9 a.m. to 5 p.m.; Sunday, 1 to 5 p.m. 706-754-3276 or 706-754-6036.

To find the campgrounds, continue north on 441 from the center and take the next paved road on the right, which goes up the hill (follow signs). At the top you will find 51 sites with full hookups for RVs and tents, and a comfort station with hot showers. There is even a hiking trail, which leads from the campground down the hill to a gorge overlook. Camping is available daily, April through October for a modest fee. 706-754-3276 or 706-754-6036.

Food and Lodging

Hickory Mountain Restaurant, located just off Highway 441 near the Co-op Craft Store, features basic, economically priced home cooking for three meals every day. Fare includes the usual breakfast items such as eggs, grits, meat, pancakes, and biscuits, and such lunch and dinner items as homemade barbecue, sandwiches, and daily specials featuring meat and three vegetables. Their dessert specialty is homemade cobbler. Everything is inexpensive. They open at 6 a.m. daily and close at 8 p.m., except on Friday and Saturday, when they close at 9 p.m. 706-754-6012.

Tallulah Falls Motel, the only motel in town, offers simple, affordable, air-conditioned/heated lodging at reasonable rates. A quaint Victorian-style gazebo on the grounds overlooks Tallulah Lake from the west side of Highway 441. P. O. Box 117, Tallulah Falls, Ga 30573; 706-754-6022.

Lakemont, Wiley and Tiger

Rabun County's southern border begins at the city of Tallulah Falls; the next townships to the north are Lakemont, Wiley, and Tiger. Back in the days of the Tallulah Falls Railroad, there was a depot in each of these towns to accommodate passenger, cargo, and mail stops along the train's daily round-trip journey between Georgia and North Carolina. In its day, the railroad was the artery carrying the lifeblood of these little communities—and, indeed, the whole of Rabun County.

Some Railroad History

From 1907 until 1961, the Tallulah Falls Railroad ran for 58 miles—crossing 42 trestles and making 19 stops—between Cornelia (where it hooked up with Southern Railroad) and Franklin, North Carolina. For 54 years, this was the major transportation and communication link between residents of Habersham, Rabun, and Macon (NC) counties and the outside world. In addition, "the old TF," as it was fondly called, provided a livelihood for many citizens who either secured work in railroad construction, maintenance, and operations, or used it to transport goods into and out of the area. As explained in *Memories of a Mountain Shortline: The Story of the Tallulah Falls Railroad* (edited by Kaye Carver and Myra Queen, Foxfire Press, 1976):

> The TF belonged to the people it served; it gave them jobs, bought things from them, took them places, brought people to see them, shipped out their farm produce, brought in things they couldn't raise or make, provided depots to gather in, kept them company, provided excitement, and even forecast the weather by the sound of the whistle. It seems there was hardly a facet of life which the railroad did not touch upon.

There were four earlier attempts to bring a line through Rabun County, but each of them failed.

Each of those early railroads–the Blue Ridge (or Black Diamond), the Northeastern, the Richmond and Danville, the Blue Ridge and Atlantic–was plagued with financial difficulties. So was the TF. It went into a one-year receivership in 1908, just eleven years after its inauguration. In 1923, it slipped into receivership for the remainder of its life. In 1933, Receiver J. F. Gray petitioned to abandon the Tallulah Falls line altogether. Although the Interstate Commerce Commission eventually granted permission for this, no action was taken because of the public support (shared by TF officials) for keeping it in operation.

By the 1950s, however, all shortline railroads were doomed to extinction by improved highway transportation, and the TF was no exception. By then she hauled only cargo, having retired her only passenger coach in 1946, and in 1954 she even ceased carrying the mail. Nonetheless, people hated to see the TF go, and her final run on March 25, 1961, stirred many emotions. Engineer Goldman Kimbrell relates, in *Memories of a Mountain Shortline:*

> The last trip the train ran was pitiful. All them little kids that had been a getting chewing gum that we'd thrown off to them, even the older people that lived along the line, was out there to see it. The last trip, it looked like all of them was wipin' their eyes. Everybody that could got in the caboose to ride the last trip. We didn't tell nobody they couldn't ride. Anybody that wanted to ride, they just got on.

Some evidence of the TF remains today–if you know where to look. Pillars from the only steel and concrete trestle on the line stand near the head of Lake Tallulah, in plain view from Old 441 (turn at the brown sign marked "Old 441" on west side of Highway 441, just north of Terrora Park and Visitor's Center). Up in Wiley, a few yards of steel rails lie trapped in pavement at Wiley Junction (Highway 441), which was one of the TF's stops. Barely visible, they run diagonally across the side road that connects Old and "New" 441 in front of the post office and convenience store. Further north in Clayton, several old boxcars are being used as residences on North Main Street, near the junction with Highway 441. (Look for the lawn covered with windmills, or whirligigs.)

Tallulah Falls Railroad

The Tallulah Falls Railroad has been preserved for posterity by the motion picture industry. Our very own mountain shortline played a part in the 1950 filming of *I'd Climb the Highest Mountain*, starring Susan Hayward and William Lundigan. In 1955, Walt Disney chose it for the filming of *The Great Locomotive Chase*, the Civil War story of Andrew's Raid, in which Union forces attempted to cripple the Western and Atlantic Railroad between Atlanta and Chattanooga, Tennessee.

Lakemont Then and Now

Of the three communities covered in this chapter, Lakemont, which lies alongside Lake Rabun, was by far the busiest railroad stop, especially in summer. That's when the tourists and "lake people" would arrive–often with servants in tow–to spend the season under the cool canopy of trees that sheltered their Lake Rabun homes. (For the history and current attractions of Lake Rabun itself, see our chapter on the lakes.)

Most of the early property owners lived and worked in Atlanta. They bought their vacation home lots from Augustus Andreae, a German immigrant who had arrived in Tallulah Falls around the turn of the century. Andreae had negotiated with the Georgia Railway and Power Company (forerunner of Georgia Power Company) to trade his inexpensive property along the Tallulah River for land above the projected flood level. This shrewd move meant, of course, that he suddenly owned frontage on the newly created Lake Rabun. His daughter Herta Schartle recalls in *Lakemont, Ga.: The Early Years,* by Ben Noble, Jr., and Olin Jackson (Legacy Communications, 1989):

> He also reserved the right to build boathouses for himself and for his assigns, and that's why the people who bought from dad don't have to get any permits from the power company to build boathouses to this very day.

This real estate coup, accompanied by an entrepreneurial spirit, led to the creation of many lakefront homes–as well as the Lake Rabun Hotel–and, for all intents and purposes, secured Augustus Andreae's place as the founder of Lakemont.

In the 1920s, "downtown" Lakemont was about half a block long and included Alley's Grocery, the post office (in a corner of Alley's Grocery), the railroad depot, the Lakemont Lodge hotel, and a couple of other small buildings. After the Tallulah Falls Railroad was dismantled in 1961, Main Street changed. The old hotel was razed during the 1960s, and the tiny Lakemont Depot was moved and used as a lakeside home, then later demolished. Eventually, a new, straighter portion of Highway 441 was constructed to the east, and through-traffic bypassed Lakemont completely.

Today, you drive through Lakemont on the scenic route called "Old Highway 441." One vestige of the town's past remains, and is worth a stop for nostalgia's sake: Alley's Grocery. Built in 1925, this country grocery is run by Lamar Alley, son of the original owners. It's still the only store serving the community, and it carries everything from hardware to groceries to fishing supplies. It's a friendly little place, and on any given day, you're likely to find there some of the locals who regularly stop to chat with Lamar.

If you're in the mood for conversation, ask them about the television and feature movies that have been made in the area. Two recent award-winners are *Foxfire* (starring Jessica Tandy, Hume Cronyn, and John Denver), the 1987 Hallmark Hall of Fame television movie that used the exterior and interior of Alley's store; and *Decoration Day* (starring James Garner), Hallmark's 1990 movie that was filmed on Lake Rabun.

Wiley and Tiger

Both of the next two communities north, Wiley and Tiger, had depots for the Tallulah Falls Railroad. We've already mentioned the old rails embedded in pavement in front of Wiley Junction, the original location of the depot. Beyond the railroad connection, local history books are silent on the subject of Wiley. In contrast, Tiger is much more a topic of history and anecdote–even down to the origin of its name.

Wiley was probably named after an early white settler, whereas Tiger– according to lifelong resident and professional storyteller Janie P. Taylor, who has been featured in *Foxfire* magazine–was named after the Bengal tiger. How, you may wonder, could an animal from the jungles of India influence the naming of a remote mountain village in Georgia?

Following England's war with France over possession of India in the 1700s, some of the British soldiers migrated to the New World, settling in the northeast Georgia mountains. "Imagine their surprise and shock," Janie P. says, "to hear echoing from the cliffs of a nearby mountain a piercing cry, as the dying scream of a woman–the same sounds they had heard the black-striped tigers make in India." These sounds evoked such powerful memories that the early settlers named the peak Tiger Mountain.

"The weird, frightening cry was, of course, not made by a tiger," Janie P. says, "but rather by a native mountain cat, a sleek, black panther, commonly called a 'painter.'" It's been many a decade since the wild cats' screams were heard around Tiger, for as civilization encroached on their territory, the elusive "painters" retreated further and further into the higher mountain elevations. Nonetheless, one little Georgia mountain–and the township that grew up around it–bear witness to their existence.

Tiger Mountain is the distinctive, pyramid-shaped peak that dominates the horizon west of town. It is visible from Old 441, but for a closer look, turn left (if driving north) at the four-way stop by the Post Office in Tiger. That is Bridge Creek Road, and less than a mile from the intersection, it skirts the base of Tiger Mountain.

Another interesting anecdote about Tiger is that it had a zoo during the early 1930s. Billboards throughout the region urged "See the Zoo at Tiger," and the town enjoyed some renown for that alone. On display were two bears, exotic birds, and mountain wildlife, such as foxes, squirrels, and raccoons. There was also a snake pit, a monkey cage, and an alligator pit–replete with a huge alligator. In one of her amusing "Tiger Tales," Janie P. tells how the alligator got loose one day. After frightening a certain little girl and her dog, then terrifying a team of mules and some men, it was finally captured and returned. "But it took eight men to load that alligator into a '34 Ford pickup!"

Things to See and Do

There are several interesting things to do and places to visit and shop in the Lakemont-Wiley-Tiger area. We list them here in alphabetical order.

Barn Hill is a gradually evolving family enterprise of antiques and collectibles on the left side of Highway 441 about 2 miles north of the Tallulah Falls bridge. (Look for the windmill, and follow signs to entrance and parking just off the highway, below the building.) They have a large selection of old farm tools, and somewhat of a general store atmosphere inside the main building which includes vintage items such as old marbles and bottles. Open seasonally, when the sign indicates so (no phone).

Four Winds Village Indian Museum and Trading Post. Located 6 miles south of Clayton on Old Highway 441 between Wiley and Tiger, this Indian museum has a fascinating array of artifacts from North and South American Indian tribes, as well as "numerous worldwide relics and oddities." Of special note are items from Georgia tribes, some of which are said to be several thousand years old: ceremonial pipes, bowls, hunting and farming tools and weapons. Newly made Indian jewelry, rugs, moccasins and so forth also are available for sale. Open daily 10 a.m.-5 p.m. P. O. Box 112, Tiger, Ga 30576; 706-782-6939.

Hidden Treasures is a recent addition to the list of antiques and collectibles shops. It is located in a house that sits just off Highway 441, about a mile north of the Pickin' Parlor on the right (look for the hand painted sign that says "Antiques & Treasures"). The day we visited, there was a small but varied selection that included pottery, porcelain, brass, silver, jewelry, kitchen utensils, magazines, and decorative arts. Owner Amy Williams assured us more inventory was on the way. 706-782-6297.

Lofty Branch Appalachian Shopping Village is a hillside "village" of working studios. Here you can buy arts, crafts, furniture, garments, collectibles, and gifts–and sometimes watch them being made, or learn how to make them yourself.

This enterprise is the brainchild of Debbie and John Koenig, hardworking, talented craftspeople who are as committed to education as they are to marketing. John, an expert timber framer and builder, holds workshops and demonstrations in traditional construction techniques. (He and his crew, incidentally, designed and constructed all the buildings at the complex.) Debbie is an award-winning weaver who also teaches weaving and spinning, and schedules other kinds of craft workshops and demonstrations at Lofty Branch. Even their young sons Josh and Zac get into the act by building and selling wooden birdhouses.

Drive into the complex and park up on the hill, then take a leisurely tour of the various free-standing studios. You'll find **Heyward Pottery & Critters,** with sculpture and functional pottery; **Simons Studio,** with miniatures, floral arrangements, gifts, and more; the **Warm Fuzzy Shop,** with handmade sweaters, wraps, scarves; **K's Kountry Krafts & Gifts,** with wooden toys, decorative accessories, pillows, wreaths, etc; the **Orchid Patch,** an "official Cabbage Patch Babyland adoption center," which is chockablock with Cabbage Patch dolls and stuffed animals.

The spacious central Gallery houses contemporary and traditional works for sale–handwoven wearables, jewelry, pottery, furniture, paintings, decorative accessories, fiber arts, etc.–created by more than 60 different individuals in an array of media from glass, porcelain, wood, and metal to paper and fiber. You'll also find a selection of easy-listening music cas-settes, books on building and gardening, and an assemblage of looms and weavers' supplies. The small eatery inside the main gallery can provide you with a snack, a piece of homemade cake or pie, a cup of coffee or tea, and cold soft drinks.

Mountain Maffick and **KristKindle Mart** are two annual festivals hosted by Lofty Branch Appalachian Shopping Village. Mountain Maffick, held the Saturday and Sunday of Memorial Weekend, is a juried show of high-quality arts and crafts in which there are more than 50 booths, plus the concessions stands, live entertainment and periodic demonstrations you might expect at any country festival. KristKindle is a somewhat smaller event where you can Christmas shop while sipping hot spiced cider in a festive atmosphere. Patterned after similar holiday fairs in Europe, Kristkindle is held the Friday, Saturday, and Sunday following Thanksgiving. Wares for sale at this festival are not limited to crafts, but they must be new items (not flea-market type). The hours for both festi-vals are 10 a.m.-5 p.m; admission is free. Both festivals are held outdoors in the permanent booths on the grounds.

Lofty Branch Appalachian Shopping Village is located 5 miles north of Tallulah Falls and 6 miles south of Clayton on Highway 441, and is open Tuesday through Sunday, 10 a.m.-5 p.m. Route 1, Box 2901, Lakemont, Ga 30552; 706-782-5246.

Smokey Mountain Stables is located on Highway 441 (on the right if dri-ving north) just north of Tallulah Falls (and 8 miles south of Clayton). Accomplished riders will be happy to know that the stables' motto is "Our trail rides are fun 'cause our horses can run." But beginning riders can rest assured they will get a sedate mount. Make reservations for one-hour, two-hour, and half-day trail rides, and overnight camping expedi-tions. The longer trail rides venture into Tallulah Gorge, but even the one- and two-hour rides make stops at picturesque lookouts. Open year-round. Weekday rides by reservation, weekends by preset schedule. Horse rentals. 706-782-5836.

This Old Place is the retail shop for **Strauss Studio** and **Tiger Mountain Weavers,** located on Highway 441 in Wiley, next to Bartow's Bar-B-Que. In addition to an attractive display of handwoven garments and acces-sories, one-of-a-kind belts and jewelry, and decorative home accessories,

Sue Strauss and Martha Plane have filled this small space with a sizable array of craft supplies (including yarn) and the popular Green Shutters Restaurant specialty foods, relishes, jams and jellies. A beautiful wooden loom is set up in the corner–usually sporting a work in progress–and a spinning wheel stands at the ready nearby. Ask them for a demonstration. If that sight inspires you to try your hand with fiber, you can sign up for lessons in weaving, as well as spinning, knitting, crocheting, and quilting. Children can sign up for special craft days (once a week in spring and fall), where they'll get to finish a whole project. Open Monday-Saturday, 10 a.m.-5 p.m.; winter hours: Thursday-Saturday, 10 a.m.-5 p.m. P. O. Box 2074, Clayton, Ga 30525; 706-782-7995.

Whippoorwill Antiques, a small white building on the left that was once a roadside tavern (just north of Dailey's Quilts & Crafts on Highway 441), has two rooms filled to the ceiling with glassware and china, books, wrought iron collectibles, kitchen utensils, jewelry, photographs, Coca-Cola memorabilia, toys, dolls, doll furniture, sheet music, vintage linens and clothing–plus some furniture. Owner Agnes Skinner says she carries "antiques, collectibles and good junk." Open daily, year-round, afternoons only. 706-782-3640.

Where to Eat and Stay

Most of the standard lodging facilities–motels, hotels, bed and breakfasts, and so forth–are in the Clayton area, but there is one new one here that is quite different.

Camp Creek Cottages owner Tommy Brown describes his enterprise as a "lumberjack campground." He and his family have built five rustic but comfortable 1940s-style camp cottages with one, two, and three bedrooms, full kitchens, whirlpool tubs, fireplaces, screened porches and open decks. These year-round, heated cottages provide privacy because they are scattered about on 24 acres of land that is, itself, surrounded by national forest. A bunkhouse provides basic sleeping room for eight, and pop-up campers and tents can be accommodated on the grounds. Brown has anticipated every recreational need with a bait and tackle shop, eatery, and canoes and flat bottom boats that can be rented for use on the area's lakes. He says there are miles of nature trails that go back along the

Chattooga River, and he has made every effort to keep the place "real natural," even to the exclusion of televisions and telephones. Camp Creek Cottages is 1.5 miles off Highway 441 on Camp Creek Road, which is 3 miles north of Tallulah Falls Bridge and 8 miles south of Clayton. Reasonable rates for cottages; bunkhouse is even less. Special children's rates. P. O. Box 300, Wiley, Ga 30581; 706-782-6611.

For a cold drink or snacks, there's **Alley's Grocery** on Old 441 in Lakemont, as well as several gas station/convenience stores along Highway 441. Wiley Junction, at the connecting road between Old and New 441 in Wiley, even has a short-order grill for breakfast, lunch, and snacks.

Bartow's Bar-B-Que is the only restaurant in this locality, and it's open for lunch and dinner daily (11 a.m. to 9 p.m.). Owner Alice Roberson has decorated this casual eatery with a pig motif, because their specialty is pit-cooked barbecue. In this end of the county, Bartow's is the only place for ribs, barbecued beef, pork and chicken and Brunswick stew. You can eat there, or request take out. Prices are inexpensive. Located on Highway 441 in Wiley. 706-782-4038.

Pig Pickin' is a new annual community festival held on the grounds at Bartow's Bar-B-Que. This three-day celebration over Memorial Weekend coincides with Mountain Maffick. Pig Pickin' features scores of booths with locally made crafts, demonstrations, games, music and general down-home fun for all ages. The star attraction is the pit barbecued whole hog, made available for "pickin'"—just like at old-time festivals. Another nostalgic touch is the Saturday night street dance. Saturday 10 a.m.-5 p.m.; Sunday 1-6 p.m.; Monday 10 a.m.-3 p.m.

Retreat Centers

Mountains have long been valued as a place to achieve spiritual renewal. Not only do churches of all denominations abound in Rabun County (and surrounding areas), but there are, in addition, several retreat centers. These draw on the sense of peace, contemplation, and communion with nature that these mountains offer.

Anapauo Farm is a retreat home for individuals, small groups, or families. Amenities on the 20-acre wooded site include include a cabin (sleeps six), guest room (sleeps two), camping platforms, trails leading to the Tallulah River, and "rest, refreshment and renewal." Owners Sally and Art Lockhart started the retreat center after Art retired from the Episcopal ministry. In addition to "unstructured" retreats, they also offer "guided" retreats. Anapauo Farm is located on the west side of Highway 441; look for their large yellow mailbox about 3 miles north of the Tallulah Falls Bridge. Star Route 320, Lakemont, Ga 30552; 706-782-6442.

Covecrest Christian Renewal Center is a United Methodist-related center for individuals, families, and groups. It is sited on 180 acres of beautiful land, with its own meadows, lakes, streams, and waterfalls. The center offers cabins with fireplaces and porch swings, as well as camping. A 10,000-square-foot conference center–with such amenities as ceiling-to-floor stone fireplaces, and walls of windows overlooking meadow and woodland–serves as the hub of activity for the international Elderhostel educational program (open to persons 60 years old and older), as well as other public seminars. Executive Director Bob Murphy, a Methodist minister, and his wife, Carole, oversee every aspect of the operation.

Each August, Covecrest is the site of a most impressive religious play. "His Last Days," which uses music and drama to depict the life of Jesus Christ, is staged around the beautiful pond and rolling grounds of Covecrest Christian Renewal Center. A locally mounted production, this has been a popular annual event since 1983. Performances are 7 p.m., Friday and Saturday nights of one weekend (frequently the first of the month), and it is suggested you bring your own lawn chair. Admission is free.

To get to Covecrest, turn at the post office in Tiger (a left if driving north on Old 441). This is Bridge Creek Road. Then drive about 6 miles and watch for the sign marking the entrance to Covecrest on the left. Route 1, Box 3117, Tiger, Ga 30576; 1-800-782-2683 or 706-782-5961.

Four Winds Village is a "spiritual, health and educational retreat" that offers bed and Continental breakfast, and primitive camping at the creek area in the rear acreage, behind the Indian museum (mentioned above). Inexpensive rates. It is located on Old 441, six miles south of Clayton between Tiger and Wiley. Four Winds Village and Essene Faithists Church, P. O. Box 112, Tiger, Ga 30576; 706-782-6939.

Clayton

Long before the white settler arrived, this entire area had been Cherokee territory, and the Indians had established a network of trading routes so extensive as to reach north into North Carolina and Tennessee, west into Alabama, and southeast into Savannah and even Florida. Historians record that five of these routes intersected at a place known in the 1700s as "The Dividings." This eventually became Clayton, and Clayton eventually became the hub for continuing travel and trade along these routes.

Clayton was established in 1829, five years after the formation of Rabun County, and subsequently designated as the county seat. It was named in honor of Georgia's first Superior Court Judge, Augustus S. Clayton. Records show that the town's land was acquired from Solomon Beck. Obadiah Dickerson, an early settler who later became a prominent citizen, laid out the town lots.

Because there was no sawmill within the county then, Clayton's first courthouse and jail were simple log buildings with handmade board roofs. A series of courthouses was built over the years, each structure slightly more elaborate and sturdier than the one before. The first frame courthouse was a white, two-story edifice built in 1879. It still stands today on West Warwoman Road, behind Savannah Place Shoppes, having been renovated for private business offices and meeting space.

By the turn of the century, Rabun County had a population of about 6,000, and Clayton had become a small town. In the center of its one-square-mile city limits sat the courthouse mentioned above—right at the top of a hill. The north-south and east-west roads (which we know today as Main and Savannah Streets), met in a square around the building. Behind the courthouse was the town well. The Blue Ridge Hotel, the area's earliest inn, stood just to the north, next to Nelson Tilley's general store. Other businesses in town included dry goods and hardware stores. Two churches, Baptist and Methodist, a schoolhouse, and several residences completed the community. With the exception of the courthouse, none of these is in existence today.

When the Tallulah Falls Railroad extended its line to Clayton, and the Bank of Clayton opened its doors in 1904, a new era of development began. The Clayton Women's Club established the first library in 1914, and, wanting to create a more progressive community, undertook to remove all the hitching posts from Main Street. At the end of the decade, the newly organized State Highway Board launched a program of modern road construction that included Clayton's east-west highway (known today as U.S. 76).

These improvements in transportation meant, among other things, an increase in tourism. The creation of Lakes Burton, Seed, Rabun, Tallulah, and Tugalo from the damming of the Tallulah River added a new element—summer residents—to the growing number of vacationers.

Commenting on Rabun County's allure, author Lillian Smith, a Clayton resident, wrote:

> Actually it is a place of quiet beauty, neither dramatic nor 'breath-taking', but of a loveliness that weaves itself into the memory and stays there. Even today it seems to most of us who know it, a little corner cut off from the restless world, and we cherish it as a place where there is still a fragment of peace … All this has been here a long time. And many have come to our mountains seeking this beauty and peace and quiet and cool-ness, and have stayed on. Or have come again and again to find what they left here the year before.

This is as true today as it was in 1946 when it was written.

It is no wonder then, that Clayton has become the hub for tens of thousands of people coming into these north Georgia mountains from every adjacent state. They come to stay a few days, a week, a month, or the entire summer and fall, to enjoy the mountains' temperate climate, the beautiful scenery, the fishing, boating, and swimming in the lakes and rivers. They come to enjoy the gracious mountain hospitality, the country dining, the countless arts and crafts shops and antique stores, the hiking trails and the waterfalls, the country music and country dancing. And they come to steep themselves in Appalachian lore.

There are really two main parts to Clayton today, the busy section on Highway 441–with its shopping centers, fast-food eateries, restaurants, service stations, convenience stores, and specialty shops–and the area known as "downtown."

Downtown Clayton

To find Clayton–the real Clayton–you need to go to Main and Savannah Streets. This is the heart of town. Here you find a typical small-town look, with one primary intersection and two-hour curbside parking–with no meters.

The architecture of the various buildings reflects practically every decade of this century. The buildings housing April Leigh's Boutique, Clayton Flowerbed, and Cotton States Insurance on East Savannah Street, for instance, were built before 1920; Clayton Baptist Church on South Main Street was built in stages over the '30s and '40s–and so on, right up to 1982, when the Savannah Place Shoppes, the row of boutique-like shops on East Savannah Street, was built, distinguished by attractively decorated, pastel-colored storefronts.

Clayton–like other mountain towns–was never affluent, and because of this, few grand homes were built in the early days. Sometimes a family would build or buy a tiny, basic dwelling, then expand it over the years as their business prospered and resources became available. Such is the history of Alton and Mary Story's lovely two-story home on the corner of Church and Hamby Streets, across from the Presbyterian Church. Mrs. Story's uncle, Colonel Clyde Holden, an attorney and Rabun native, bought the original four-room house around the turn of the century. The Colonel and his wife, Annie Rickman Holden (also a Rabun native), expanded it in the '20s, and had the four redwood Corinthian columns that distinguish the front porch shipped from Chicago in the '30s.

In downtown there are a variety of shops: florists; card, craft, book, gift, and antique shops; drug, department, furniture, appliance, and hardware stores; art galleries and photography studios and shops; stores that sell apparel for men, women, and children; and even a travel agency.

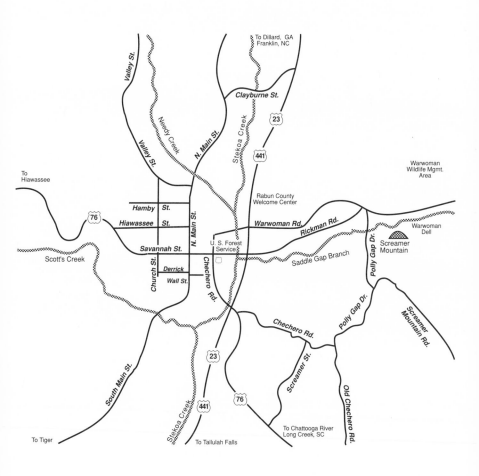

Valley St.

Needy Creek

Valley St.

To
Hiawassee

76

Hamby St.

Hiawassee St.

Savannah St.

Scott's Creek

Church St.

Derrick

Wall St.

N. Main St.

N. Main St.

Stekoa Creek

To Dillard, GA
Franklin, NC

Clayburne St.

23

441

Rabun County
Welcome Center

Warwoman Rd.

Rickman Rd.

U. S. Forest
Service

Saddle Gap Branch

Chechero Rd.

Warwoman
Wildlife Mgmt.
Area

Warwoman
Dell

Screamer
Mountain

Polly Gap Dr.

Polly Gap Dr.

Chechero Rd.

Screamer
Mountain Rd.

23

South Main St.

Stekoa Creek

441

76

Screamer St.

Old Chechero Rd.

To Tiger

To Tallulah Falls

To Chattooga River
Long Creek, SC

The merchants sponsor **Annual Sidewalk Sales,** usually in May and October. These are conducted with a festival atmosphere, and in addition to the tables and racks of merchandise that line the sidewalks, there are food and live entertainment. There is also an annual **Christmas Parade,** usually held the first Saturday in December.

You can park and stroll and shop downtown. Folks are friendly here, so don't be surprised if they speak or at least nod when they pass by.

Clayton's year-round population is, even today, only around 2,000; the county population around 11,000. The residents, many of them, are descendants of the pioneer settlers from the early 1800s, and their names–Bleckley, Cannon, Dickerson, Gillespie, Holden, Kelly, Miller, Rickman, Wall, and others–remain prominent in the area. Many of these families still live in the mountains in and around Clayton–Black Rock, Screamer, Germany–some in the original homesteads.

Clayton's Famous Women

When talking about the town's past, local historians like to bring forward the names of two important Clayton women: Celeste S. Parrish, a pioneer in the field of education, and author Lillian Smith, a pioneer in human rights.

"Miss Celeste," as she was known, was born in Virginia in 1853, orphaned by the age of 15, then sent out into the world to make her own way. She tried to teach at a country school, and what may have begun as an act of survival quickly became her life's passion.

Despite the social resistance to educating women, Celeste advanced her education by studying at night, and in 1896, earned a Bachelor of Philosophy degree from Cornell University. She joined the faculty at Randolph-Macon Woman's College in Lynchburg, Virginia, and taught mathematics, philosophy, psychology, and pedagogy. In 1902, she became head of the Department of Pedagogic Psychology at the State Normal College in Athens (later the University of Georgia).

Named one of Georgia's first Supervisors of Rural Education in 1911, and charged with bringing mountain schools up to national standards, Celeste began making the rounds–"by stage, by wagon." During this time, she fell in love with the Clayton area and established a home here.

Celeste's accomplishments included helping to get bills passed that fostered the incorporation of vocational education in both the public school system and in the University of Georgia and its branches. Of the many organizations she founded (or was active in), one of the best known is the American Association of University Women.

Celeste Parrish died in 1918 at the age of 65, and was laid to rest in the Baptist cemetery behind Clayton Baptist church (South Main Street). In his eulogy, State Superintendent Brittain called her "Georgia's Greatest Woman." That solitary phrase is inscribed beneath the name and birth and death dates on her granite grave marker.

Just three years before Miss Celeste's death, eighteen-year-old Lillian Smith moved from Florida to Clayton with her parents and seven brothers and sisters. In 1920 her father founded the Laurel Falls Camp on Screamer Mountain, the first summer camp for girls in Georgia. "Miss Lil" ran it from 1926 until it closed in 1948.

In the 1930s Miss Lil and Paula Snelling published a liberal journal (later known as *South Today*). It was the first ever to publish prose and poetry by black writers. During this time, Smith turned to writing for herself, and in 1944 published *Strange Fruit*. The novel was simultaneously a bestseller–selling at the rate of some 20,000 copies a week–and the most controversial book of its day. The story dealt with the explosive issues of interracial relationships, prejudice, and even lynching, and as a result, was banned in several cities.

Over the next 20 years, until cancer took her life in 1966, Miss Lil authored seven more books related to human rights and dignity. Numerous awards were conferred upon her, including several honorary doctorates. She has been called "a central figure in the then-dawning civil rights movement."

With the exception of times that she traveled, Miss Lil spent most of her life in Clayton. It is a tribute to the fair-mindedness of the citizens of Clayton that while most did not share her opinions, the town as a whole continued to accept her as one of their own. Hundreds of people attended her graveside service at the family home on Screamer Mountain. They included college presidents, writers, musicians, domestics, farmers, neighbors–people from all walks of life. The simple granite tombstone reads:

LILLIAN SMITH

DEC. 12, 1897–SEPT. 28, 1966

DEATH CAN KILL A MAN

THAT IS ALL IT CAN DO TO HIM

IT CANNOT END HIS LIFE

BECAUSE OF MEMORY

Antiques and Collectibles

Junction Hollow Antiques features items in country, primitive, and Victorian styles, such as quality reproductions, used furniture, mirrors, accessories, silver, china, tools, quilts, kitchen items, and sports collectibles. Owners Paul and Juanita Berry formerly had Berry Patch Antiques in Lighthouse Point, Florida. Open Tuesday through Sunday, 10 a.m.-5 p.m., May to November. Located in a brick house on the right, about one mile north of Clayton on Highway 441, next to the Farm Bureau office. 706-782-7216.

Mountain Mama Antiques owner Janice Massee says her store carries "everything from A to Z." By this she means: farm equipment, furniture, jewelry, glass, books, china, lamps, kitchenware, pictures, clocks, ironware, dolls, vintage hats, kerosene lamps, collectibles, wreaths, and baskets. Open year-round; closed Tuesday and Wednesday. Hours are 1 p.m. "til," which usually means until dark. (In the summer, that might be 9 p.m.) Located about a mile north of Clayton on Highway 441, on the right, past Junction Hollow Antiques and the Farm Bureau office. 706-782-6232.

Mountain Peddler carries an extensive collection of jewelry, china, glass, silver, paintings, engravings, kitchenware, guns, decorative accessories, and furniture of all styles and from all periods, American and European. Owners Tommy and Beanie Ramey make frequent trips along the Eastern

Seaboard to replenish the store's supply of antiques. Open year-round; closed Sunday and Wednesday. Located on East Savannah Street several doors east of Main Street. 706-782-4633.

S. & S. Dillon, Ltd., carries fine-quality antiques: furniture; glass, porcelain, rare books, paintings, art pottery, folk art, accessories, and "eccentricities." This is a small shop, but owners Steve and Sherlene Dillon keep it filled with excellent American, European and Asian pieces from various eras. Open year-round, Monday through Saturday, 10 a.m to 5 p.m. (Sunday by appointment). Located in Depot Center, across from the Chik'n Coop restaurant on Highway 441 South. 706-782-4393.

Timpson Creek Millworks & Antiques, Ida Mae's and Marche d'Or are three shops under one roof. Together they sell jewelry, decorative accessories, antiques, American and French folk art, and faithfully reproduced furniture made by master craftsman Dwayne Thompson–who also does custom furniture work. You will also find a selection of French and Southern American specialty food items: jams and jellies, mustard, barbecue sauce, salsa, dips, spices, and more. Located 7 miles west of Clayton on U.S. 76, just before Charlie Mountain Road at Lake Burton. Open April through October, daily except Wednesday. Timpson Creek and Ida Mae's: 706-782-5164; Marche d'Or: 706-782-7731.

Book Shops, Gift Shops, and Galleries

Allen's Books & Crafts has a selection of jewelry and gifts, including crystals. Books range from children's books to best-sellers, with sections on genealogy and the metaphysical. They also carry books with a local and regional focus, and magazines of all types. Open year-round. Located in Depot Center, across from Chik'n Coop Restaurant on Highway 441. 706-782-7190.

Carnes sells homemade jams, jellies, condiments, relishes from a colorful little roadside stand where the Carnes family's property meets the road. In winter when the stand is closed, a sign guides you up the driveway to their house where you can purchase their products. They're well known for their Plum Nutty spread, but the other creations, such as chow chow and relishes, will interest you too. Located on the west side of North Main Street (Old 441), about a mile from town.

Gifts from Debbie features a wide selection of porcelain, glass, baskets, brass, potpourri, and gift items. Open daily. Located inside Deal's Drug Store, next to Winn-Dixie in the Village Shopping Center on Highway 441. 706-782-3813.

Golden Lotus Emporium specializes in spiritual and metaphysical books, Bibles, cards, incense, and jewelry, and is open year-round. Located just south of town on Highway 441, next to Coldwell Banker Hal West Realty. 706-782-2690.

M & M Book Store carries a complete line of paperbacks, hardbacks, bestsellers, children's, and inspirational books. They have a large selection of books of local and regional interest and also carry used books and magazines. Open year-round. Located on North Main Street, by the Clayton Cafe. 706-782-6296.

Main Street Gallery specializes in contemporary American folk art and fine paintings, furniture, garments, jewelry, and accessories. Helen Meadors, Jeanne Kronsnoble and Susan Belew own this shop–talented craftswomen all–and it reflects their lively senses of humor as much as their aesthetics. Don't expect typical country crafts: you'll find no geese with bonnets or ruffled calico wreaths here. What you will find are paintings by Georgia artists like Sarah Rakes, rustic furniture by Don Bundrick, handwoven wearables and throws by Meadors and Belew, and necklaces, bracelets, and earrings by an array of American artisans. Items such as these you might expect to find in big city galleries at double the price. Closed Wednesday, Sunday and between Christmas and New Years. Located three doors north of the intersection at Main and Savannah Streets, on the west side of Main Street. 706-782-2440.

Mary George Poss Art Gallery & Gift Shop is owned by well-known Clayton artist Mary George Poss, whose paintings are rendered in both impressionist and realist styles, using either watercolor or acrylics. Her work has been exhibited throughout the South and in Europe, and her prints and originals hang in many homes and business establishments throughout the region. Collectors enjoy her florals and especially her paintings that recreate scenes from 19th-century Rabun County. Recent works include a limited edition print of the turn-of-the-century Burton community, which was submerged when Lake Burton was created.

In addition to selling her fine limited-edition prints, this shop offers an array of elegant gifts, from potpourri and baskets to porcelain, ceramic, and glass items. In one corner is a permanent Christmas shop, featuring decorative and hostess items for the holidays. Open year-round; seasonal hours. Located in Savannah Places Shoppes, East Savannah Street downtown. 706-782-2387.

Reeves is something of a landmark here, and for good reason. Since 1928 it has provided one-stop shopping for furniture, gifts, housewares, sporting goods, and garden and building supplies—to say nothing of the most complete array of hardware and electrical items anywhere. Locals brag, "You can buy *anything* at Reeves."

The gift area features porcelain, glassware, brass and silver, baskets, silk flowers, candles, cards and stationery, table linens, and towels. It is outfitted for the holidays with an array of Christmas ornaments, gifts, and hostess items. Open daily except Sunday. Located on the corner of Main and Savannah Streets. 706-782-4253.

Other Places to Visit, Things to Do

The **Rabun County Welcome Center** is in an attractive, rustic cabin on Highway 441. As an official Georgia welcome center, it's filled to the brim with free maps and printed material about the state in general and the mountain region in particular. The staffers will greet you with a smile and answer your questions with authority. Open Monday-Friday, 9 a.m.-5 p.m.; Saturdays in October, 12-5 p.m. Located on the right just north of the intersection with U.S. 76 West. P. O. Box 761, Clayton, Ga 30525; 706-782-4812.

U. S. Forest Service, Tallulah District Office, has excellent maps—most are free, some have a nominal charge—of the Chattooga River, hiking trails, and camping and recreation areas in the Chattahoochee National Forest. They can also give you information on hunting and fishing, which are allowed in the National Forest and state wildlife management areas.

Rabun County Welcome Center

The office is located in the green building on the corner of Chechero and East Savannah Streets, one block west of Highway 441. P. O. Box 438, Clayton, Ga 30525; 706-782-3320.

"Tut's" Hang Glider Heaven is the enterprise of Frances "Tut" Woodruff. Although from Atlanta, Tut adopted Rabun County as her home decades ago. A woman with bountiful energy and entrepreneurial spirit, she has been gradually expanding this mountain property. What began as a site for semiannual hang-gliding competitions has been enhanced with the addition of completely furnished rental log cabins, hiking trails and a game preserve with llamas, bears, deer, and more. Plans are even underway to construct a hang-gliding flight simulator.

The three-day hang-gliding competitions themselves are open to spectators (moderate fee) and organized like outdoor festivals, with lots of entertainment, live music, food, and family fun. Call for their schedule and spend a day watching the fliers sail their colorful "kites," as they're called, from the top of the mountain down into the center of the park. The kites marked "Tut's Fliers" belong to the team Ms. Woodruff sponsors in competitions all over the world. She herself made the *Guinness Book of World Records* as the oldest solo hang glider, but these days only flies in tandem (two people per kite).

Get to Hang Glider Heaven by turning east (left if driving south) off Highway 441 on Seed Tick Road (two miles south of Clayton), then follow the signs. Stop first for information at the log cabin office on the corner of Seed Tick Road and Highway 441. P. O. Box 1470, Clayton, Ga 30525; 706-782-9908 or 6218.

Annual Events

Staying in Clayton can put you within reach of any fairs or festivals in the region. Clayton itself has a topical fair each March, and a Christmas parade each December. Check with the Chamber of Commerce for dates and locations. P. O. Box 761, Clayton, Ga 30525; 706-782-4812.

The **Conservation Fair,** held on a Saturday in March, is an educational event that tries to increase public awareness of the environment and the need for careful use of limited natural resources. More than 30 different organizations and clubs–such as the Friends of the Mountains, National Forest Service, Trout Unlimited, Rabun Beautiful–set up exhibits on everything from the preservation of trout streams to solar energy and recycling.

Special emphasis is given to educating children about the importance of conservation, and a contest is held to see who has brought the best "Litter Critter" created from roadside litter. Musicians and storytellers provide entertainment throughout the day. This is an educational and fun family afternoon for which there's no admission. (Usually held in the banquet room of the Chik'n Coop restaurant, South Main Street.)

The **Christmas Parade** in downtown Clayton is a small but earnest event with floats, music, entertainment. Each year has a different theme, and various prizes are awarded to the floats that best carry it out. Some 5,000 people turn out for this popular local event, which is usually held the first Saturday in December.

The "Wild and Scenic" Chattooga River

One of the last free-flowing streams in the Southeast, the Chattooga River serves as a natural border between Rabun County, Georgia, and South Carolina. An act of Congress in 1974 proclaimed the Chattooga "Wild and Scenic," preserving this river and a quarter-mile corridor along both sides so that its primitive beauty can be enjoyed by present and future generations.

Headwaters of the Chattooga are actually in the mountains of North Carolina. From there it flows southward some 50 miles to end in placid Lake Tugaloo, dropping nearly one-half mile in elevation along the way. And along that way are rapids—from Class 1 (very easy) to Class 6 (extraordinarily difficult). Sections I and II, where tubing is permitted, are for beginners—and for those who would rather not tangle with the more turbulent waters. Sections III and IV contain the most exciting rapids, and only experienced boaters should travel there independently.

In addition to its reputation among white-water boaters, the Chattooga River is also known as the location for the filming of the movie *Deliverance*. If you take a rafting trip with any of the outfitters, chances are you'll hear tales of the production company's experiences on Chattooga, and if you travel Section IV, you might even recognize where some of the scenes were filmed.

Three professional rafting companies are licensed by the U.S. Forest Service to conduct excursions on the river. Their guides are highly skilled and know every bend and every rock and every rapid in the river. They also know how to prepare you for the trip, and will accompany you along the way. Regular trips start in the $30/person range (group rate) for weekdays, and vary by Section. Multi-day river trips cost the most, and weekday mini-trips the least. If you're interested in a guided trip, be sure and call ahead for reservations; these folks stay booked.

Southeastern Expeditions – U.S. 76, east of Clayton. 1-800-868-RAFT

Wildwater Ltd. – U.S. 76, east of Clayton. 1-800-451-9972;
        in SC: 803-647-9587.

Nantahala Outdoor Center – Bryson City, NC; 704-488-6900.

There's lots of beautiful scenery: the cascading waterfall just off the river where Long Creek joins the Chattooga with a flourish (Section IV), thick stands of mountain laurel and rhododendron, sheer rock cliffs, and gigantic river-worn boulders. Wildlife is frequently sighted, and includes deer and hawks. If you venture down Section IV, where *Deliverance* was filmed, you'll get to see Deliverance Rock, so named for the boat load of expensive cameras and equipment it claimed during production.

If you haven't the inclination to go white-water rafting, there's a nice, safe, dry vantage spot on the river you can visit. Drive about 15 minutes out of Clayton on Highway 76 East until you come to the bridge and the South Carolina border. Just past it on the left, you'll see the entrance to a paved parking lot and rest station. Park there, then follow the marked, paved trail down the (steep) bank to Bull Sluice, which is a Class 5 rapid. Afternoons you can witness the progress of rafting expeditions, in which as many as six, six-person rafts participate.

Wildlife Management and Scenic Areas

The Forest Service, in cooperation with the state, manages three wildlife refuges in Rabun County. The **Lake Burton Wildlife Management Area** is near the northwestern shore of that lake, but at present it has no features for public use.

The **Coleman River Wildlife Management Area,** a little further northeast of there, was developed in honor of "Ranger Nick," the area's first forest ranger (Roscoe Nicholson). This is in the vicinity of Tate City, one of the county's oldest settlements, and it is also the location of the Tallulah River's headwaters. A Scenic Area is tucked between Tate Branch and the Coleman River, and offers camping, fishing, and hiking. Hikers here encounter large, old-growth timber, and enjoy the picturesque Coleman River, which tumbles through high boulders. The Tate Branch and Tallulah River provide good trout fishing, and campers can revel in the remote mountain scenery. To get there, take U.S. 76 west from Clayton for 8 miles. Turn right (north) on the paved county road (by the Persimmon Fire Department) and continue for 4 miles, then turn left on F.S. 70 and drive 1.25 miles.

The **Warwoman Wildlife Management Area,** less than five minutes drive east of Clayton, has centuries worth of history. Its name derives from the legend of the Cherokee Warwoman, an elder prophetess who came to the area each spring to foretell the tribe's future. Local legend has it that when the Cherokees were being forcibly removed in the 1830s, the Warwoman buried her divining crystals somewhere in the forest, to keep them safe.

Earlier, Quaker naturalist William Bartram had traversed this area on his 1776 journey through the mountains. His diaries document waterfalls and plant life still present today. They are visible along the nationally known, 37-mile **Bartram Trail,** established in 1978, which passes through what is now the **Warwoman Dell Recreation Area.**

In the next century, cuts and grades (still visible today) were completed through the Dell to accommodate the ill-fated Blue Ridge or Black Diamond Railroad, which was abandoned due to the Civil War.

More recently, the area has been a popular picnic spot. In the 1930s, the Civilian Conservation Corps (CCC) built massive log picnic shelters in the dell. The Forest Service renovated this historic picnic area in 1988, thanks to private contributions and a federal grant. Today you can walk beneath ancient hemlocks and admire some 150 botanical species that thrive in the cool, moist dell. There are picnic shelters, tables, benches, and grated fireplaces, plus nature trails and informative markers. No camping is allowed.

To visit the dell, drive about 3 miles east of Clayton on Warwoman Road and look for the sign on the right. Turn in and park, or if the gate is closed, park on the road and walk down into the dell. Across the highway on the left you can pick up the Bartram Trail, or hike back in to see Becky Branch Falls (see "Waterfalls" further on).

Hiking Trails

Several organizations sponsor seasonal wildflower walks, and you can contact the Chamber of Commerce (706-782-4812) for a schedule. Most of these walks are free of charge, along easy-to-moderate trails, and require only that you bring your own lunch. Register for one at the Hambidge Center west of Dillard. The nominal fee includes a complimentary lunch.

In addition, there are more than 65 miles of National Forest trails just within the Tallulah Ranger District, headquartered in Clayton. And that's not including the 79 miles of Appalachian Trail, or those in state or private parks.

You can obtain an excellent, free booklet with maps, *Trail Guide to the Chattahoochee-Oconee National Forests*, at the USFS Ranger Station on Chechero Street. Some of the trails it includes that are near Clayton are:

Appalachian Trail. 79 miles in Georgia, 9 along western border of Rabun County; U.S. 76 West 16.5 miles to Dicks Creek Gap parking lot.

Bartram Trail. 37 miles; loops from North Carolina line across Rabun Bald to Chattooga River; across from Warwoman Dell, 3 miles east on Warwoman Road, or 11.2 miles on Warwoman to Ga 28, then east 2.2 miles to signs at Chattooga River.

Chattooga River Trail. 10.7 miles; U.S. 76 East 9 miles, at Chattooga River.

Coleman River Trail. 1 mile; begins at Coleman River Bridge; U.S. 76 West 8 miles, right on Persimmon Road for 4 miles, left on F.S. 70 for 1 mile, park on right just before bridge.

Holcomb Creek Trail. 1.3 miles; loops around Hale Ridge Road; Warwoman Road east 10 miles, left on F.S. 7 (Hale Ridge Road) for 9 miles.

Minnehaha Trail. 0.4 miles; leads to Minnehaha Falls near Rabun Beach Area; Lake Rabun Road.

Oakey Mountain ORV Trail. 6.2 miles; near Lakes Burton and Rabun; U.S. 76 West 6.8 miles, left on Charlie Mountain Road to dead end, right on Bridge Creek Road 2 miles to deadend, right for 1.6 miles to entrance on left.

Rabun Beach Trail. 1.3 miles; leads to Angel Falls, near Rabun Beach camping area; Lake Rabun Road.

Raven Rock Trail. 0.8 mile, west bank of Chattooga to Raven Rock Cliff; Highway 441 South 8 miles, left on Camp Creek Road 1.4 miles, left on F.S. 511 for 2.6 miles, left on F.S. 511-B (F.S. 511-B recommended for four-wheel drive vehicles only).

Sutton Hole Trail. 0.3 mile; west bank of Chattooga River; U.S. 76 East 7 miles, right on F.S. 290 for 0.3 miles, left on F.S. 290-A to deadend (F.S. 290-A recommended for four-wheel drive vehicles only).

Three Forks Trail. 9.5 miles; from summit of Rabun Bald to Chattooga River; Warwoman Road east 16 miles, left on F.S. 86 for 4 miles to John Teague Gap.

Warwoman Dell Nature Trail. 0.4 mile; Warwoman Dell Recreation Area; Warwoman Road east 3 miles.

Before you set out to hike, it is wise to leave information of your general plans with someone. Experienced hikers recommend that you: carry drinking water; have rain gear with you (this area has one of the highest annual rainfalls in the U.S.); carry a trail map; and wear comfortable walking shoes.

Waterfalls

There are numerous waterfalls in the north Georgia mountains. Several of these are in the Clayton area, and you will find maps and additional directions for finding them at the Welcome Center. (Other Rabun County falls are described in chapters corresponding to their location.)

Angel Falls. 50 feet high, second falls 0.5 mile upstream; Rabun Beach Recreation Area, Lake Rabun Road.

Becky Branch Falls. 25 feet high; across from Warwoman Dell Recreation Area; Warwoman Road east 3 miles to trail on left.

Dick's Creek Falls. 60 feet high; where Bartram Trail crosses Dick's Creek Road at the Chattooga River; Warwoman Road east 6 miles, right on Dick's Creek Road (recommended for four-wheel drive vehicles in bad weather) 4.4 miles to Bartram Trail crossing, park and walk 200 yards north along trail.

Holcomb Creek Falls/Ammons Creek Falls. Two falls, with observation deck at Ammons Falls; Warwoman Road east 10 miles, left on Hale Ridge Road (F.S. 7) for 9 miles to trail at intersection with Overflow Road.

Martin Creek Falls. A series of 3 falls along Martin Creek in Warwoman Wildlife Management Area; Warwoman Road east 3.5 miles, left on F.S. 152 for 0.5 mile, hike up west side of creek.

Minnehaha Falls. 50 feet high; below Seed Lake Dam on upper end of Lake Rabun.

Panther Creek Falls. 65 feet high, in Panther Creek Recreation Area; Highway 441 3 miles south of Tallulah Falls.

Tallulah Falls. Three falls (16 to 96 feet high) remain in Tallulah Gorge, a fourth is visible during winter or heavy rainfalls; Highway 441 in Tallulah Falls.

Please exercise caution when visiting any waterfall. As beautiful as they are, the rushing water and wet, lichen-covered rocks are treacherous, and people have suffered injuries–and fatal falls–trying to get just one step closer.

Horseback Riding and Stables

In addition to the horseback riding and stabling opportunities at the stables in Dillard and Wiley, you can enjoy a Georgia mountains vacation with your own horse. The **Willis Knob Horse Trail and Camp,** which was constructed in part by local volunteers, is a Forest Service facility located near the Chattooga River, east of Clayton. The 15-mile loop trail adjoins the Rocky Gap Horse Trail in South Carolina to make 27.5 miles of some of the most scenic horseback-riding trails to be found in the Southern Blue Ridge. Winding through mountains separated by deep valleys, the trail passes through several types of forest environments, providing gorgeous views as it descends into the Chattooga River corridor. Two fords permit riders to cross the river from one state to the other.

The camp has eight campsites. Part or all of the camp can be reserved, but only one group can occupy the facility at a time. There are toilet facilities, a campfire area, two ten-horse stalls (with a spring-fed watering trough), cooking grills, picnic tables and lantern posts. To get to Willis Knob, go east from Clayton on Warwoman Road for 12 miles. Turn right on Goldmine Road (F.S. 157). Continue past Woodall Ridge Day Use Parking Area; camp is 2 miles further on the left. For more information and reservations, contact the Tallulah Ranger District Office: P. O. Box 438, Clayton, Ga 30525; 706-782-3320.

For privately owned, overnight stabling just west of Clayton in the beautiful Persimmon Community area, contact the **Chattahoochee Horse Motel,** Route 2, Box 2357, Clayton, Ga 30525; 706-782-4385, or **Persimmon Valley Farm,** Route 2, Box 2333-H, Clayton, Ga 30525; 706-782-5469.

Restaurants and Other Places to Eat

Clayton's restaurants can accommodate just about any taste and any budget–whether you're in the mood for something light to eat on-the-run, or want to relax over a candlelit meal with a glass of wine. In addition to the places we mention here, there are also several fast-food chains and small, locally run eateries.

Mixed drinks are not served in Rabun County, but some establishments
have beer and wine licenses. We suggest you call ahead and inquire.

The majority of restaurants here do not take reservations; we've indicated
those that do. The busiest time of year is October–leaf season–and then
our best advice is either plan to eat a little earlier, or make a reservation.

Baker's Dozen Bakery is a family-run bakery that offers an array of cookies, cakes (like Hershey-Bar Pound Cake!) and pies, plus breads, dough-
nuts and pastries. Freshly brewed coffee and some tables and chairs make
it easy to enjoy a quick breakfast right there. They're open 6 a.m. to
6 p.m., Monday through Saturday. Located in Depot Center, Highway
441 South. 706-782-5215.

Betty's Hungry House Cafe #3 serves three meals a day of "Home
Cooking at Its Best." Their extensive breakfast menu includes country
ham, sausage, bacon, eggs, pancakes, grits, biscuits and gravy, and more, in
combination plates or as side orders. Sandwiches include burgers, barbecue, clubs, BLTs, and more. They have a soup and salad bar, and a daily
special with meat, two vegetables, bread, coffee/tea. Dinner includes
entrées of chicken, pork, fish and beef. Inexpensive. Take out available.
Open 6 a.m.-8:30 p.m. daily. Located in Depot Center, Highway 441
South, across from the Chik'n Coop restaurant. 706-782-9900.

Burrell's Junction features an array of modestly priced lunch and dinner
items such as steaks, prime rib, seafood, trout, and chicken. They also
have soups, salads, a salad bar, sandwiches, burgers and desserts. Daily
lunch specials. Beer and wine are served. There are pictures on the walls
commemorating Clayton's Tallulah Falls Railroad days. A gift shop adjacent to the dining room sells crafts and gift items handmade locally, books
by regional authors, and a selection of homemade jams, jellies, and condiments. Hours are 11 a.m.-2:30 p.m. and 5-8:30 p.m.; closed Sunday after
2:30 p.m. and all day Wednesday. Located on Highway 441 South, in the
Village Shopping Center. 706-782-2828.

Clayton Cafe has the exterior look of a 1950s cafe, but the interior was
updated in 1990. The inexpensively priced fare includes homemade soups,
cakes and pies, sandwiches, and burgers. Daily specials offer choice of
meat, three vegetables, dessert, and coffee or tea; dinners include potatoes, salad, and bread. Open 6:30 a.m. to 11 p.m., Monday through

Saturday (open Sundays, April through October). Located on North Main Street. 706-782-5438.

Chik'n Coop Restaurant has the most varied menu in town–from hearty to light (dine in or carry out). Although they're known for their chicken, you'll find beef, pork, and seafood as well, all reasonably priced. A soup and salad bar with more than 40 selections is available lunch and dinner, as are menu items such as appetizers, sandwiches, entrées–and their special corn fritters. They add a hot buffet with choice of meat and several vegetables during lunch. Their Friday night special is an Italian buffet. On Sunday, owners Pat and Judy Marcellino open the spacious banquet room from 11 a.m. to 2:30 p.m. for an extensive–yet inexpensive–hot and cold buffet featuring several meats, numerous vegetables, and a salad bar. Open 11 a.m. to 8:30 p.m., Wednesday through Saturday, and for lunch on Sunday. (Catering available.) You can't miss the restaurant on the west side of Highway 441 South, adjacent to the Village Shopping Center. 706-782-3437.

Green Shutters Restaurant began life as a produce stand in 1934, and sold apples and cider from an orchard on the hill behind the house. In those days, the highway in front of it was the main route between Tennessee and Florida, and the produce stand quickly expanded into a restaurant for hungry travelers. Mrs. Maude Fisher, Rabun County's first Home Demonstration Agent, cooked the meals on a wood stove. Her techniques were handed down to the present owner, Steve Mazarky, which is why the restaurant's motto is "The home of wood stove cookery in North Georgia."

The quaint, two-story wood and stone building clings to the side of the road. The top floor–at street level–houses a gift shop, the bottom, the restaurant. In the gift shop is an array of decorative accessories and gift items, and the restaurant's own homemade pickles, relishes, jellies, and other specialty foods.

Downstairs in the restaurant are two rooms. One is fully enclosed and has a fireplace, which is used in fall. The other is a covered, screened "porch." Breakfast, lunch, and dinner are served "family style," meaning bowls and platters of food are placed on your table, and refilled, if you like, when empty. For breakfast, expect country ham, bacon, sausage, scrambled eggs, hot biscuits, their own special cinnamon biscuits, and homemade jelly.

Lunch and dinner feature meats such as fried chicken and country ham, four or five in-season vegetables, hot biscuits and cornbread and fresh fruit cobbler. Friday night's special is barbecued ribs; Saturday night's is southern fried quail. This place is popular, so we encourage you to make reservations on weekends, especially in October. Parking is very limited; if you're coming as a group, we suggest a car pool.

Open weekends in April, daily except Tuesday, May through October. Hours are 8-10 a.m.; 11 a.m.-2 p.m.; 5-9 p.m. Located about a mile south of Clayton on Old 441, before you get to Tiger. 706-782-3342.

Julia's Southern Nights Restaurant is open for lunch and dinner 11 a.m.-2 p.m. and 5-10 p.m. "Fine Dining" is their motto, and they feature steaks, fresh fish and seafood, and chicken. Entrées come with choice of potato or rice, salad and vegetable. A basket of warm miniature bagels and cream cheese is brought to each table. There are inexpensive daily specials, plus an Early Bird Special between 5 and 7 p.m. Beer and wine are available. Prices are mostly moderate. Located a half-mile south of town on Highway 441. 706-782-2052.

Lynn's Buffet (at Henry's Restaurant)–open only for lunch–offers plentiful down home cookin' in a casual atmosphere. The buffet consists of choice of meat, nine vegetables, salad bar, dessert, coffee or tea. Sandwiches on the menu include generously sized "Henry Burgers." All breads and desserts are homemade. There's a big buffet for Sunday lunch. This has been a popular place with the locals ever since Lynn Watts' daddy opened it 20 years ago. Open 11 a.m.-2 p.m.; closed Saturdays. Inexpensive. Located in Henry's Restaurant, a mile south of town on Highway 441. 706-782-3533.

Main Street Soda Shop, inside Clayton Drug Store, is an early '60s-style soda fountain/luncheon counter. You can buy magazines, paperback books, toiletries and sundries, have a prescription filled, then take a seat on a vinyl-padded stool to have a sandwich or an ice cream soda. Daily sandwich specials include chips, medium drink or iced tea; there is also a diet salad plate. Takeout available. Inexpensive. Closed Sunday. Located on the corner of Main and Savannah Streets. 706-782-3211.

Stonebrook Restaurant serves lunch and dinner daily. The lunch menu includes sandwiches, daily specials with potato and salad, and a hot buffet with two meats, vegetables, dessert and salad bar. For dinner there are appetizers, soup, salad bar, entrées of beef, seafood, chicken, and fish, and homemade cake and pie. Moderately priced. Wine list available. Open 7 a.m. to 9 p.m. in season; 11 a.m. to 9 p.m. during winter. Located next to the Stonebrook Inn on Highway 441 South. 706-782-2214.

The **Stockton House Restaurant** offers a varied menu in a cheerful, bright atmosphere and is one of the few restaurants in the region to pamper the diner with linen tablecloths and napkins, fresh flowers and a wine list. Large front windows provide a charming view of Screamer Mountain and a rolling pasture dotted with cattle. They serve a hot, all-you-can-eat buffet at lunch (choice of one meat, three vegetables, bread and dessert), or you can order soup, salads, sandwiches and omelettes from the menu. Dinner is from the menu, which includes steaks, prime rib, chicken, pork chops, fish and seafood, and some pasta dishes. All prices are very moderate. This 1950s-style brick home was converted into a restaurant in 1986, and has ample parking with handicapped access in the rear. Open daily, year-round, for lunch (11 a.m.-2 p.m.) and dinner (5-9 p.m.); Sunday buffet lunch. Located 1 mile east of Clayton on Warwoman Road. Reservations encouraged during season. 706-782-6175.

Lodging

In and around Clayton are a number of bed-and-breakfast inns, cabins, cottages, chalets, lodges, and motels.

Most of the time, lodging can be booked a week or less in advance. There is one time of year, however, when overnight accommodations here—and throughout the mountains—are nearly impossible to obtain on short notice. This is during the "leaf season" in October. Do book your October stay well in advance; two months ahead is none too early. Here is a list of the better-known accommodations.

English Manor Inns, a bed-and-breakfast operation just 1.2 miles east of Clayton on Highway 76, is the largest privately owned "cluster inn" east of the Mississippi. Here are six free-standing "Inns" on a 7.2-acre secluded garden park developed and operated by English and Susan Thornwell. All the rooms have private baths, many have fireplaces, and there are five lavishly decorated suites. Several suites have their own whirlpool tubs, or you can rent the large in-ground hot tub secluded in its own building (by the hour). From the common rooms to the bedrooms, you are surrounded by antiques, many of which are Thornwell heirlooms. Despite the size of English Manor (120 capacity), and the "old money" or traditional English decor, this is a warm and friendly establishment designed to be intimate and romantic. (All rooms have coffee makers and TVs; telephones are in each inn, but not each room.)

Breakfast is served in the main building between 8:30 and 11 a.m. Through the week it consists of homemade granola, fresh fruit, homemade cakes, hot spiced applesauce with apricots, breads, juices, coffee and tea. On weekends it expands into brunch where you might savor cheese soufflés, creamed chicken and puff pastry, homemade roast beef hash, and potato pancakes and applesauce in addition to the usual juices, fruit, breads, coffee and tea.

Unique to this Inn are their Mystery Weekends, where guests can play characters and participate in the investigation of "Sir English's murder." For these, full gourmet meals are provided. Rates are lowest between January and Memorial Day. Well-behaved pets accepted. P. O. Box 1605, Clayton, Ga 30525; 1-800-782-5780 or 706-782-5789.

A Small Motel & Lodge is a cheerful Mom & Pop-type six-unit motel with fireplaces, cable TV, air-conditioning, and a four-bedroom lodge (house) with kitchen and fireplace. Hosts Hank and Mad Dearborn provide you with free coffee. Inexpensive. Well-behaved pets accepted. Located on Highway 76 East, just off Highway 441. Route 3, Box 3025-D, Clayton, Ga 30525; 1-800-786-0624 or 706-782-6488.

Blue Ridge Motel has cottages, motel rooms and efficiencies with fully furnished kitchenettes. Features include daily maid service, cable TV, heat/air-conditioning, and a private picnic area with a barbecue pit. This spruced-up, family-run business is just outside the center of Clayton, and its rustic, wooded setting keeps it quiet and private. Reasonable rates; open year-round. Only 1/2 mile north of Clayton on North Main Street. Route 1, Box 3399, Clayton, Ga 30525; 706-782-7315.

Commodore's Motor Inn on Highway 441 South, has telephones, cable TV with free HBO, heat and air-conditioning and king-size beds in each of its units. Highway 441 S, Clayton, Ga 30525; 706-782-4269.

Heart of Rabun Inn has 65 rooms with cable TV, individual heat and air-conditioning, and a swimming pool. Highway 441, Clayton, Ga 30525; 706-782-4258.

Kathwood Inn (formerly Old Clayton Inn) is one of the oldest inns in the area, and the only one in downtown Clayton. The two-story building with an old-fashioned rocking-chair porch was completely renovated in 1989. It has 52 rooms and 5 suites, and is open year-round with moderate, seasonal rates. P. O. Box 1557, Clayton, Ga 30525; 706-782-4207.

Stonebrook Inn is set back off the highway on a grassy knoll, has a heated swimming pool in the front yard, and is surrounded by a well-maintained and landscaped yard. This is the newest lodging in Clayton, and owner Warren Beck has taken every measure to ensure that it has the appointments and hospitality of an inn rather than the impersonal feeling of a "motel." The 48 luxurious rooms have king- or queen-size beds, cable TV, free HBO. Handicapped and nonsmoking rooms are available, as is a complimentary Continental breakfast. Moderate, seasonal rates.

The **Stonebrook Restaurant** next door, which we've described elsewhere, serves three meals May through October, and lunch and dinner, November through April. Located on Route 441 South. P. O. Box 341, Clayton, Ga 30525; 706-782-2214.

Tut's Cabins, are located at Hang Glider Heaven, which we described earlier in this chapter. These new, completely furnished log cabins have one, two, three, and four bedrooms with private baths and wood stoves. They are available by the night, weekend, week, or month, and the rates vary by cabin, season, and length of stay. Advance deposit required. Open year-round. Located 2 miles south of Clayton on Seed Tick Road. P. O. Box 1470, Clayton, Ga 30525; 706-782-9908 or -6218.

Mountain City and Rabun Gap

Just north of Clayton along Highway 441 are the incorporated cities of
Mountain City and Rabun Gap, which lie in the fertile Little Tennessee
River Valley. This is the location of the Eastern Continental (or Blue
Ridge) Divide, where waters drain either southward into the Savannah
River and on to the Atlantic–or northward into the Tennessee-Mississippi
Gulf system.

It was here, in this relatively level expanse, that some of the county's first
white settlers established homesteads in the early 1800s. As historian
Andrew Ritchie reveals in *Sketches of Rabun County History:*

> The great pioneer preacher, Bishop Asbury, who traveled
> through the mountains on horseback, said in his diary, 'These
> men are not back here in these mountain valleys seeking reli-
> gion, they are back here looking for good bottom land.

And, indeed, they found it. Even today, this is where most of the county's
agricultural activity occurs. Acres of cabbages–the primary cash crop–are
planted and harvested in the rich, black loam that stretches from
Mountain City through Dillard.

The valley and its ring of lush, wooded hills provide picturesque views
year-round, whether you stay on Highway 441 or venture off on side roads.
Most of the commercial attractions are clustered along the main route.

Just west of Highway 441 lies a beautiful, self-contained valley within a
valley: Wolffork. This area was originally named "Wolf Fork," after the
pioneer practice of catching marauding wolves by placing a trap under a
fork in a tree from which a piece of meat was hung. And in the mountains
ringing that valley on the north is the creek, Keener's Creek, that gives
rise to the Little Tennessee River.

Albert and Carson Beaver visited Wolffork Valley one spring, and guided by Adam Keener, great-grandson of the valley's pioneer settler Abraham Keener, they traced the origination of the Little Tennessee River for their book *Valley So Wild, a Folk History* (East Tennessee Historical Society):

> More little tributaries darted like Cherokee children out of laurel and rhododendron thickets to rock-hop down to the main stream [Keener Creek], now no more than four feet wide ... The creek wound on up into the narrow hollow to collect the cold clear product of the last spring up the mountain, the first spring of the Little Tennessee.
>
> Back down in the meadow where Adam Keener had pointed, it was 100 yards through foot-high orchard grass and over a barbed wire fence to the joining of Billy's Creek and Keener Creek. Six feet downstream Little Garland Branch is the first stream to enter the river, and but for those six feet it would be a three-way confluence.

Mountain City and Rabun Gap also have a state park, interesting shops, a historic bed-and-breakfast inn, a water-powered gristmill and the internationally known Foxfire program.

Black Rock Mountain State Park

At an elevation of 3,640 feet, this is the highest state park in Georgia. Sheer granite cliffs, for which it is named, look down on Clayton like silent sentinels. From the visitor's center erected beside them you can enjoy the panorama that sweeps south of Rabun County and east into South Carolina. Other overlooks in the 1,502-acre state park (and on Black Rock Road leading to the park) provide jaw-dropping mountaintop views of the southern Appalachians and even the Great Smoky Mountains. On clear days, visibility can reach 80 miles.

Originally, the park land was privately owned, but back in the 1930s it was donated to the state. Governor Herman Talmadge dedicated it as a state park in 1952, and in the years since then, Black Rock has been a popular stop for tourists and residents alike.

Park facilities include 10 year-round rental cottages (5 have fireplaces, 5 wood stoves, all are air-conditioned), 53 tent and trailer sites with full hook-ups, 11 walk-in campsites, a 10-mile trail system, a 17-acre lake (fishing only), 2 picnic shelters and a playground.

The visitor's center (on Black Rock Road on the way to the cabins and campgrounds) features interesting exhibits including a stuffed, 320-pound black bear and several other wild animals, and a small but growing display about mountain heritage. They also sell books about the area and have a rack of free brochures describ-

Overlook of Black Rock Creek State Park

ing other interesting places in the region. You may also like to inquire about their interpretive nature programs, scheduled during spring and fall, which are open to the public. The center is open 8 a.m. to 5 p.m. daily.

To get to Black Rock State Park, drive 3 miles north of Clayton on Highway 441 into Mountain City, and turn left on Black Rock Road at the state park sign. Follow signs to the visitor's center all the way at the top. The park is open from 7 a.m. to 10 p.m. daily. Black Rock State Park, Mountain City, Ga 30562; 706-746-2141.

Foxfire:
A Mountain-Grown Success Story

For most people, the name Foxfire is associated with the series of best-selling books about southern Appalachia that were published by Double-day. How these books came into being and what they developed into is a story in itself.

What began as one young English teacher's attempt to create a meaningful classroom experience for some bored ninth- and tenth-graders has
evolved over the years into an approach to instruction that is currently
being applied in hundreds of American classrooms–in every subject,
grades Kindergarten through 12. This is how it started.

In 1966, Eliot Wigginton, or "Wig," as his students call him, came to
the mountains from his college training in the north, prepared (or so he
thought) to teach ninth- and tenth-grade English at the Rabun Gap–
Nacoochee School. His first weeks were a disaster. Most of his students
didn't want to read or write; some barely could. Boredom and hostility
prevailed.

Realizing that the traditional method of teaching English was just not
going to work, Wigginton drew the students into a discussion, over several
periods, about what made learning enjoyable and how learning was
retained. Out of this came the idea of creating and producing a magazine.
The students hadn't the faintest notion about how to write one, let alone
put one together, but Wigginton assured them they could and would learn.

Initially they thought to create a literary magazine, printing artwork and
prose and poetry from literary figures along with contributions from the
students. For additional material, they decided to write about some of the
"old ways" of their elders. To do this, they learned how to use a tape
recorder and Wig's 35-mm camera, and began to interview the older members of the community–often their own grandparents. The stories they
documented in words and photographs included planting crops by the
phases of the moon or signs of the zodiac; home remedies; superstitions
and ghost stories; signs by which the weather was predicted; how moon-
shine was made; slaughtering, curing, and smoking hogs; dressing and
cooking wild game; soap making; cabin building and chimney building.
The students transcribed the tapes, developed the photographs, and wrote
articles about the stories.

That was the end of Wigginton's teaching problems ... and the beginning
of Foxfire magazine. The fledgling publication, named after a lichen that
grows on decaying organic matter in damp, dark mountain coves and
glows in the dark, was issued quarterly and, within a year, had attracted
considerable attention. The students gradually phased out the idea of publishing a literary journal in order to focus on the wonderful wealth of
material they could glean from talking with kinfolk.

As *Foxfire* magazine gained a following, it soon came to the attention of editors at Doubleday publishing company, who negotiated with Wigginton and his high schoolers to publish a collection of the articles, *The Foxfire Book*, in 1972. Its meteoric rise as a best-seller led to the publication of another volume, then another, and another until the series culminated in ten volumes–plus the anniversary book *Foxfire: 25 Years*–selling more than seven million copies and remaining, to this day, the most popular series in the history of Doubleday.

Offshoots of the books' popularity include the acclaimed play which ran on Broadway in 1982, and the Emmy-winning, 1987 Hallmark Hall of Fame television movie–both of which starred Jessica Tandy and Hume Cronyn.

The "Foxfire approach" is based on the principle that students learn more efficiently when they have a genuine voice in planning what happens in their classrooms, when they produce a product that will be valued by a real audience outside the classroom, and when the state-mandated academic agenda is engaged in a meaningful way, not just through teacher-initiated coverage of the material. In this way, the project chosen by the students–for example, the publication of *Foxfire* magazine–becomes the delivery system for the classroom knowledge. Locally, the Foxfire approach is used in several language arts, music, and

Foxfire Museum

radio/video classes at Rabun County High School, as well as in elementary school classes throughout the county.

Elsewhere in Georgia and across the United States, colleges and universities sponsor graduate-level Foxfire courses for teachers. Hundreds of Foxfire-trained teachers are currently working with thousands of students–and helping to test and refine the pedagogy.

You can learn more about this remarkable effort by visiting Foxfire's **Museum of Appalachian Artifacts** and the Foxfire Fund offices, on Highway 441. This is the first driveway south of Black Rock Road (on the left if driving north), diagonally across from Log Cabin Crafts.

The museum–of which eighty percent was conceived and built by students–is housed in a half-dovetail, notched log structure behind the office buildings (free admission, but donations gratefully accepted). Here you will find nearly 200 items that symbolize mountain culture: tools for hunting, trapping, farming, cabin making, blacksmithing; a handcrafted wagon; household and housekeeping items such as a spinning wheel and reeler, gourd dipper, handwoven baskets, brooms; and even some furniture. The gear-and-stone assembly from a mid-19th-century gristmill are on display as well. Each item is either an Appalachian original that was written about in the *Foxfire* magazines or books, or else it was made by an Appalachian craftsperson during a teaching demonstration for Foxfire students.

In the adjacent sales office, you can pick up free brochures about Foxfire, purchase any of the student products such as the books, cassette tapes and so forth, and sign up for a subscription to *Foxfire* magazine, which is still produced quarterly by Rabun County High School's Foxfire students. The museum and sales office is open Monday through Friday, 9 a.m. to 4 p.m., Saturdays 10 a.m. to 4 p.m. during tourist season. Mailing address: Foxfire Fund, Inc., P. O. Box B, Rabun Gap, Ga 30568; 706-746-5828.

Shopping and Browsing

Some excellent craft and antique shops, a weaver's studio and a specialty foods shop/garden are located in Mountain City and Rabun Gap. Here they are.

Blue Ridge Home Crafts, Inc. If you enjoy creating crafts, this shop may have the supplies you need. They stock supplies for macrame, cross-stitch and needlepoint, chair bottoming and basket weaving, as well as a full line of yarn and a large selection of instruction books. Ask about their craft classes. They're open year-round, Monday through Saturday, 8 a.m.-4:30 p.m., and are located just north of the Fina station on Highway 441 in Mountain City. P. O. Drawer L, Mountain City, Ga 30562; 706-746-6924.

Co-op Craft Store. This shop is the newest of the three retail outlets for the Georgia Mountain Arts Products, a large craft cooperative formed in 1969. Like its sister shops in Tallulah Falls and Clarkesville, it is filled to the rafters with reasonably priced, authentic mountain crafts such as quilts, toys, wood crafts, softsculpture, pottery, fiber arts, jewelry, and so on. Many of the craftspeople represented in this co-op have been featured in the Foxfire magazine and books.

You can visit the shop year-round, Monday through Saturday 10 a.m. to 5 p.m., and Sunday 12:30 to 5 p.m. It is located in a log cabin on Highway 441, across from Rabun Gap–Nacoochee School. Mail orders accommodated; P. O. Box 305, Rabun Gap, Ga 30568; 706-746-5990.

Log Cabin Crafts. This little log cabin houses a carefully chosen selection of handcrafted gifts and collectibles. The works are by some 30 regional artists, and all media are represented, from glass and wood to fiber and pottery. Owners Hilda and Bill McCarter pride themselves in featuring several exclusive lines, such as the Original Hildie Doll, designed and made locally for their shop, and Country Scene pottery.

There are hundreds of effectively displayed items. The McCarters also carry locally made jams and jellies and other Georgia specialty foods. Two of the most popular ones are rosy peach jam (with a hint of banana) and apple cobbler jelly.

Log Cabin Crafts is open daily May through October, 10 a.m.-5 p.m.; Sundays 12:30-5 p.m. and weekends in April and November through Christmas. Mail-order is available year-round. The shop sits right on the edge of Highway 441 in Mountain City, across from Black Rock Road. P. O. Box 6, Mountain City, Ga 30562; 746-2991.

Mountain City Antiques & Collectibles. Here, in a tiny one-room, 1928 building, two families offer a wide range of items such as glassware, furniture, lamps, household items, dolls, pictures and books. Some are antiques, some collectibles, but all goods are carefully chosen by Betty and Cobb Williams and Pat and Dave Patch.

The shop is open 9 a.m.-5 p.m., daily except Friday, May through October. It is located on Highway 441 in Mountain City, on the left side of the road (if driving north) just north of Black Rock Road. Parking is between the shop and the Fina station next door. Mail: c/o Williams, P. O. Box 391, Clarkesville, Ga 30523.

Penny's Garden. Tucked back off the highway is a charming place where fragrant herbs are grown and then concocted into a variety of unique culinary delights that are pleasing to the taste, the scent, and even the sight: gourmet herbal vinegars, jellies, and jams in imaginative combinations such as Raspberry-Lemon Verbena. There are also live herb plants and scented geraniums, and sachets, potpourris, dried flower arrangements, and wreaths made from flowers grown in Penny's Garden. Carrying the Penny's Garden label, the culinary products are now becoming widely known and marketed throughout the Southeast and further.

Owners Penny and Don Melton also sell garden accessories and books to help you with your own projects back home. Inquire about their schedule of herbal and floral workshops and seminars.

Penny's Garden is open Monday through Saturday, 9 a.m. to 5 p.m. To find it, take Darling Springs Road (north of Log Cabin Crafts) from Highway 441 in Mountain City. This becomes Black's Creek Road. Continue for .6 mile; Penny's Garden will be on the left. Call or write for their free mail-order catalog. P. O. Box 305, Mountain City, Ga 30562; 706-746-6918 (garden) or 706-746-2298 (home).

Sylvan Falls Mill. Located out in Wolffork Valley, this mill is snuggled into a little hillside right next to the rushing waterfall that drives the wheel–a most picturesque site. Present owner/operator Dick Davis, who lives in the mill house, runs it nearly every day (closed Sundays), April through October, even though he's retired. You can buy little sacks of whole wheat flour and corn meal that have been ground right there. And, of course, you can photograph this vivid symbol of yesteryear.

Sylvan Falls Mill

A sign on the front of the building reads.

> The first grist mill was constructed on this site in 1840 of
> wormy chestnut and remained in use until the 1930s. The
> present mill wheel was installed in 1946 after being in use in
> Tennessee since 1930. The 27-foot overshot waterwheel was
> constructed in Hanover, Pennsylvania, and generates approxi-
> mately 25 H.P. The mill was remodeled into living quarters in
> 1978 with additional work being done in 1985. The beauty of
> the site is preserved for your and our enjoyment and we want
> you to feel welcome.

To get there, take Wolffork Valley Road (across from Don's service station
on Highway 441 just north of Mountain City). Drive about 2.25 miles,
then turn left on Taylor Chapel Road and continue about 500 yards. Both
roads are paved, and you will see signs for the mill at the intersections.
Route 1, Box 548, Rabun Gap, Ga 30568; 706-746-2806.

The Cover Up Handweaving Studio. Professional weaver Sharon Grist
creates fine handwoven gifts which are available through select local
shops as well as through her own mail-order catalog. Among her most
popular items are table runners, placemats and napkins, baby blankets,

and customized bed coverlets and afghans. Grist's work usually leans toward the traditional, but she also creates contemporary-looking wall hangings on commission. Several can be seen in local banks and meeting facilities.

Although her studio is not open to the public, she will take appointments for personal consultations during which you can commission her to weave a custom coverlet or special art piece for your home or office. Call or write to request a catalog or schedule an appointment. Route 1, Box 216, Rabun Gap, Ga 30568; 706-746-2231.

The Rocking Horse. This cute little white house with blue trim enjoys a new life as a craft shop. All of its rooms are filled with locally made, reasonably priced crafts: dolls, toys, wreaths, decorative accessories, and so forth. Owner Mary Williams is also the spark behind the annual festival, which we mention further on.

A large sign announces the store from the Highway 441 curb, but the building itself sits back a bit, so look closely. It's next to Jim's Service Center in Mountain City, on the right going north. P. O. Box B, Mountain City, Ga 30562; 706-746-6979.

Rabun Gap–Nacoochee School

You can't help but notice the school's impressive brick buildings and scenic, rolling campus on the left driving north on Highway 441. Although it isn't open to the public, it is a prominent landmark, and its history is worth relating.

Up until the turn of this century, formal education just wasn't available to mountain children. The rough terrain and absence of adequate roads, combined with the demands of obtaining food, clothing, and shelter, made organized "book learning" all but impossible. As historian Andrew Ritchie wrote:

> Although little groups of children were taught from three to five months in little log houses or weatherboarded shanties and in as many as 35 places, all public school property of the county was officially reported in 1900 at less than $5,000. There was no

railroad and no graded or paved highways. The census of 1900 showed that one-fifth of the voters could neither read nor write.

However, Andrew Ritchie and his wife–both descendents of some of the first white settlers of Rabun Gap–were determined to change all that. After much travail, they founded the Rabun Gap Industrial School in 1905.

Two years earlier, in 1903, a similar effort had been undertaken in Nacoochee Valley some 50 miles away. There, the Presbyterian Synod of Georgia had opened a public school called Nacoochee Institute. Like the farm school at Rabun Gap, poor boys and girls of the mountain region attended and were taught farming and homemaking skills along with the three R's.

Over the next two decades, each school developed in similar–but separate–ways. Then Fate intervened.

Within one month's time, fire had ravaged the buildings and swept through the campuses of both schools. It was then the two Boards of Trustees saw greater possibilities in union, and voted to merge the schools on the Rabun Gap site. Thus, in 1927 the Rabun Gap–Nacoochee School (RGNS) was born.

For many years, RGNS served as a private/public high school for students in the northern part of Rabun County, and it even enjoyed a ten-year stint doubling as a junior college. This is where, in 1966, Eliot Wigginton began his teaching career, and where he and his ninth- and tenth-grade English students originated the Foxfire program (now conducted at the Rabun County High School).

When Rabun County's consolidated high school was built in Tiger in 1976, RGNS became completely independent. It retains its Presbyterian connection to this day through affiliation with the Synod of the Southeast.

Today the coeducational, college preparatory school has some 250 students who have come here from all over America–and foreign countries–to attend grades 7 through 12. About 50 of the students commute from the surrounding communities, while the rest live on campus in the dormitories. Rabun Gap–Nacoochee School, Rabun Gap, Ga 30568; 706-746-5736.

The Blue Ridge Divide
Arts & Crafts Festival

This is an annual October weekend event (check with the Rabun County Chamber of Commerce in Clayton for exact date) held in the parking lots along the east side of Highway 441 in Mountain City (by the Rocking Horse and Log Cabin Crafts). Since its inception in the late 1980s, this festival has grown in the number of participating artists and craftspeople as well as in attendance.

Some of the wares you're likely to see include handmade and hand-painted baskets and wooden toys and decorative items; fabric arts such as crocheted lace collars, hand-painted or appliqued sweatshirts, vests and jackets, quilts, pillows and afghans; original paintings and jewelry.

Live entertainment provides diversion throughout the weekend, and one of the most requested bands in the area usually performs here. The Young at Heart Band is made up of local AARP members who perform at numerous public events throughout the summer and fall seasons.

These twenty-or-so fun-loving seniors—wearing navy slacks, red-checkered shirts and straw "skimmers"—belt out old sing-along standards, like "East Side-West Side," on kazoos cleverly disguised with various and sundry kitchen and household utensils. An electric piano and guitar (and occasionally a fiddle) lend support to the plungers, funnels, mops, pie plates, etc., that masquerade as instruments.

Mountain City Flea Market

This is a standard, open-air flea market—the largest in this area—where anyone can rent a table and peddle their wares. This is not (fortunately) a clothing discount outlet, but rather, you can expect to find a never-ending variety of items, new and old, from fresh produce to costume jewelry to such "treasures" as vintage dolls and toys, guns and knives, tools, kitchen utensils, glassware and porcelain—not to mention handmade pillows, quilts, and decorative accessories.

Collectors will be happy to learn that more than a few antiques and collectibles dealers rent booths here throughout the season. In fact, behind the covered pavilions parallel to the highway, are two small, permanent, free-standing buildings that also house antiques.

The flea market is open every Friday, Saturday, and Sunday from May through October. Weather permitting, it may even open in April and stay open into November. The hours are roughly 9 a.m. to 5 p.m., although most peddlers pack up around 4 p.m., sometimes earlier on Sundays. If you're serious about antiquing, get to the flea market early, when folks are just unpacking their wares (about 7:30). Otherwise, the dealers who routinely cruise through here may beat you to your bargain.

The York House

What may be the oldest Georgia inn to be in continuous operation (since 1896), is located just three-quarters of a mile north of Mountain City, a quarter mile east of Highway 441 on York House Road. The picturesque bed-and-breakfast, known as **The York House,** is listed on the National Register of Historic Places, and stands as a visible reminder of Rabun County's heritage.

More than a century ago, in the 1850s, Bill and Mollie Gibson York's two-story log cabin and farm was part of the original 1,000-acre Gibson plantation established in the Little Tennessee River Valley. Toward the end of the century, the Tallulah Falls Railroad was extending its line through Rabun County, and the railroad surveyors were sent into the valley. As was the custom of the times, they lodged at Bill and Mollie's cabin.

Anticipating increased travel, Bill added rooms to the cabin and opened the York House as an inn in 1896. After the railroad was completed, the York House earned its own railroad stop, known as "York Siding," just a short carriage ride from the inn.

Business prospered, and in 1907 "Papa Bill" and "Little Mama," as the Yorks were called, added an "L" extension, creating the structure seen today. The original log cabin, however, was never lost. It is encased in the walls, forming what are now the lobby, parlor and two guest rooms.

Papa Bill and Little Mama ran the inn through 1916, and their heirs maintained proprietorship until the late 1970s. The York house has since undergone several restorations, but it retains its historic, turn-of-the-century look and character.

Giant trees–thought to have been planted by Papa Bill–shelter this two-story inn, and a backyard creek adds charm to the quiet, pastoral setting. Many couples have been inspired to take their wedding vows among the pines that tower over the old spring house in back. Porches on two levels span the front of the structure, providing private entrances to the 13 guest rooms, each with a private bath. An inviting sitting room/lobby on the main level has a fireplace at each end. The only public telephone is located here.

Proprietors Phyllis and Jimmy Smith have furnished each room with 19th-century beds and armoires. Bed linens and accessories in romantic contemporary prints and florals complement the "heritage" look.

The competitive room rate includes an ample and varied Continental breakfast served in the room on a silver tray. The most elaborate room, the Honeymoon Suite, has its own fireplace, remote-controlled color television, four-poster cherrywood bed (double) and matching armoire, and a velvet settee. A complimentary, chilled bottle of champagne awaits the occupants. P. O. Box 126, Mountain City, Ga 30562; 706-746-2068.

Other Overnight Accommodations

If you travel with a recreational vehicle, or prefer camping out, two Mountain City locations can help. Black Rock State Park, which we have already described, has rental cabins, tent and trailer sites, and camping in pioneer and primitive style. And just off Highway 441, the Mountain City R.V. Park can accommodate your recreational vehicle. P. O. Box 69, Mountain City, Ga 30562; 706-746-6985.

Dillard

When you come to the town of Dillard, you will notice that there are many mentions of this name, as in Dillard House Inn and Restaurant, John and Earl Dillard's Place Restaurant, Dillard's Best Western, and many others.

This is not at all coincidental. These Dillards are all descendants of John Dillard, who settled the town shortly after the Revolutionary War and after whom the town is named.

Born in Culpepper County, Virginia, John Dillard served in the Revolutionary War under the command of his cousin, Captain Thomas Dillard, Jr., also from Culpepper. Their battle campaigns brought them to north Georgia where they were in conflict with Indian warriors. When the war was over, John Dillard bought 1,000 acres of land south of the North Carolina border and settled there. Other colonials from Virginia and North and South Carolina followed, and when a town was created it was named for its first inhabitant.

Following the war, John Dillard spent the remainder of his life in the picturesque valley. He died in 1842 at the age of 82 and was buried in the Head of Tennessee Baptist Cemetery in the little town that carried his name. This cemetery–one of the first in the county–exists today, just off Highway 441 adjacent to the Dillard House, and on a rise overlooking the valley. John Dillard's marble tombstone, a gift from the government, can be seen from the road in the second row of tombstones, halfway down from the church. It reads:

AUG 12, 1760
JOHN
DILLARD
LIEUT. VA. MIL.
REV. WAR
JUNE 5, 1842

The grave to the left, marked with simple hewn stones at foot and head, belongs to one of his many children, his son James. The barely visible inscription carved on the headstone reads:

JAMES DILLARD
WAS BORN
DEC 1792
DIED 1861

Succeeding generations of Dillards married descendants of other early Rabun County settlers–Dickerson, Carter, Ritchie, Kelly, Garland, Grist, McKinney, Gibson, Neville–thereby building a network of kinfolks that encompasses many of the names still prominent in the valley today–and memorialized on numerous tombstones in the Head of Tennessee cemetery. Some town landmarks even reflect this lineage. For example, the Highway 441 bridge over Betty's Creek in Dillard was named in honor of Dr. Lester Neville, an esteemed county physician from earlier this century–who was the great great grandson of John Dillard.

Shopping and Browsing

Appalachian Gallery is a small shop that carries an assortment of original paintings and signed, limited-edition prints by regional and national artists such as Ralph Taylor, Stephanie Robinson, Charles Fracé, and Ray Harm. They also offer custom matting and framing. Located on the west side of Highway 441, near John & Earl's Restaurant. Open year-round. 706-746-9936.

Appalachian Trader Antiques, formerly located in the old courthouse building in Clayton, has a large, varied, and interesting selection of antiques and collectibles. There are primitives; glassware and porcelain; cast-iron items; toys; crockery; quilts; pottery; old bottles; books; paintings, prints and photographs; jewelry; vintage hats, dresses, purses and linens; and there is even some furniture. Owners Bev and Jerry Rose feature the collections of eight different dealers, all on one level. Open daily except Wednesday, 10 a.m.-5 p.m. or later. Located across from John and Earl's Restaurant. 706-746-5194.

Dillard Mini Mall is an emporium of antiques, collectibles, crafts and custom decorative painting. Owners Henri and Steve Graves have gathered more than 15 different dealers together to fill the 9,000-square-foot building with an array of items. Rather than just a succession of booths, each dealer's area is artfully arranged so that you have the impression of being in one very large exhibition hall, and can browse around and across the aisles, encountering an endless variety of items from different periods, different countries: loveseats, bedsteads, bureaus, tables, chairs, and other furniture; player, upright, and grand pianos; linens and lace; glassware and crystal; silver services and flatware; porcelain dinnerware, sculpture and decorative accessories; jewelry; paintings, etchings and prints; and Norman Rockwell memorabilia. Also featured at the Mini Mall is the eye-catching, one-of-a-kind, handpainted furniture and cabinetry created by Henri Graves, whose work is finding its way from the Georgia mountains into homes and offices throughout the South. The Mall is open daily, year-round, and is on the east side of Highway 441, just past Valley Pharmacy. 706-746-2127.

Dillard Village Antiques, across the highway from the Mini Mall, has three separate shops under one roof. The entrances for **Country Collectibles, Village Peddler,** and **Partners 'N Plunder**–each owned separately–share one long front "porch," which is crowded with kids' sleds, wagon wheels, school desks, milk cans and farm implements, and more. Inside, the shops feature additional primitives, kitchen collectibles, kids' lunch boxes, glassware, porcelain, furniture, old advertising signs, toys and dolls, and a large selection of Coca-Cola collectibles. They're open Friday, Saturday and Sunday, January through March; every day but Wednesday, April through December. 706-746-5156.

Fence Rail, one of the area's oldest craft shops, first opened its doors in Clayton in 1972. Mr. and Mrs. Gilbert specialize in carrying high-quality, handmade quilts (twin, regular, king/queen), the majority of which are made locally. Buy one of them, and they'll consign the quilter to make matching pillows, valances, or wall hangings. Also available are quilted placemats, pillows and accessories, woven rugs and coverlets, soft-sculpture animals, baskets, and cinnamon-scented brooms. Open 10 a.m. to 12 p.m., then 2 p.m. to 5 p.m. every day except Sunday, when the hours are 2 p.m. to 5 p.m., and Wednesday, when they're closed. 706-746-5843.

Heritage Handweavers is the shop founded by mother and daughter weavers Ruth Williams and Lynnette Zoellner. They produce high-quality handwovens such as rugs, placemats, tablecloths, dish towels, throws, and wearables, plus they sell a generous selection of locally made crafts such as dolls, doll furniture, baskets and birdhouses. It is just north of the Farmers' Market on Highway 441. Shop hours are 9:30 a.m.-4 p.m., Monday-Saturday; 1-4 p.m. on Sunday.706-746-2086).

Julia's specializes in "Quilts and Other Mountain Crafts," which you'll find displayed in several large rooms on the left-hand side of the open-air Farmer's Market. Owner Brian Leach features locally made quilts in every size, pattern, and price; wooden bowls, toys, and games; hand-loomed placemats and rugs; coverlets and throws; baskets; soft-sculpture animals; and unpainted furniture such as rocking chairs, shelving, tables, and so on. Located on Highway 441 just north of the entrance to the Dillard House. Open daily, 10 a.m-5 p.m. 706-746-5754.

Mountain Mall Gems & Gifts has an unusual combination of gems and stones (cut, tumbled or rough), jewelry, ceramic and soft-sculpture dolls and animals, silk flower arrangements, quilts, and pillows, Christmas decorations (ornaments, wreaths, etc.), and even more. It is located next to the PigglyWiggly, on the east side of Hwy, 441. Open year-round, Monday through Saturday. 706-746-5170.

Pine Cone Antiques of Dillard carries a general line of antiques, including glass, porcelain, silver, lamps, mirrors, pictures, formal furniture, and so on. The shop is small but filled with a wide selection of excellent pieces from many periods, both American and European. It is located in the right half of the Valley Pharmacy building, on the east side of Highway 441. Open April through December, 9 a.m. to 5 p.m. daily. 706-746-2450.

The Linen House carries discount, brand-name linens and towels plus a wide and attractive selection of regional country crafts and gifts such as dolls, wood crafts, potpourri, scented soaps, cookbooks, etc. Located across the road from and just north of the Best Western. Open daily; seasonal hours. 706-746-5397.

The Merry Christmas Shop and Country Junction contains more than 20,000 Christmas ornaments, as well as handcrafted wreaths and tree decorations, Christmas pillows, tree skirts, and plush animals. As you might expect, there's a selection of Christmas collectibles by such makers as Snow Village and Fontanini. Just inside to the left and a few steps down on the lower level is **Country Junction,** which features quilts, pillows, dolls, stuffed animals, baskets, hand dipped candles, locally made crafts and home accessories and gifts including collectibles such as the Cat's Meow Village, Effanbee, Precious Moments and Goetz. They also have a selection of cookbooks and humor books. Opposite John & Earl's Restaurant. Open year-round. 706-746-5899.

Valley Cherishables offers "a delightful collection of old things used in new ways," which encompasses classic tools, antique furniture, vintage books, glassware, and dolls. Owners Alice and Bill Brooks have also amassed a huge collection of authentic old quilts, and sell one-of-a-kind gifts made from olden day fabrics. A specialty is their Santa doll, which has a country look. Their "Country Boutique" features novelty gifts such as feed-sack wearables, bonnets, quilted sweatshirts, and T-shirts. Open year-round. Opposite John & Earl's Restaurant. 706-746-9991.

Lodging and Dining Combinations

Dillard House Inn and Restaurant. What began as an overnight inn for travelers almost a century ago has since grown into a year-round family resort with farm zoo, horse stables, tennis courts, swimming pool, and whirlpool tub. From Memorial Day through October, there's nightly enter-tainment–bluegrass music, clogging, storytelling, gospel singing–in Henry's Playhouse on the grounds.

A gift shop is stocked with regional items: books about the area (including the *Foxfire* series); cookbooks featuring regional cooking; locally produced crafts, gifts, t-shirts and sweat shirts; plus the famous Dillard House hams, bacon, preserves and peanut brittle.

Guests can choose from accommodations in the Oaklawn, Meadow, and Blueridge sections of the motel, as well as luxurious suites, and elegant cottages. A few rustic rooms are available in the restored, antique-filled original Dillard House. Rates vary by season and accommodation.

Dillard House

The Dillard House Restaurant is known far and wide for its mountain cookin' served family style–that means platters and bowls of steaming food crowd your table and can be refilled. Breakfast (served until 10 a.m.) is an event unto itself–fit for a "mountain man." But then, so are lunch and dinner. Meals feature farm-grown vegetables, eggs, chicken, specially cured hams, sausages, and bacon, plus a wide assortment of jellies, relish, fresh-baked breads, and homemade desserts. The large, casual dining room has a wall of sunroom-style glass that offers views of the Rabun Gap valley. Prices are moderate. Open 7 a.m. to 8:00 p.m Monday through Friday; open until 8:30 p.m. Saturday and Sunday.

Behind the restaurant's parking lot, adjacent to the farm zoo, is the Dillard Stables, which conducts a variety of different rides: Scenic Farm (1 hour), River (1 hour), Waterfall (2.5 hours), and Mountain Top (half-day; snacks provided).

There are also Picnic Rides, which include a Dillard House lunch served on picnic tables alongside the Little Tennessee River (1.5 and 3 hours). Folks in a hurry can take a 30-minute Trail Ride around a portion of the Dillard House Farms (when horses are available). More adventurous souls can sign up for an overnight camping trip, riding on wilderness mountain trails in the National Forest, and eating hearty "gourmet campfire" meals prepared by the guides (2 days, 1 night). Children not yet ready for trail riding can be led around the fenced ring by a parent, when an appropriate horse is available (15 minutes).

Inquire at the stables for the various rates, schedules, and age requirements for each ride, and plan to make reservations in advance.

Carrie Dillard, grandmother of the management who founded the present
business in 1917, would undoubtedly be proud to know that her family has
served more than five million guests to date. P. O. Box 10, Dillard, Ga
30537; 1-800-541-0671 or 706-746-5348, or FAX: 706-746-3344.

Quality Mountain Valley Inn and Restaurant. This inn, which opened
in 1987, has a pool and 40 tastefully decorated rooms (rates vary by season; inquire about special promotions).

A small gift shop in the front of the restaurant features jams, jellies, and
condiments, books, some T-shirts or sweatshirts, crafts and decorative
accessories–mostly with a Georgia mountains theme.

The restaurant has booths and tables inside, and an open back porch
where tables are available in nice weather. The "country gourmet" menu
items include appetizers, soups, sandwiches, salads, burgers, and entrées.
From 11:30 a.m. to 5 p.m. daily there is a large salad bar and a hot buffet
featuring one or two meats such as roast beef, fish, chicken, ham, five or
six freshly cooked vegetables, homemade yeast rolls, and homemade
dessert such as cobbler, pudding, cake or brownies. The dinner buffet is
available after 5 p.m., and is more elaborate than the one at lunch;
entrées from the menu include chicken, steaks, and seafood. Prices are
moderate. Open daily; take out available. Reservations accepted. Highway
441, Dillard, Ga 30537; Inn: 706-746-5373; Restaurant: 706-746-5932.

Dillard's Best Western and John & Earl Dillard's Place Restaurant. The
motel has 68 spacious, nicely appointed rooms and suites with rocking-
chair porches and peaceful mountain views. Free satellite TV with HBO.
Some rooms have refrigerators. Special features include a swimming pool,
whirlpool tub, tennis courts, and trout pond.

The restaurant serves three meals a day, every day. They're known for
their mountain food: pit-cooked barbecue, ham, pork chops, chicken,
steaks, fish, fresh vegetables, and homemade bread, pies, jellies, condiments. Popular deep-sea fish and shellfish dishes have been added to the
menu in recent years.

The decor is "mountain casual," with sturdy wooden tables and chairs. A fireplace in the back room–ablaze during the winter–makes for cozy dining. Paintings of mountain scenes hang on the walls; they're by well-known regional artists. Photographs on the walls of the middle room were taken during the filming of *Deliverance* and *The Long Riders*. Incidentally, this area has been the location for a number of other television and feature length movies: *Angel City, Blast Fighter, Chatwill's Verdict, Decoration Day, The Double McGuffin, Four Seasons, Foxfire, Grizzly, Kelsey and Son, Long Walk into Forever, Million Dollar Dixie Deliverance, Whiskey Mountain, and World of Audubon*.

The breakfast menu lets you order a lot or a little, from steak and eggs to a couple hot fresh biscuits. In between are country ham, bacon, grits, gravy, etc. Lunch and dinner fare ranges from sandwiches, brunswick stew, and a vegetable plate, to entrées such as barbecued meat, steak, and fish, to desserts. Daily specials. Moderate prices. No reservations. Highway 441, Dillard, Ga 30537; 706-746-5321.

Moon Valley and Moon Lake Cafe is located west of Dillard off Betty's Creek Road. The Moon family offers year-round lodging for individuals or groups in cabins or in a medieval-style "castle" on a wooded hill. Moon Valley is peaceful, secluded, and picturesque. Dinner, by reservation, is in the rustic lakeside cafe. In warm weather you dine by the water; in cold, by the fireplace. The fare is billed "gourmet," and entrées are preselected when you make reservations. Rates vary. Route 1, Box 680, Rabun Gap, Ga 30568; 706-746-2466.

Other Places for Good Food

Johnson's Cupboard Cafe, about a half-mile north of the Best Western on the right, serves "all-American homestyle" food from 6 a.m. to 2:30 p.m, Monday through Wednesday, 6 a.m. to 8:30 p.m., Thursday through Saturday. Closed Sunday. Selections range from omelettes, quiches, and burgers, to sandwiches, salads, and soups. Daily specials include "international fare." Prices are moderate; takeout available. 706-746-5700.

JoAnn's Bakery & Delicatessen, "The Sweetest Place in All These Hills," offers an amazing variety. In addition to fresh bakery treats such as candies, pastries (Danish, French, German, Greek), cookies, cakes, pies, and breads, there are deli meats and cheeses (domestic and imported). As if that weren't enough, JoAnn also makes a selection of homemade gourmet dinners that are frozen and ready to serve two to four people. Open daily, 11 a.m. "til dark-thirty." Located across from John & Earl Dillard's Restaurant. 706-746-5707.

Valley Pharmacy, on Highway 441 just north of the Farmer's Market, recreates the old drugstore/luncheon counter concept in a late-1950s-vintage brick building. Here you can have a prescription filled while you shop for toiletries and sundries, or sit on a vinyl-covered stool to have a sandwich and an ice cream soda. The food includes soups and chili, sandwiches and the whole gamut of soda fountain specialties, all inexpensively priced. Open 9 a.m.-6 p.m., Monday through Saturday. 706-746-5335.

Lodging

The Dillard area offers a number of overnight accommodations in addition to the inn/restaurant combinations mentioned above.

Chalet Village is a "village" of contemporary rental chalets scattered among the woods off Georgia 246, just north and east of Dillard. These chalets vary in size from the cozy two-person "Honeymoon" cottages (with loft bedroom and whirlpool tub) to multiroom units suitable for small groups. Each chalet has a fireplace, complimentary firewood, complete kitchens, maid service, and color TV. Some have hot tubs. Guests also enjoy the swimming pool, tennis courts, and trout pond. Seasonal rates. P. O. Box 329, Dillard, Ga 30537; 706-746-5321.

Slick Rock Cabins are comfortable two-bedroom cabins that are modest in construction, but have fireplaces, efficiency kitchens, TV, porches, and decks. Linens, dishes, and utensils are furnished. Best of all, they offer breathtaking views of Dillard Valley. Cabins are available by the weekend, week, or month; rates vary accordingly. They're located two miles northeast of Dillard on Highway 246. No pets allowed. 706-746-5716.

Dillard R.V. Park is across the road from the Best Western. Register at Valley Supply Company. P. O. Box 160, Dillard, Ga 30537; 706-746-2713.

Betty's Creek

To the west of Dillard is Betty's Creek Valley, one of the most beautiful in the entire region. And in this valley are a number of exceedingly interesting places.

But first, a word or two of history.

The Betty's Creek area was the birthplace of the first white male born in Rabun County. According to Nancy J. Cornell's account in *A North Georgia Journal of History*, by Olin Jackson (Legacy Communications, 1989), George Washington Anderson McKinney was born on April 14, 1826, to William and Margaret Anderson McKinney. The McKinney's log home sat on a rocky hilltop overlooking a portion of the Cherokee ceremonial grounds, and their Indian neighbors took great interest in the happy event:

> Soon after his birth, the Cherokees arrived at the McKinney house in full ceremonial robes. They reportedly came into the house and danced around the infant's cradle. Picking him up, they carried him down the hill to their ceremonial grounds (now part of the Rabun Gap-Nacoochee School). With rituals befitting the occasion, the Indians made George a blood brother. After the ceremony, they carried him safely back to his mother.

Andy's Trout Farm. The idea of catching captive fish in a "trout farm" pond will most likely do something to the insides of true trout fishermen who glory in their skill and delight in the exhilarating experience of casting for trout in a rushing mountain stream. However, there are folks who do not want to be "bothered with all that," who like to cook freshly caught trout, and who do get a bit of a tingle when feeling a two- or three-pound trout taking the bait. Those who are so inclined will find Andy's Trout Farm to their liking. There are several ponds and a 3-acre, well-stocked lake in a lovely 350-acre mountain setting. Andy's staff will supply fishing poles and surefire bait, or you can bring your own. No license is needed, and there is no limit. You pay by the pound for the trout you catch, and if you wish, the staff will clean them so they're ready to cook. Andy's Trout Farm also has one- and two-bedroom housekeeping cabins. Prices are moderate.

To get to Andy's from Dillard, go west on Betty's Creek Road about 5 miles and follow the signs. P. O. Box 129, Dillard, Ga 30537; 706-746-2550.

Copecrest Square Dance Resort. Square dancers come here from all over the country (and other parts of the world) to participate in Western-style square-dancing sessions and clinics. These are the real aficionados, the "pros." There are also housekeeping cabins here for the square-dance participants. The turn-off for Copecrest is the same as for Andy's Trout Farm. The Copecrest Resort is not open to the public, but individuals or groups with special interests may be welcomed. Guests of Andy's Trout Farm (adjacent) can watch the square dancing. P. O. Box 129, Dillard, Ga 30537; 706-746-2134.

Hambidge Center for the Creative Arts and Sciences is primarily a retreat for individuals with special creative interests and talents, but it also sponsors various exhibits, classes, and nature walks. It is one of the fewer than 25 such retreats in the United States and Western Europe.

The Hambidge Center was established in 1934 by Mary Crovatt Hambidge, a noted weaver, in honor of her late husband, artist Jay Hambidge, who is best known for his creation of the design system called Dynamic Symmetry.

Here's how it all started. During the 1930s and '40s, Mary organized the Weavers of Rabun, a collective of local weavers trained to card, spin, dye, and weave wool and silk. So exceptional was their work that a shop on New York City's Madison Avenue carried it, and President Truman ordered all the draperies and upholstery for the Presidential yacht, Williamsburg, to be made from their fabric. Furthermore, the Weavers of Rabun won a gold medal at the Paris Exposition of 1937.

But in addition to this interest, Mrs. Hambidge always envisioned developing a self-sufficient community for talented artists who would build homes and studios there, remaining sheltered from the problems of city life and drawing inspiration from beautiful natural surroundings. With the help of friends, she acquired the 600 beautiful and scenic acres on Betty's Creek Road for this purpose. This exact vision never materialized, but she was able to create a retreat embodying the spirit of her dream, offering residencies of two weeks to two months, May through October, to professionals from all disciplines. Freed of daily chores and decisions, these individuals are enabled to focus, in seclusion, on the project or concept on which they are working.

The Hambidge Center opens its doors to scientists, educators, and business leaders as well as artists. In this way, a potter can meet a neurologist, who can meet a composer, who can meet a botanist, who can meet a sculptor or engineer or painter, allowing for cross-pollination of ideas.

Since the residency program was established in 1974, the Hambidge Center has awarded some 400 fellowships to individuals from nearly every state in the U.S. and half a dozen foreign countries. Former Hambidge Fellows include Eliot Wigginton, founder of Foxfire; the late Olive Ann Burns, author of *Cold Sassy Tree;* and Richard Cytowick, M.D., a neurologist, whose breakthrough work on synesthesia earned a Pulitzer prize nomination.

The public is welcome to hike the miles of marked nature trails at Hambidge, which are accessible year-round (from May through October, register in the office first). And several public programs are scheduled from spring through fall. These include a series of guided nature walks and special art exhibitions. The nature walks are guided by local naturalist Marie Mellinger, who plans each around a different topic such as Cherokee lore, wild edibles, fungi, ferns, and such. Attendance is by reservation only (modest fee includes lunch).

Several times during the season, the works of one of the resident artists or of a guest artist are exhibited. Each exhibition opens with a reception for the featured artist and a covered dish dinner (no fee; no reservations necessary). The shows hang in the gallery for several weeks, and can be visited during the center's regular hours (free admission, but donations gratefully accepted). Past shows have included sculpture, fiber arts, paintings, and contemporary American folk art.

Call the center for schedules and information. It is open Monday through Friday, 9 a.m. to 5 p.m., May through October. To find it, drive 3.5 miles west on Betty's Creek Road, and look for the driveway on the right marked by a sign and stone pillars. P. O. Box 339, Rabun Gap, Ga 30568; 706-746-5718.

Just a little further down Betty's Creek Road is the historic **Barker's Creek Mill,** which belongs to the Hambidge Center. This is one of two water-driven gristmills in Rabun County, and was built in 1944 for Mary Hambidge. It is the last mill to have served the residents of Betty's Creek Valley. Master stone mason Claude Darnell, a lifelong resident of this community, did the rock work, and was one of the millers. Claude's son-in-law, David Elgin, was the last full-time miller in the late 1970s.

Since then the mill has had several restorations and a series of part-time millers. Today it is open the first Friday and Saturday of each month. Freshly ground corn meal and grits are available for purchasr. To visit the mill, drive half a mile past the Hambidge Center entrance and look for the sign on the left. You can't see the mill from the road; it is at the bottom of a short dirt driveway.

Annual Festivals

The whole town of Dillard hosts two very popular weekend festivals every year, which are located around the Farmer's Market.

The Great Cabbage Festival in July celebrates the humble vegetable that has long been the major cash crop in this area. Festivities begin with a parade and go on to include a "cabbage cook-off," (cooking contest) and a "cabbage run" (5K foot race). All the local stores participate. You'll find booth after booth of crafts and food, and live entertainment is scheduled throughout the weekend.

Incidentally, taste a Rabun County cabbage if you can. Newcomers to this area are often skeptical when they hear locals bragging about the wonderful flavor. Then they taste for themselves and find that "our" cabbages are definitely sweeter–whether raw or cooked.

The Homemakers' Harvest Festival, which has been an annual event for more than 35 years, occurs over three consecutive weekends in October. All of Rabun County's homemakers' clubs plan and host this down-home festival. You'll find booths and tables laden with handmade crafts, furniture, fresh produce, honey, and the favorite preserves, pickles, relishes and baked goods made by some of the best homemakers around. As with the

Great Cabbage Festival, there's also entertainment by local individuals and groups.

For exact dates and schedule of events for both festivals, contact the Rabun County Chamber of Commerce. P. O. Box 761, Clayton, Ga 30525; 706-782-4812.

Rabun Bald and the Bartram Trail

A few miles east of Dillard looms the second tallest peak in Georgia–Rabun Bald, 4,696 feet high. The main ridgeline here marks the Eastern Continental Divide, so most of the streams of this peak flow into Warwoman Creek, then the Chattooga, and finally into the Savannah River on their way to the sea.

Because the Cowee Mountains rise to its north, and the protected Chattooga River corridor lies below it to the east, Rabun Bald can support big game such as bear, mountain lion, and deer. Some say wild boar roam here.

From the observation tower atop the peak, you have 360 degree views of the Blue Ridge Mountains and foothills. Warwoman Wildlife Management Area stretches to the south, South Carolina's Lake Keowee glitters in the east, and Whiteside Mountain's sheer granite face touches the clouds in the northeast near Highlands, North Carolina.

It's best to explore this area armed with maps from the U.S. Forest Service office in Clayton. For the **shortest hike to the summit**–about 2 miles–take Highway 246 from Dillard. Drive about a mile past the entrance to Sky Valley (about 7 miles total), and turn right onto Hale Ridge Road (F.S. 7) beside the Scaly Mountain, North Carolina, Post Office. Drive for about 2 miles (pavement ends) and take the right fork on F.S. 7-A, Rabun Bald Road (F.S. 7 continues left). Go 1.3 miles and take a left fork (toward Beegum Gap). Continue 0.3 miles to a parking area on the right (across from two stone driveway posts), then walk up the primitive road onto the marked Bartram Trail. Follow that to the summit of Rabun Bald.

The Bartram Trail is a 37-mile National Recreational Trail, so once you are at the summit of Rabun Bald, if you are prepared for a moderate to strenuous hike of about 17 more miles, you can follow the trail into the Warwoman Wildlife Management Area and Warwoman Dell. From there, you can hike another 17 or so miles as the trail loops back to the east and north, along the Chattooga River into South Carolina.

To start at the Bartram Trail's northernmost point in Georgia, take Hale Ridge Road (F.S. 7), the right turn off Highway 246 at the Scaly Mountain Post Office. Drive about 2 miles (pavement ends), and at the fork, keep to the left (F.S. 7-A goes to the right). After another mile, you will see the Bartram Trail sign on the right side of the road.

Sky Valley

SKY VALLEY

In the 1960s, a local developer bought acreage in a pastoral, secluded valley near the Georgia-North Carolina border. Not only was the land scenic, but he believed the conditions–2,200- to 4,240-foot elevation, plus a hill with a 250-foot vertical drop–might just lend themselves to skiing.

They did, and in 1970 local craftsmen built a unique, rustic-but-contemporary, 22,000-square-foot lodge adjacent to the ski slopes. The following year, Sky Valley Resort opened, and made headlines as the southernmost ski slope in the United States.

Over the next few years the 2,400-acre development expanded to include a championship 18-hole golf course, six tennis courts, two ski slopes, and a junior olympic pool–making it a "four-season resort." Later, single-family homes, condos, and timeshares were added.

In 1978, the city of Sky Valley was incorporated and since then has grown into a well-run, residential community with several hundred homes. The privately owned Sky Valley Resort operates within the city of Sky Valley.

Sky Valley Resort offers many recreational opportunities, and under the right conditions, you might be able to ski in the morning and play golf in the afternoon!

The golf course and driving range are open year-round, weather permitting. The course has a green fee which varies by day and time (twilight is least expensive). Members (homeowners and non-residents) have special rates. There is a per-person cart charge.

The ski slopes and lift are open December through February, as weather permits (call for fees). You can rent the necessary equipment on the premises. Since annual snowfalls are light, the resort uses snow-making equipment when the temperature falls below 28 degrees.

Throughout the season the resort hosts public events, including a fire-works show every July 4, arts and crafts and antiques shows, plus weekly guided hikes. A snack bar, restaurant, and lounge serving mixed drinks are located in the lodge.

To get to Sky Valley Resort, take Highway 441 to north Dillard, then turn right on Highway 246. Drive about 4 miles and follow signs to the entrance. Sky Valley Resort, Sky Valley, Ga 30537; 706-746-5301.

Sky Valley Resort Rentals can put you in a privately owned, fully equipped condo or chalet overlooking the golf course or secluded in the forest. Amenities include decks, fireplaces, washer/dryer units, cable TV and telephones. They can accommodate from one to ten people; golf and group package rates are available upon request. Sky Valley, Ga 30537; 706-746-5301, ext. 223 or 402.

The Lakes

Before the development of hydroelectric dams in northeast Georgia, there was on the Tallulah River a mighty waterfall said in many ways to be as spectacular as Niagara Falls. The Cherokee Indians named the falls Tallulah meaning *terrible*. By the beginning of the twentieth century, the falls had become such an attraction that thousands of visitors from around the country were coming to see it.

Even before the turn of the century, developers of natural resources were eyeing Tallulah Falls as a great potential power source. General A. J. Warner, formerly a field general in the Union Army during the War Between the States, was one of the first people to introduce the idea of harnessing the waters of Tallulah for hydro power. When Gen. Warner visited the site around 1900, he is said to have remarked that, with the exception of Buffalo, New York, no city in the country was more advantagously situated with respect to the development of hydroelectric power than Atlanta.

Ten years later, a predecessor of Georgia Power Company, the Georgia Railway and Power Company, proceeded with plans for a powerhouse and dam. After a lengthy environmental controversy in the state over the development of the river, which would destroy the great falls, the project finally proceeded. People came from miles around for a last glimpse of the falls and to view progress on the dam and tunnel that would carry water to the powerhouse. In that day, the project was considered one the most remarkable engineering achievements anywhere.

By 1913, the Tallulah Dam and one unit of the power station was completed and electricity flowed for the first time over power lines to Atlanta. The dam created a new 63-acre lake (Lake Tallulah) with 3.6 miles of shoreline. The following year, additional generators were installed, and the Tallulah Falls hydro development was declared to be the biggest in the United States, with the exception of Niagara.

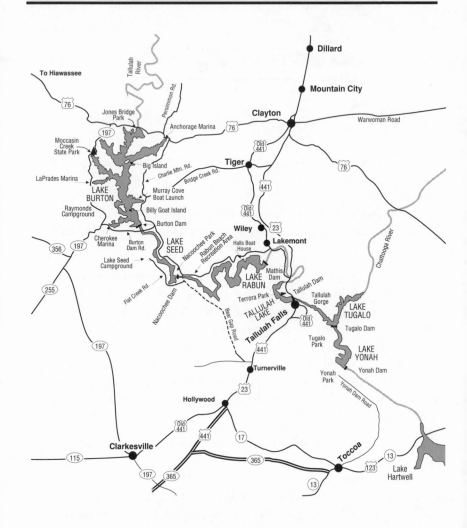

Rabun County's Mountain Lakes

Over the next several years, the power company constructed five more reservoirs, dams, and powerhouses. Today, all six projects are listed in the Georgia Register of Historic Engineering Sites.

Lake Burton, by far the largest of the six northeast Georgia reservoirs, lies at an elevation of about 1,867 feet. With 62 miles of beautiful shoreline, it covers 2,775 acres and holds over 5 billion cubic feet of water.

When the power company began acquiring land within the area planned for the reservoir that was to become Lake Burton, it was necessary to purchase the little town of Burton and the surrounding lands, including the homesteads of 65 families. The Burton community was located near what is now Goat Island, not far from Burton Dam. The company also moved the remains of persons buried in the old Burton cemetery to a new location.

During the process of purchasing land from individuals, the only instance where condemnation proceedings were required was the case of a property owner who claimed to have a gold mine on his place.

Burton Dam was completed in 1920, seven years before the power station. When water went over the dam for the first time in 1920, the reservoir filled at such an unexpectedly rapid rate that the company was unable to remove all the houses within the area. A few of them, along with a schoolhouse, floated off downstream.

Down river from Lake Burton lies Lake Seed, a small, narrow body of water formed by Nacoochee Dam, completed in 1926. Lake Seed has 240 acres and 13 miles of shoreline.

The next lake in the chain, Lake Rabun, was created upon completion of Mathis Dam in 1915. This 834-acre reservoir has 25 miles of shoreline, much of it lined with stately homes and estates built in the 1920s and 1930s.

The fourth lake is Lake Tallulah, and the fifth is Lake Tugalo. Construction of Tugalo Dam, begun in 1917, was halted by conditions created by World War I. Work was resumed and completed in 1922. Lake Tugalo covers 597 acres and has 18 miles of shoreline.

Lake Yonah, the last lake in the Tallulah River development, is actually situated on the Tugalo River at the point where Georgia and South

Carolina meet. The Yonah project, which has 325 acres and nine miles of shoreline, was completed in 1925.

With the exception of Lake Tugalo, which is undeveloped, most of the lands bordering the lakes are leased to individuals by Georgia Power. Some shoreline property is privately owned. Houseboats and boats with restrooms or sleeping quarters are prohibited on all the north Georgia lakes.

When the dams were completed and the water began to rise behind them, many acres of riverside farmland were covered by deep, blue-green reservoirs. Each reflects the magnificent hues of the hills and mountains surrounding it.

During the decades since, the lakes have had an important impact on life in the northeast Georgia mountains. Prosperity came to Rabun and Habersham counties through growing tourism and the construction of hundreds of lakeside homes and boathouses. In Rabun County, the lakes have been projected to be the fastest growing area through the end of this century.

For the visitor, the lakes offer opportunities for swimming, boating, water skiing, picnicking and camping. Nearby are numerous waterfalls and hiking trails, including the famous Appalachian Trail.

There is good fishing in the north Georgia lakes and in the streams that feed into them. During hunting season, hunters find an abundance of deer, ruffed grouse, and other game in the wildlife management preserves of the Chattahoochee National Forest.

On all the lakes there are places to picnic, camp, and launch a boat. There are marinas on two lakes, Burton and Rabun. Lake Rabun offers several rustic and interesting inns as well as individual cabins which provide a pleasant atmosphere for a weekend break in the mountains. Lake Burton offers cabins and country cooking.

Along the winding highways and secondary roads encircling the lakes, you'll find some intriguing shops carrying such items as handmade pottery and wood-carved decoys. Along these roads, the scenery is beautiful and ever-changing. In the spring, dogwood, flame azalea, mountain laurel and rhododendron bloom along with an array of wild flowers on the shorelines and in the woods. In the fall, gold, rust and red leaves of dogwood, hickory, maple, oak, sourwood and tulip poplar paint the mountainsides.

Lake Burton

On Lake Burton, once primarily a fishing lake, are many homes built by
area residents and by people from Atlanta and elsewhere in Georgia,
Florida and many other states. From the crooked roads surrounding this
lake (Highway 76, Highway 197, and Charlie Mountain Road) you can
catch only an occasional glimpse of the water. What you see are serene
mountain views, apple orchards, rolling farmland, and pastures of grazing
cows and horses. You can see the old Burton Dam from Burton Dam Road,
just off Highway 197. When traveling this road from Clarkesville, go 23
miles and turn right onto Burton Dam Road at Brooks Lil General Store.
From Clayton, go 10.7 miles on Highway 76 West, turn left onto Highway
197, and continue for 8.3 miles. Turn left at Burton Dam Road and Brooks
Lil' General Store. The dam is a short distance away on the left.

The way to really enjoy the beauty of Lake Burton is in a boat. If you
don't have a boat of your own or a friend with one, then consider a
pontoon boat rental at LaPrade's. See directions on how to get to
LaPrade's under the LaPrade's heading of the next section–Food, Lodging
and Marinas.

The lake has 62 miles of shoreline, and you could easily spend an entire
day riding along the shore. However, here are a few suggestions for making
your boat trip more pleasurable. (See map.) Note that LaPrade's is located
on the west side of the lake at the end of a cove called Wildcat Creek.
From here, drive your craft to the main body of the lake. This should take
no longer than 15 minutes. Now, look for Big Island, the only island in
this area of the lake. Once you spot the island, there are several interesting routes you can take: (1) Circle Big Island and ride east down Timpson
Cove. The Anchorage Marina is located at the end of this cove. (2) Turn
left in front of Big Island and travel north to and beyond Jones Bridge
which crosses the north end of the lake. (3) Turn right at Big Island and
continue straight ahead to Burton Dam.

Along the shoreline, in any direction, you'll see homes and boathouses,
old and new. Houses range from old cabins nestled in the woods to elegant
two- and three-story homes with elaborate gazebos and landscaping and
boathouses that themselves resemble homes.

The lake tends to be more calm from early to mid-morning and after about 6:00 p.m. During the week, there are fewer boaters and skiers. If the weather is clear to partly cloudy, a special late afternoon treat is to watch the sunset from Big Island. (Bring your camera.) Stop your boat near the island. You'll be sure to have company. This is a favorite summer pastime of many Burton fans. As the day ends, the mountains and hillsides below the sun become dramatic silhouettes. Hues of red, pink, yellow, and orange fill the skies and reflect in the blue-green water. From this same spot, on a clear day, you can also get a nice view of Charlie Mountain, overlooking the lake on the east side of Big Island. Behind Charlie Mountain is Glassy Mountain, topped by a U.S. Forest Service tower.

Even on a cloudy day with misty rain, a boat ride can be a pleasurable experience – if you're properly dressed and there is a top on your boat. On those days, few boats are present to disturb the water, and fog adds a mystical quality to the lake and the nearby mountains.

Food and Lodging

LaPrade's is a landmark, known far and wide for some of the best country cookin' in the north Georgia mountains. *Reservations are a must.* The dining room is a quaint, old weatherbeaten single-story structure atop a hill overlooking Lake Burton. This is a family style situation where you sit at tables the length of the dining room with people you've never met. You'll spend a part of your mealtime passin' the biscuits and cornbread, fried chicken, country ham, and garden fresh vegetables to others around you. The folks you'll meet are always nice, and the food is delicious and filling!

Aside from a few rental houses and cottages, LaPrade's' rustic cabins are just about the only accommodations available on Lake Burton. The cabins are freshly painted in green and white and have front porches, gas heaters, and bathrooms. Towels and linens are furnished. Cabin rentals include three meals as well as on-site access to swimming, fishing,and other lake activities. To rent a cabin, *you must make reservations.* One night's deposit is required in advance; no credit cards accepted. On weekends, rentals are available for a two-night minimum; on holiday weekends, the minimum is three nights.

LaPrade's

Innkeeper Robert Nichols explained that John LaPrade built a camp on the present site in 1918 to house and feed engineers and workers who were building Lake Burton and Burton Dam. When the Lake Burton reservoir was completed several years later, he turned LaPrade's into a fishing retreat. Since that time, it has evolved into a rustic mountain resort. The Nichols family operates three farms that supply food for the dining room.

LaPrade's is open from April 1 to December 1. It is located on Highway 197 across the road from the lake. When traveling from Clarkesville on this scenic road, drive for about 23 miles to Brooks Lil General Store, followed by the Rabun County line. Continue for another 3 miles, and you'll see LaPrade's marina on the right and the cabins and restaurant on the hill on the left. From Clayton, follow Highway 76 about 10.7 miles to the point where it intersects Highway 197. Turn left, continue for 5.5 miles, and look for LaPrade's on your right. Office, lodging and gift shop, 706-947-3312. Marina and boat rentals, 706-947-3003 or 1-800-262-3313.

Laurel Lodge. A short distance off Highway 197 and near the Rabun County line is another place for homestyle cooking and short orders on weekends only during the summer. The owners say you will *always* need reservations. It's best, too, to ask what is being served on a particular night. On Friday night (6:00 to 8:00 p.m.) dinner is served. Lunch on Saturday (11:30 a.m. to 1:30 p.m.) is mostly hamburgers and hot dogs.

During much of the summer, Saturday night (6:00 to 8:30 p.m.) is steak and shrimp night. On Sunday, you can enjoy a family style noon-day meal, as long as you made a reservation the day before.

Laurel Lodge has five very rustic cabins (with no restrooms), a swimming pool, and a campground with full RV hookups. To reach Laurel Lodge when traveling on Highway 197 from the Clarkesville area, continue north for 1 mile after passing Brooks Lil General Store on your right. Very near the Rabun County line, turn right onto Laurel Lodge Road. There are signs here to the lodge and to Cherokee Landing. Continue for a short distance on this unpaved road until you see Laurel Lodge on your left. 706-947-3241.

Raymond's Campground is an RV park on Highway 197 very near the turn to Laurel Lodge. There are 97 RV hookups here; all are three-way. Reservations are accepted up to two weeks in advance. Open April 1 to November 15. The campground is located 7.9 miles from where Highway 76 intersects Highway 197 and just 0.4 miles from the turn onto Lake Burton Road. 706-947-3420.

Marinas, Boat Rentals, and Boat Launches

Anchorage Boat Dock is a place where you can launch a boat or store your boat for the winter. You can also purchase gas, snacks and fish bait. Fishing boats (with 9.5 horsepower motors) can be rented by the day. Reservations needed on weekends. To reach Anchorage from Clayton, drive west on Highway 76 for 6.8 miles. Turn left at Charlie Mountain Road. Take the next right turn, and you'll see Anchorage a short distance away on your left. 706-782-5193.

Anchorage Outboard, next to Anchorage Boat Dock, rents pontoons in the summer. Call 706-782-3013 for prices and reservations.

Cherokee Landing, which has a boat launch, does not rent boats. Snacks and fish bait may be available. To reach the landing, look for the signs at Laurel Lodge Road on Highway 197 very near the Rabun County/Habersham County line. Turn off on this road and follow the signs. 706-947-3411.

LaPrade's is one of the best marinas on Lake Burton. You can launch your boat free of charge, or you can rent a variety of water craft. Choose from an aluminum fishing boat (with 8-horsepower motor), a 24-foot pontoon boat (with 55 horsepower motor), a Grumman lake canoe, or a row boat, or pedal boat. For this season's rental rates, call 706-947-3312. LaPrade's marina also offers boat storage over the winter.

Mark's Marine rents pontoon boats for $100 a day from mid-May through the summer. Take Highway 76, 6.8 miles from Clayton to Charlie Mountain Road. Turn left here and then an immediate right. Mark's Marine is on the left. 706-782-5565.

Burton Fish Hatchery Boat Launch. From Clarkesville on Highway 197, the hatchery is 20 miles. The hatchery and the launch are on the right just before you reach Moccasin Creek State Park. From Clayton, go 10.7 miles on Highway 76 to Highway 197. Continue for 3.8 miles to the hatchery. 706-947-3112.

Murray Cove Boat Ramp. This gravel ramp for small boats is located in a fairly remote area near Wood's Store on Charlie Mountain Road. From Highway 76, take Charlie Mountain Road for 1.5 miles. (See map.) Turn right on Bridge Creek Road and continue for 0.5 miles to Wood's Store. If you do not see the sign for the ramp, inquire at the store. 706-782-5593.

Swimming and Picnicking

Timpson Cove Beach, on Charlie Mountain Road, is a small recreation area with Lake Burton's only swimming beach. Built and maintained by Georgia Power, the beach has a modern bathhouse with restrooms and small sandy beach with a view of Timpson cove and homes across the way. The swimming area is roped off, and there is a dock for sunning. No lifeguard on duty. To reach the beach, follow Highway 76 from Clayton for 6.8 miles. Turn left on Charlie Mountain Road and continue for less than a mile. The beach is on the right; parking is on the left.

Jones Bridge Park has a couple of covered picnic tables overlooking the lake. No restrooms or swimming area. The park is 8.9 miles west of Clayton on Highway 76.

Moccasin Creek State Park

Long a favorite of campers, **Moccasin Creek State Park** is situated on
Lake Burton next to the fish hatchery on Highway 197. The 32-acre park,
open year round, is so popular for camping that during the spring, summer,
and fall, reservations are required one month in advance for 12 selected
sites. There are a total of 52 camp sites, each with electrical and water
hookups.

Other features are hot showers, restrooms, and a playground and pavilion
on the waterfront. Volleyball, basketball, and horseshoes all are available
in the park. Camping fees are $7 a night for trailers and RVs, and $6 for
tents. There is also a $5 reservation fee.

Good fishing is nearby, and the park sells fishing and hunting licenses. On
the park property, fishing in Moccasin Creek is restricted to children 11
years old and under, and to adults 65 and older. A fish-cleaning house on
park property is available to registered campers.

A specially designed fishing pier is available to wheelchair-bound visitors
and other handicapped persons. Anyone, regardless of age, who possesses a
Georgia disability fishing license is authorized to fish from the pier and
other sections of Moccasin Creek.

Trout Fishing Derby. In June of each year, during National Fishing
Week, a kids' trout fishing derby is held for up to 200 participants at
Moccasin Creek Park. There are prizes for various age categories for the
most fish, the biggest fish, and so on. Local merchants donate fishing rods
and other prizes for this event.

Lake Burton Arts & Crafts Festival. Another event at the park is the
Lake Burton Arts & Crafts Festival. Held the last Saturday in July, the
festival features 50 vendors from all around the area. The work of each
artist or craftsman has been screened by the festival commmittee. You'll
find handmade furniture, leather and silver crafts, oils, watercolors, and
much more.

Trails in the Park. On park property, across the road from the camping
area, there are two trails along Moccasin Creek. The wildlife trail is a
1 mile loop which almost anyone could take without strain. The terrain,
which is almost completely flat, follows and then crosses a small tributary

to Moccasin Creek and then takes you through a pleasant meadow. Along the way, the Forest Service has erected interesting signs and structures. There is a "bat house" with information about the value of bats in destroying insects. And there is a bluebird house with information about how America lost so many bluebirds in the 1950s through the use of pesticides. The other trail, which is moderately difficult, is about 2.5 miles in length. Along the trails are two small waterfalls.

To reach Moccasin Creek State Park traveling from Clarkesville, drive almost 29 miles north on Highway 197. From Clayton, take Highway 76 west for 10.7 miles and turn left on Highway 197. Contininue for 3.8 miles until you see the park on your left. The park is open every day from 7:00 a.m. to 10:00 p.m. For more information, call 706-947-3194.

Lake Burton Fish Hatchery

Lake Burton Fish Hatchery raises 350,000 rainbow trout each year for use in stocking streams for public fishing in northeast Georgia. During your visit, you can walk around the pools and view the trout, which range in length from four to nine inches. In ponds on the site, the hatchery raises catfish. These are used for kids' fishing events, held in Georgia and elsewhere across the nation.

The hatchery, which is operated by the Georgia Department of Natural Resources' Fisheries Management Section, is open 8:00 a.m. to 4:00 p.m every day. The staff is very helpful should you have any questions about trout or hatchery operations. Tour groups are welcome. From Clayton, take Highway 76 west for 10.7 miles and turn left on Highway 197. Continue for a 3.8 miles until you see the hatchery on your left. For information, call 706-947-3112.

Fourth of July Fireworks

The most exciting event at Lake Burton takes place every year on the Fourth of July. The Lake Burton Civic Association sponsors a fireworks display in the vicinity of Goat Island, not far from Burton Dam. The display attracts hundreds of boats from all over the lake. While you may be able to find a viewing spot on one of the dirt roads near the lake, the best view, of course, is from a boat.

Lake Seed

Formed by Nacoochee Dam, Lake Seed is one of the smallest in this chain of mountain lakes. With just 13 miles of shoreline and a narrow, snakelike shape, it resembles a river in some areas. The lake is fine for fishing and small motorboats but is too small for water skiing.

You can view Lake Seed by turning onto Burton Dam Road off Highway 197 at Brooks Lil General Store near the Rabun County/Habersham County line. This road, which borders both Lake Seed and Lake Rabun, quickly changes to Lake Rabun Road. However, there are no obvious signs for these roads.

Lake Seed is nice for sailing and canoeing. There are no marinas or restaurants on the lake, but there is a boat launch and a primitive campground. Seed is a quiet, peaceful retreat compared to the lakes on either side of it which, in summer, are busy with motorcraft.

Boat Launches, Picnicking, and Camping

There is one boat ramp on Lake Seed's east side. Traveling on Lake Burton Road from Brooks Lil General store at Highway 197, go 5.8 miles. You'll see the boat ramp on the right.

Lake Seed Campground. On the west side of the lake is a primitive campground maintained by Georgia Power and is located in a remote setting off a rough, winding, graveled road. This is a rather difficult drive, and a pickup or four-wheel-drive vehicle is recommended. To get there from Highway 197, follow Lake Burton Road (which becomes Lake Rabun

Road) from Brooks Lil General Store for 7.3 miles. Just past Nacoochee Dam and Nacoochee Park, turn right, cross the river, and then bear right onto Flat Creek Road. Shortly, you'll see the old dam again. Continue for several miles (at least 30 minutes) on the graveled road to the campground. Adjacent to the campground is a small beach (without a lifeguard), a picnic area, and latrines that do not flush. No water is available.

Nacoochee Park, just downstream from Nacoochee Dam, is a lovely, scenic place for a picnic. It is located on the river and just below the dam. The park is well maintained by Georgia Power and has rest rooms. From Highway 97 at Brooks Lil General Store, follow the Lake Burton (Lake Rabun) Road 7.3 miles. The park is on the right.

Lake Rabun

From the road, Lake Rabun is the most scenic of all the lakes. There are two ways to reach the lake. One is to follow the Lake Burton (Lake Rabun) Road from Hwy. 197 at Brooks Lil General Store. Coming from this direction, you'll begin to see the lake after driving 7.5 miles – shortly after passing Nacoochee Dam and Park.

Probably the most traveled route to the lake is from U.S. 441 just north of Tallulah Falls. After passing Georgia Power's Terrora Visitors' Center, continue north on 441. Immediately after you cross the Tallulah River on the Paul Green Bridge, look for a U.S. Forest Service sign directing you to the Lake Rabun Recreation Area and a highway sign pointing to Lake Rabun. Turn left here and continue on this road (old Georgia 441), which parallels the Tallulah River, for 2.3 miles. At this point, you are just south of Lakemont. Bear left at the intersection, where you'll see signs all pointing left to the Barn Inn, Lake Rabun Hotel, and other places. This is Lake Rabun Road. All of the inns, restaurants, and other establishments discussed here are on this road.

Lake Rabun Road winds left and right for several miles, offering numerous scenic vistas of the shoreline and the mountains. It is difficult to keep your eyes on the narrow road as you try to peer over or through a continuing series of fences and rock walls bordering the charming estates and old homes. Most of the homes – some with tennis courts – are on large lots

Lake Rabun

that were surveyed soon after the lake was built. For generations, names like Nunnelly and Branch have been on the same mailboxes. Like Lake Burton, Rabun is alive in summer with ski boats and jet skis.

Lodging and Dining

All lodging on Lake Rabun is located on Lake Rabun Road. The first four lodges listed here are less than two miles from the turn onto Lake Rabun Road from old Georgia 441 in Lakemont. All are across the street from the lake.

Forest Lodges offers five rental cabins. The cabins are in a quiet area under the trees and away from the road. Each is constructed of wood in a simple barn style and has a deck. Each cabin has color TV and is fully equipped for housekeeping. Call for rates and reservations. Long-term rentals are available in winter. From old Georgia 441 in Lakemont, follow Lake Rabun Road for 0.1 mi. At the Forest Lodges sign, turn right and proceed to the office. 706-782-6250.

The Lake Rabun Hotel offers a rustic but most interesting lodging experience. Built in 1922, it was financed by an Australian named August

Andrea, who soon took over ownership and operation of the hotel. There are 16 modestly furnished, bright and airy rooms, some with private half-baths but without telephones. Owners Bill and Jan Pettys and manager Eddie Edwards will make you feel right at home. The Pettys have added electric heat and made other improvements, including cable TV in the gathering areas. For the first time in its history, the hotel is open year-round.

The hotel maintains its original old-fashioned charm. As in decades past, guests enjoy a continental breakfast before the fireplace on seasoned old couches and chairs. Some light fixtures and furniture have been cleverly crafted from the twisted limbs of native mountain laurel and rhododendron. In the gathering room you will find is an interesting collection of old books and magazines.

Outside, tall hemlock trees shade stone pathways and a picnic area for guests. There are many varieties of wildflowers and mosses. It is a setting that blends harmoniously with the adjacent Chattahoochee National Forest. Rooms are reasonable. To reach Lake Rabun Hotel, drive 1.6 miles on Lake Rabun Road from the turn at old Georgia 441 in Lakemont. The hotel is on the right. For more information and reservations, call 706-782-4946.

The Lake Rabun Inn has 17 rooms with private baths. There are two eight-bedroom lodges with fully equipped kitchens and fireplaces. Across the street on the lake is a dock for guests. Special rates for church groups and senior citizens. Open May to December. Rates on summer weekends are moderate. From old Georgia 441 in Lakemont follow Lake Rabun Road for 1.1 miles. The inn is on the right. Call 706-782-5780 for reservations.

The Barn Inn, once a dairy barn, has been remodeled into a hostelry that is ideal for family reunions, business gatherings, or simply a weekend retreat. It retains its barnlike shape, and furnishings are early American. The seven guest rooms have queen-sized beds and private bath. The gathering area has comfortable furniture and a stone fireplace. Continental breakfast is served each day in the dining room. Follow Lake Rabun Road 0.8 mi. from old Georgia 441. The inn is on the right. To reserve a room or the entire lodge and to inquire about rates, call 1-800-633-8524 or 706-782-5094.

Rabun Beach Cabins has three rustic cabins, each with full kitchen, a double bed, and two single roll-aways. No TV or phone. Cabins can be rented weekly. Inquire here about boat rentals. To reach the cabins, turn onto Lake Rabun Road at old Georgia 441 in Lakemont and continue for 5.6 miles. The cabins are on the right. 706-782-4887.

Rabun House Restaurant, directly across the road from Lake Rabun Hotel, is the only eating establishment on Lake Rabun. The restaurant is open for business three meals a day, seven days a week. The decor, with blue and white checked tablecloths and burlap curtains, is simple but cheery. Breakfast includes egg dishes, bacon, and other typical items. Lunch features include burgers, sandwiches, steaks, and fries. During the evening hours, Rabun House is a steak house with choice steaks, giant baked potato, and salad. Prices are moderate. Hours are 7:00 a.m. to 10:00 p.m. From old Georgia 441 in Lakemont, drive 1.6 miles on Lake Rabun Road. Rabun House is on the left. 706-782-7310.

Rabun Beach Recreation Area

Rabun Beach Recreation Area, located entirely within the Chattahoochee National Forest and operated and maintained by the U. S. Forest Service, is open from early June through Labor Day. This is an excellent playground for the family, providing camping, swimming, and hiking . To get there, follow Lake Rabun Road about 5.4 miles from old Georgia 441 in Lakemont. The main entrance to the camping area is on the right; the swimming and picnicking area and boat launch are on the left. Many summer visitors fish from the shore at the site of the boat launch.

The recreation area has a short, sandy beach with sunning dock and roped off swimming area. There are lakefront picnic tables under the trees. A lifeguard is on duty during the summer.

In the campground are 50 campsites on lush, rolling forest land. Trailers and motor homes are permitted; however, no hookups for water or electricity are provided here or in any Chattahoochee National Forest recreation area. In the campground and also on the beach are restrooms with cold showers. For more information about rates for camping and recreation area hours, call the U.S. Forest Service office in Clayton. 706-782-3320.

Hikes to WaterFalls

Angel and Panther Falls. Within the camping area of the Rabun Beach Recreation Area are trails to two waterfalls – Angel Falls and Panther Falls. Both are on the same trail, and you can reach them within an hour from the starting point inside Area 2 of the campground. If you do not see the signs to the trail head, ask the U.S. Forest Service employee on duty. The well-maintained trail parallels a stream known as Joe Branch over moderate to fairly steep terrain. You'll cross a few footbridges en route to the falls. Both falls are beautiful in their own right, and they offer a quiet place to appreciate nature.

Minnehaha Falls, probably one of the most majestic in Georgia, is also one of the most underrated. The falls drop about 100 feet over magnificent boulders. From old Georgia 441 in Lakemont, follow Lake Rabun Road for 6 miles. Turn left at the sign for Nacoochee Park. Cross the bridge and continue for 0.3 mile. At the Bear Gap Road sign, continue straight ahead for 1.5 miles on the graveled road (Bear Gap Road) that borders Lake Rabun. Look for a small U.S. Forest Service hiking sign on the right. This is the trail head.

Park your car on the left side of the road and take the brief (less than 15-minute) walk to the falls. The fern-lined trail climbs steeply upward through a damp thicket of rhododendron and mountain laurel to a pleasant cove at the base of the falls.

Be careful here and at other waterfalls. A step off the trail may be treacherous. Note: Bear Gap Road may be rough during inclement weather.

Marinas

Hall's Boat House and Lakemont Marine is Lake Rabun's only marina. There are boat slips for rent year round, and one pontoon boat is available for rent for about $100 a day. The store at Hall's has groceries and snack foods as well as boat and ski supplies. From Hall's pavilion over the lake, you can see a number of the beautiful old homes and boat houses that line the lake. Sometimes, on holiday weekends during the summer, the pavilion is the site of live country music and buckdancing (a popular local dance). Follow Lake Rabun Road from Lakemont for about three miles. Hall's is on the left. 706-782-4981.

Lake Tallulah

Lake Tallulah, a little gem of a lake, borders U.S. 441 at the bridge at Tallulah Falls. There are just a few homes on the shoreline. Most were built many years ago and are now partially hidden by the lush forest around the lake. You can view the contour of this small but beautiful lake from Terrora Park. Also, you can get a different perspective by driving for a short distance around the lake on the road just south of the dam at Highway 441.

Terrora Park, operated by Georgia Power, is a beautifully maintained 300-acre park on the lake. Visitors here will find a white sandy beach with a bathhouse and concession stand. There are campsites with electrical hookups, a comfort station with hot showers, two pavilions, charcoal grills, lighted tennis courts, picnic tables, and hiking trails. For the kids, the park also has a playground with a sand foundation. Situated on the edge of the forest, the playground has several slides and different types of swings as well as monkey bars.

The lake is stocked with trout, and fishermen can try their luck from a fishing pier in the park. A paved walkway to a Tallulah Gorge overlook is accessible by wheelchair.

There is a modest charge for overnight camping and for pavilion reservations. Most other park facilities are free. From the first of June through Labor Day, the park is open seven days a week from 10:00 a.m. to 7:00 p.m. From September through May, hours are 8:30 a.m. to 5:00 p.m. The beach is closed Monday and Tuesday. For more information, call 706-754-3276.

Lakes Tugalo and Yonah

The remaining two lakes in the northeast Georgia chain are relatively undeveloped. The east banks of both lakes border South Carolina. Lake

Tugalo is accessible only by driving for several miles down a partially paved road. At Tugalo Park, you'll find a primitive camping area for trailer and tent camping, restrooms, drinking water, a picnic area with grills, and a boat launch. Bank fishing is also available. Lake Tugalo is the only lake with no homes. It remains much as it was in the 1920s. To reach Tugalo Park when traveling north on Highway 441, turn right onto old Georgia 441 (now a loop road), just south of Tallulah Falls. Take an immediate right turn on the road to Tugalo Park. Follow this road 5.5 miles to the park.

Lake Yonah, which has a few privately owned homes, is accessible from Yonah Dam Road. From Toccoa, at the intersection of Highway 17 and Highway 184, continue north for 12 miles on Highway 184. This road, which becomes Yonah Dam Road, will lead you directly to Yonah Park, located just below Yonah Dam. There is a picnic area with grills, drinking water, and a boat launch.

Fishing in the Lakes

In the years following the creation of the lakes, trout thrived. But, according to fish biologist Anthony Rabern, the trout began to disappear in most of the lakes as they aged and there was less oxygen in the water.

Long before the lakes were created, says Rabern, there were bass, crappie, and other species in the rivers that would form the lakes. Today, the lakes have self-sustaining populations of bass, bream, catfish, crappie, and yellow perch. Wall-eyed pike are stocked in the lakes to help control the shad population.

Marvin Jowers, a long-time Clayton resident and businessman, has fished four of the northeast Georgia lakes for the past 44 years. In terms of "good fishing," Jowers ranks Lake Rabun first, Burton second, then Seed and Tallulah.

"Some people who come to fish at Lake Burton or Lake Rabun for the first time have no luck and go away saying, 'There's no fish in those lakes,'" says Jowers. "Chances are, they went fishing on a summer day – not the best time. Motor boats are everywhere on the lakes in summer, and they disturb a good afternoon of fishing." He adds that it's best to fish with someone who knows a particular lake's fishing "hot spots."

The best months for fishing, Jowers advises, are February through May, and September through November. Though winter can be a good time to fish, the marinas are all closed on Lake Burton during that time and there are no available boat rentals. Also, launching your own boat between November and March is made difficult because Georgia Power routinely lowers the water in Lake Burton and some other lakes by eight or more feet.

As for bait, Jowers uses minnows for crappie and yellow perch and crickets for bream. During the spring months, when spring lizards are plentiful, they are the best bait for catching large mouth bass. Several stores near the lakes offer a variety of fish bait. Three of these are **Crestview Grocery** and **Glassy Mountain Grocery,** both on Ga. Highway 76 near Charlie Mountain Road between Clayton and Lake Burton, and **Brooks Lil General Store** on Highway 197 at Burton Dam Road, very near the Rabun County/Habersham County line. Fishing licenses are available at these stores and at many area hardwares and other businesses and at Moccasin Creek State Park.

For more information about any of the lakes, call or visit **Terrora Visitor's Center** *in Tallulah Falls. The Georgia Power staff will be happy to answer any questions you may have. 706-754-3276 or 745-3036.*

Interesting Drives and Shops
Near the Lakes

On Highway 197, en route from Clarkesville to the lakes, are several intriguing shops and other points of interest. This beautiful drive follows the course of the Soque River much of the way. At one point, a tributary to the river crosses directly over the road.

Alley's Chapel, just 3 miles from Clarkesville, is a charming little United Methodist Church restored to its original 1864 appearance with white paint and a tin roof. The chapel occupies a rather picturesque vantage point atop a grass-covered knoll and flanked by large white pines, graceful oaks, and a small cemetery.

Inside the chapel, old pine pews are brightened by red fabric seat covers. Hymnals and old hand fans are strewn about. An old upright piano sits by one of the tall windows. On the rear wall hangs a picture of Jesus. Sitting

Mark of the Potter

here in this sanctuary, one's mind seems to wander to thoughts of mountain folk singing and "ole time religion."

Mark of the Potter, another landmark, is located on the Soque River near the little community of Batesville. The shop carries handcrafted, contemporary pottery by local artists as well as handmade crafts in wood, metal, and ceramic jewelry, handblown glass and woven items. In the studio, you can watch owner Jay Bucek and other potters at work. All of the stoneware here is wheel thrown, and each pot is an original.

The building in which the shop is housed was once Grandpa Watts' Grist Mill. The original mill, built in 1930 for grinding grain and corn into meal, has been restored and is listed as a National Historic Site. From a porch over the river, visitors can see and feed mountain trout in their natural habitat. Open daily (except Christmas) from 10:00 a.m. to 6:00 p.m. Mark of the Potter is just south of the intersection of Highway 255 and 197. 706-947-3440

Batesville General Store, which proclaims to have "the best biscuits in Batesville," is at the intersection of Highway 255 and Highway 197, in the heart of tiny Batesville. Owned by Don and Margie Nelson, the store was originally constructed in 1870 and rebuilt in 1922.

The store retains its charm from the early days. You can order delicious items from the grill. For breakfast, choose from eggs, bacon, gravy, ham, steak, sausage, and hash browns. Lunch mainstays include hamburgers, hot dogs, and a variety of delicious sandwiches including barbecue, grilled cheese, turkey, fish, and roast beef. Homemade desserts may include banana pudding and cinnamon rolls. While waiting, you can browse the aisles for homemade jams and jellies and a variety of handmade gifts and groceries. In the summer, patrons can sit outside on picnic tables. Meals served every day. 706-947-3434.

The Wood Duck, next door to Batesville General Store, is where Frank and Norma Brown and Neal and Johni McElroy have a fascinating studio and shop. The Browns and the McElroys, who came here to escape the "rat race" of the city, create beautiful hand carved, hand painted wood duck decoys and other wildlife subjects. You can watch them at their work in the studio. The Wood Duck also carries handmade baskets, wreaths, needlecraft, original paintings, and Christmas decorations. Located in Batesville at Highway 197 and 255. Call 706-947-3032 for hours of operation.

Uncle Tom's Gifts. This small shop is adjacent to LaPrade's marina on Lake Burton. The friendly ladies who run the shop will show you a variety of home-cooked jams and jellies, and crafts made by people from the area. From the Rabun County/Habersham County line on Highway 197, continue north for 3 miles. The gift shop is on the right.

An interesting side trip on your visit to the lakes is the drive from Georgia 197 down Highway 356 toward Helen and Unicoi State Park. This road passes through some lovely country. Shortly after you turn onto Highway 356, a range of beautiful mountains beyond Helen comes into full view.

As you drive in the direction of these mountains, you pass through miles of unspoiled, rolling countryside, some of it wooded, and serene valleys of open farmland with herds of cattle grazing near old barns. There are few

signs of habitation along this entire stretch, except for farm buildings and
a few homes.

The Appalachian Trail

The famous Appalachian Trail, which reaches from Georgia to Maine, has
an entrance on U.S. Highway 76 about 18 miles west of Clayton. When
you see the familiar blue and white hiking trail sign, park on the right side
of the road and enter the trail on either side.

Section 6 of the trail, on the right, proceeds north through thick vegetation toward North Carolina. You'll climb upward for 1.3 miles before descending to a narrow dirt road at Tom Cowart Gap. The trail rises and then
dips once again through lush forests to Plumorchard Gap. The shelter at
Plumorchard Gap is a couple of hundred yards to the right of the trail.

Section 5 of the trail, on the left side of Highway 76, is said to be the second longest segment of the Appalachian Trail between paved roads in
Georgia. This is an ideal two-day backpacking trip.

Region Two

Toccoa
Hollywood and Turnerville
Demorest
Clarkesville

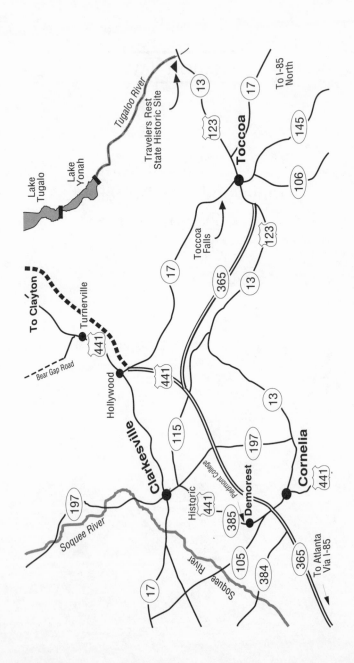

Toccoa

Established in 1874, **Toccoa** (tuh-KO-uh), was later named the county seat of Stephens County. The county itself was established in 1906 and named after Alexander Stephens, a Georgia legislator and U.S. Senator who served before and after the Civil War.

Like other mountain towns, Toccoa had a humble beginning, originating as a coaling station for the Atlanta-to-Charlotte railroad in the post–Civil War period. Prior to 1873, Toccoa was known as Dry Pond because of a large pond (near the intersection of Pond and East Tugalo Streets in the center of town) which would evaporate in the summer heat. When city fathers sought incorporation, however, they fancied a more picturesque name, and appropriated "Toccoa" ("the beautiful") from the Indian name for the 186-foot waterfall preserved within the city's limits.

Toccoa is in the foothills about 25 miles southeast of Tallulah Falls (Rabun County), where the mountains really begin. Spring comes to Toccoa about two weeks earlier than in does in Rabun County's towns of higher elevations, so if you visit here in early April you will see the city blossom forth in white and pink dogwoods and azaleas of every hue.

Toccoa offers several events and places of interest worth attending and visiting.

Steam Engine Excursion and Annual Festivals

A bit of Toccoa's history lives on today through its early and continued association with the railroad.

Every May and October, the town indulges in railroad nostalgia with a special **Steam Engine Excursion** between Atlanta and Toccoa. For this popular event, Toccoa lays out the welcome mat. While the train refills with water, its 900-some passengers have a two-hour stopover during which they can explore the town. Railroad buffs, especially those fascinated by the steam engine, enjoy this opportunity to ride–or at least witness–the real thing in action. (Since Toccoa is located on the main line of the Norfolk-Southern Railway, Amtrak–the East Coast's modern passenger train–makes daily arrivals and departures here.)

Toccoa stages two annual festivals around the downtown mall to coincide with the train's arrival. They provide plenty of entertainment in the form of booths filled with crafts and foods, exhibits, and live music. The **Currahee Arts & Crafts Festival** is held from 10 a.m. to 4 p.m. on a Saturday in May, and the **Fall Harvest Festival** is held during the same hours on the last Saturday and Sunday in October.

Toccoa's Optimists Club hosts an annual July 4th Celebration complete with food, live music, old-fashioned games and contests–and of course, fireworks. Festivities run all day and the fireworks begin at dark.

For more information, contact the Toccoa-Stephens County Chamber of Commerce: P. O. Box 577, Toccoa, Ga 30577; 706-886-2132.

Traveler's Rest

This State Historical Site, situated some six miles east of Toccoa off an old country road, was by turns a frontier cabin, stagecoach inn, early post office, and hospitable plantation home.

Traveler's Rest was built on Tugaloo (TUG-a-loo) Valley land granted to Major Jesse Walton in 1785. Several people were involved in its construction and subsequent expansions.

The fourth and last man to own it, Devereaux Jarrett, bought the inn (and several pieces of adjacent land) in 1833. He quickly developed it into a thriving plantation, expanded the structure, and opened it to the public as an inn, trading post and post office–while using it as the Jarrett family home. At this point it acquired the name "Traveler's Rest."

For three generations, the property remained with the Jarretts. Early in the twentieth century, when it ceased to be an inn, the family began

Traveller's Rest

calling it "Jarrett Manor," a name you'll hear locals use. Devereaux's granddaughter, Mrs. Mary Jarrett White, lived there her entire life, and sold the building with 2.9 acres of land to the State in 1955. Many prominent Georgians are descendants of Devereaux Jarrett, and Mrs. White herself made history as the first Georgia woman ever to cast a vote–on November 4, 1920.

To get to Traveler's Rest, go east on U.S. 123 from Georgia 17 in Toccoa, which is a right, if traveling north. (On the left just as you turn on 123 is the Toccoa-Stephens Chamber of Commerce building.) Continue east on U.S. 123 for about 6 miles, and look for a modest sign on the right that says "Traveler's Rest ¼ mile." Its arrow indicates the unmarked road to the left. It's easy to miss the turnoff, so be on the lookout. Traveler's Rest is only a short distance further, at the bend in the road.

The huge, rustic inn sits beneath giant trees, looking today much as it did to the last stagecoach traveler. The time-darkened, wooden structure is two stories tall, and has an open, 90-foot-long front porch. On the way to the entrance you pass a stone mounting step on the left, placed there to assist women who rode sidesaddle.

Inside, you are greeted by a guide who will take you on a tour of this historic house and grounds, helping you get a sense of what life was like more than a century ago for a plantation family—as well as travelers.

You visit every floor—from attic (with its hand-numbered rafters) to cellar kitchen—and all the rooms in between. All have hand-hewn wood paneling, and although the inn is not fully furnished, most rooms have at least one piece of handmade furniture, which is either from the Jarrett family or appropriate to that era. The main parlor and a small side room display such things as a stone fireplace with carved wooden mantel, a highboy, small spinning wheel, corner chair, antique tools and pieces of hardware, horse-grooming tools, weaving and spinning implements, and an 1856 atlas. In the Jarrett's bedroom on the first floor, you learn that the children all slept in the same room as their parents. The babies' cradle—still there—was hewn from a hollowed-out tree trunk. The largest room on the second floor has several bedsteads with coverlets from the period, and you learn that the male travelers who couldn't afford first-class accommodations (i.e., a private room), slept here, dormitory style.

The inn's original ledgers reportedly show the names of some illustrious guests, among them John C. Calhoun, and Georgia's Confederate governor Joseph E. Brown, who spent his wedding night here. Another traveler, G. W. Featherstonehaugh from England, wrote of his stay:

> ... I got an excellent breakfast of coffee, ham, chicken, good bread and butter, honey and plenty of good new milk for a quarter of a dollar. The landlord cultivated an extensive farm, and there was a fine bottom of good land near the house. He was a quiet, intelligent, well-behaved man, a great admirer of Mr. C. (John C. Calhoun), and seemed anxious to do what was obliging and proper, more from good feeling than for the poor return he chose to take for his good fare. What charming country this

would be to travel in, if one was sure of meeting with such nice clean quarters once a day.

There are several outbuildings on the grounds: the milk house (only the stone foundation remains), the mammy's log cabin, and the two-story structure that contained the weaving shed and the silkworm house. (To give you an idea of the operating scale of this plantation, the Jarretts employed a woman whose full-time job was tending to the silkworms during their six-week cycle from birth until the time they spun their cocoons.)

A final point of interest is the mysterious stone marker on the back lawn. It bears all manner of signs and symbols that were scratched onto its surface, and is presently being researched in an effort to learn its age, purpose, and creator. If it is Indian in origin, authorities agree that it predates the Cherokees.

This building—very likely the oldest standing structure in northeast Georgia—was designated a National Historic Landmark in 1966. It is open for tours year-round as a Georgia Historical Commission Site. Tuesday-Saturday, 9 a.m.-5 p.m.; Sunday, 2-5:30 p.m. Closed Mondays, Thanksgiving, and Christmas Day. Nominal fee; discounts for groups of 15 or more. Address: Route 3, Toccoa, Ga 30577; 706-886-2256.

Toccoa Falls

The **Toccoa Falls** are located on the campus of Toccoa Falls College, but there's no need to feel like a trespasser when you visit. The students, faculty, and staff are accustomed to having streams of visitors at the falls each year.

You can hear the falls from the parking lot. Certain times of the year, you can even glimpse it. However, to really appreciate this falls—which is taller than Niagara—pay the token fee ($0.50) to the attendant in the gift shop, go out the back door into the park, and walk the trail.

The short, slightly sloping gravel path is smooth and manageable for anyone, and there are benches along the way. To the right of the path courses the stream into which the falls empty.

Toccoa Falls

As you round the final bend, the roar masks all other sounds, and the majestic, 186-foot falls suddenly comes into full view. The water doesn't fall in a solid sheet, but rather in pieces, like lace, which is exactly how it is often described. Huge boulders surround the pool at the base of the falls.

There is a tragic note in the history of Toccoa Falls. On the morning of November 6, 1977, the dam holding back the lake above the falls broke, releasing forty acres of water to plummet over the precipice and rage through the park, down the valley, and through the campus. In its wake, 39 people were dead and 60 injured. Today, there is no visible reminder of the incident, save for a tall granite memorial and commemorative placards in the park.

At the entrance to the park there is a small gift shop and restaurant.

The Gate Cottage Restaurant is open only on Sundays from 12 to 2 p.m. (closed during August), and serves a buffet lunch with meats, fresh vegetables, tea or coffee and fresh baked bread, and homemade desserts for under $10. Call for reservations and private parties. 706-886-6831, ext. 214.

To get to Toccoa Falls, take Georgia 17 driving north from Toccoa. As you leave the commercial district, the road goes down a long, steep hill, where it widens to two lanes at the bottom. There, a gray brick sign on the left announces Toccoa Falls College. Turn in; follow the signs to the falls, staying to the left.

Simmons-Bond Inn

This "asymmetrical Victorian" mansion was built in 1903 by James Simmons, a lumber baron who also had a prosperous furniture business. His daughter, Louise Bond, eventually inherited the home and was the first to open it to boarders. It remained in the Bond family until the 1970s, and subsequently was restored and converted into an inn.

The present owners, Joni and Don Ferguson, maintain it as a bed and breakfast inn, with a restaurant that is open to the public.

The two-story structure, which is on the National Register of Historic Places, is a treat for anyone who appreciates Victorian architecture. From the porch, you step into a grand entryway featuring a fireplace and a sweeping stairway crowned with a seven-foot window of stained glass. Everywhere you look there's something special to see, such as the original fireplaces—nine of them—intricate woodwork, interior oak columns, bay windows, brass chandeliers, and stained and beveled glass. High ceilings add to the grandeur.

The restaurant occupies the first floor, and the three overnight guest rooms are upstairs (Moderate rates; corporate and longterm rates available). The largest room, "The Suite," offers a queen-size bed set in a curved alcove, and a private bath featuring an original pedestal sink. (Incidentally, this was the first house in Toccoa to have indoor plumbing.) The "Pink Room" and the "Blue Room" share a large bathroom at the end of the hall.

Overnight guests receive a complimentary Continental breakfast. The dining room opens to the public for lunch and dinner. Lunch (Sunday through Friday, 11:30 a.m.-2:30 p.m.) includes soup, salads, hot and cold sandwiches, the inn's special quiche, and homemade desserts. Dinner—which is only served Saturday night, 5-10 p.m.—features prime rib, Chicago-style shrimp DeJonghe and the Inn's quiche, along with several other entrées. All prices are moderate. Reservations are encouraged.

To visit the Simmons-Bond Inn, go north on Georgia 17 past the intersection of U.S. 123 (where the Chamber of Commerce is located). At the "T," turn left onto Tugalo Street and drive several blocks until you see the Courthouse and City Hall buildings. The inn is just past but adjacent to them, and easily seen. Follow signs to the parking lot. 130 W. Tugalo, Toccoa, Ga 30577; 706-886-8411.

Henderson Falls Park

This is Toccoa's 25-acre, in-town park and recreation site. It has play areas, an amphitheater, tennis courts, picnic pavilions—and even a waterfall and little stream. Restrooms, a pay telephone and soft drink machines are also available.

Paved walkways make it easy to stroll about the rolling grounds and admire the attractive plantings and native trees, many of which have been labeled. Since it is a public park, there are these regulations: no alcohol;

no cars, motorcycles, bicycles, or skateboards outside the designated parking area; no dogs without leashes.

To get to the park, take North Pond Street (a right if you're driving north on Georgia 17 past the Chamber of Commerce). After passing Toccoa Elementary School, bear left at the Henderson Falls Park sign. At the next "Y," bear to the right, staying on Henderson Falls Road, and in about half a mile the tennis courts come into view. The park entrance is there, on the right.

Book Store

Rollins Books and Gifts. Rollins stocks a wide assortment of popular books but also has a strong collection of books about Georgia. Located at 144 E. Doyle St., Toccoa, Ga; 706-886-3955.

Hollywood and Turnerville

Hollywood and Turnerville are not much more than two little, old country crossroad towns on Highway 441, on the way to Tallulah Falls, driving north. Traveling through this area you will begin to know you are really coming into "mountain country."

This stretch of the drive yields an array of colorful shops offering everything from fishing supplies and daylilies to peanuts and antiques. In order going north, you will find: **Hollywood Live Bait,** a tiny old store with fishing supplies and bait; **Hollywood's Kountry Korner,** a brightly painted and elaborate produce stand that sells peanuts prepared in every way, fried pork rinds, ice cream cones, pit barbecue, sorghum, and honey; **Bill's Dish Garden,** with all manner of concrete lawn and garden ornaments, including bird baths and statuary; **Trading Post,** with handmade wooden items, such as baskets, furniture, etc.; **Stewart Gardens & Craft Center,** which specializes in daylilies you can select right from the garden and also has a shops featuring handmade crafts, quilts and souvenirs; **Magnolia Antiques and Flea Market,** a one-room shop with floor-to-ceiling shelves of glassware, china, kitchen utensils, porcelain collectibles, Christmas ornaments, silver, etc., and a yard full of flea-market items such as outdoor furniture, metal signs, bottles.

Appalachian Camper Park, on the left one mile further north on Highway 441, offers cottage and trailer rentals, along with a fish pond, swimming pool and hiking trails which, as owners Joyce and Don Hammond put it, "pamper the camper." Nightly rates vary by service (water and electricity or full hook-up). Open April through October. Route 2, Box 2144, Clarkesville, Ga 30523; 706-754-9319.

Beyond the Panther Creek Recreation area, which we describe later on, are other little shops: **Nature's Greenhouse,** with plants, shrubs, pottery, flowers and concrete items; **Country Heritage Furniture,** with original reproductions; and **Joyce's Peanut Shop,** which offers that popular nut in every form and concoction, along with fresh produce, cider, and other items. One-half mile past the peanut shop there is a **Rest Area** with picnic tables. There is no view here, but it is well shaded.

As a further note, you'll see many farms and houses throughout the mountains which offer fresh produce for sale. At some of these, you do the picking; at others the fruits and vegetables are already harvested. This can be an excellent way to obtain locally grown produce, and at prices well below those of grocery stores.

Glen-Ella Springs

Glen-Ella Springs was a resort hotel in the late 1800s and early 1900s. Like many others in the area, it fell on hard times and was abandoned. A few years ago Bobby and Barrie Aycock discovered it, and enamored of its history, decided to buy and restore it. This they have done, retaining most of the original structure–and all of the charm. In addition to the modern conveniences, they have added a swimming pool.

The 16 guest rooms and suites have private baths, air-conditioning and porches with rocking chairs. Some rooms even have TV, fireplaces and whirlpool tubs. Despite these modern luxuries, the whole ambiance on the tranquil 17 acres is reminiscent of days gone by.

A complimentary Continental breakfast is provided for all hotel guests, but the dining room, which has fireplaces, is also open to the public. It serves a fine and varied menu of American and Continental dishes such as mountain trout with fresh herbs, chicken, prime rib, veal, pasta, and homemade breads and desserts. The hotel is open year-round. Dinner is served Tuesday through Saturday from 6 to 9:30 p.m. You may bring your own wine or alcohol. Reservations are recommended. Route 3, Bear Gap Road, Clarkesville, Ga 39523; 1-800-552-3479 or 706-754-7295.

To get to the inn, drive about 3.5 miles north of Hollywood, and in Turnerville, look for their small billboard indicating to turn left on New Liberty–Turnerville Road (paved). From there follow the signs and turn right on Bear Gap Road. This is a dirt road, but it is well maintained.

Panther Creek Trail
and Panther Creek Falls

This beautiful natural preserve is one of the best known and most pictures-que and scenic of all the hiking trails in the north Georgia mountains.

The trail begins at the **Panther Creek Recreation Area,** 3.5 miles south of Tallulah Falls on Highway 441. You will see the Recreation Area sign along the highway on the left side, driving north. Turn in, go through the gate and drive down into the paved parking area. (Do not park along the roadside.) The Recreation Area has a restroom and picnic tables (some are sheltered). During winter, its gate is locked, but the trail–which starts on the opposite side of the highway–is always open.

Before taking you on the trail, let us tell you about what you will be expe-riencing along the way. This is a nature lover's heaven. In the spring you can see trout lilies, violets, trillium, trailing arbutus, dwarf iris, and gay-wings. These wildflowers blossom beneath and around such flowering trees and shrubs as dogwood, service berry, Carolina bells, horse sugar, mountain laurel and rhododendron. Summer shade and fall color displays are provided by poplar, hemlock, white pine, red maple, oak and hickory trees—some of which stand more than 100 feet tall. At the very end of the trail, near the Tugaloo River, is a Protected Botanical Area in which many diverse plant species grow. Among them are some calcium-loving plants uncommon to this region, such as the chinquapin oak. Their exis-tence is credited to the presence of a narrow band of limestone which runs through the area.

Panther Creek itself has rainbow trout and redeye bass and is classified as a secondary trout stream. It drops in a series of picturesque cascades and shoals on its way to the Tugaloo River.

You start the trail at the wooden markers across the highway from the Recreation Area. The first mile or so rolls along rising and falling terrain, providing an easy to moderate hike. The sound of rushing water tumbling over rocks grows ever closer, and after about a mile, you come to the con-fluence of Little Panther Creek and Panther Creek. A little way further, just after you step around some large stone outcrops, you get to ford the stream itself. Soon afterward, the stream and the trail both smooth out for a distance.

The high shoals you come to next, about 2.5 miles in, are just that: High Shoals Falls. Many people mistake them for the real falls. Although they are enjoyable by themselves, if you persevere for another mile, you'll pass a group of outcrops and find the real Panther Creek Falls just beyond.

About 65 feet high, **Panther Creek Falls** is really a series of falls with a slide in the middle. The trail follows the upper falls along the edge of a mammoth rock outcropping, then descends, rather steeply, to the base of the falls. The force of the water has formed a large, deep pool here. It is from this vantage point that you can best appreciate the scene. Although always an impressive sight, the falls are at their breathtaking best during winter and spring, or following a period of rain, when water levels are their highest.

After the falls, the trail continues for another 2.5 miles or so to the end, but is very steep and strenuous. Because it is infrequently traveled, the trail from here on is less defined. Only sure-footed, experienced hikers should continue, but those who do will be rewarded with views of more cascades, cliffs, and gigantic boulders. The trail ends near where Davidson Creek joins Panther Creek, at the Habersham and Stephens County lines, about 6 miles from its start at Highway 441.

Demorest

Demorest is a little town about 5 miles east of Clarkesville. There are a few points of interest in and near Demorest.

The town itself came into being as a political entity in 1899. But the locale and environs were settled a decade or two before then.

According to a local historian writing in 1936, "A small band of people from Massachusetts, New Hampshire, Ohio, and Indiana came here to establish a prohibition town. The town was established with a distinct moral purpose in view. The city ordinances were very strict in regard to whiskey, gambling and prostitution. In all land deeds the clause was included that foreclosure of the land was to be the penalty for 'the practice of any of these evils on the property.' "

But there was more on the minds of these early settlers than morals. According to this same historical account, these men and others bound themselves into a company known as the Demorest Home, Mining and Improvements Company, with the purpose of initiating and encouraging industry. This eventuated in the formation, within a few years, of a hoop factory; a factory producing school desks, chairs and church pews; a knitting company; a foundry and machine works; a saddle tree factory; a spoke factory; a brick and tile kiln and others.

Only one of these businesses still stands today, or at least, a descendant of the original business, the Flor Saddle Tree Company, which we will cover later on in this chapter.

Describing further the original town and its activities, the historian writes:

> At one time there was a rock dam which formed two large lakes; one of them has now filled up. A pavilion that the young people came for dances and entertainment. Motor boats, sail boats, bateaux and steamers were on the lake in the early '90s. The

steamer "Estes" carried people pleasure riding upon both lakes. It was equipped for sixty passengers.

When we read the sentence or two about the "moral history" of the town to some of the present residents of Demorest, they chuckled in amusement, adding their own witticisms. When we read them the description of the lakes and the steamer *Estes* that carried 60 people, they shook their heads in disbelief. In fact, the body of water that is there now is not too much more than a pond. The stone dam is still there and so is the one remaining lake, but it is just a pretty, meandering, small lake or large pond and one can hardly imagine that it could ever have accommodated craft larger than canoes or row boats. The lake is behind the Piedmont College buildings, and it may be approached by way of some side streets. Stop at any local shop, or the college itself, and they will direct you.

The Town

Today, the center of the town consists of one short street with two story buildings and stores on both sides. You'll spot Steffi's Store sign at the corner, opposite the bank. Turn in and park. The building in which Steffi's store is housed was built in 1916 as were all the others on the same side of the street.

Steffi's Store sells handcrafted furniture, pottery, baskets, decoys, handwoven placemats and afghans, wreaths and dried-flower arrangements. When you enter, you'll be amused to see a large tabby cat in a chair, its head moving about contentedly. This mechanical toy has come to be known as the landmark for Steffi's Store. The store and its variety of goods are much larger than they appear when you first enter. There's another huge room to the left. The motif throughout the store is, of course, country, and all the handcrafted furniture (tables, hutches, closets, chairs, cabinets, beds, etc.) come from Georgia Pine Crafters in nearby Mount Airy. The pottery is the work of 60 artisans from all over the country and the woven articles are by Churchill Weavers and Kennybrook Weavers. 706-778-9128.

Next to Steffi's Store, on the left—and you may miss it because it is so small—is the quaint **Tin Pan Alley,** which has nothing to do with New

York and the street of buildings housing the publishers of popular music in the 1920s and 1930s. It is, in fact, a kitchen shop with kitchen gadgets (both utilitarian and decorative), gourmet coffees, baskets and the like.

Piedmont College

Piedmont College, located a very short distance north of the center of Demorest on Highway 441, was established in 1897, not too long after the town was settled. In contrast to its rather drab surroundings, the college's 50-acre campus is very attractive, with administrative and academic halls, chapel, library, dining hall, student centers, and dormitories, a gymnasium and athletic field, tennis courts and a nine-hole golf course. It offers a wide range of courses leading to a Bachelor of Arts and a Bachelor of Science degrees as well as teacher preparation programs and preprofessional courses. It is a Christian-oriented college affiliated with the Congregational Churches of America. However, it admits students of any race, color, and national or ethnic origin. Piedmont College makes a special effort to keep its rates affordable and to help students financially with scholarships, athletic grants-in-aid and work-study programs.

Flor Saddle Tree Factory

Across the highway from Piedmont College, and just a little to the north, is the saddle tree factory. There is a sign at the front of the building reading "Edward Flor Saddle Tree Factory 1883." The present owners say this sign came from the original building. But neither the present building nor the site are those of the original factory. However, the interior is very much like one might imagine it looked back in the 1880s. The manufacture of saddle trees (saddle frames) at this factory is even today a handwork process, with the lathe and the band saw as the only pieces of machinery. The operator of the factory will, on occasion, conduct tours through the factory, but one should not expect to have this happen on a drop-in basis, because of the disruption of business. Our tour was conducted personally by Mr. Earl Watson, who had been working in this firm for the past 60 years, and whose father, Alvin Watson, and uncle, John Rusk, worked with the original company.

The Habersham Winery

The Habersham Winery is located on Highway 365, 4 miles south of the Demorest exit. This winery has several lines of wine that compare quite favorably with those of the larger and better known vintners of California and New York. Its output is tiny compared to that of the large wineries, but it is intended mainly for local and tourist consumption. Travelers are invited to visit and taste and to tour the winery through every step of the wine-making process. The winery is open to the public Monday through Saturday, 10 a.m. to 5 p.m. Groups of 10 or more should make reservations. P. O. Box 476, Baldwin, Ga 30511; 706-778-WINE.

The vineyard, about 32 acres, is located several miles north of the town of Clarkesville. To get there, take Route 197 north out of Clarkesville (a very short distance north of the town square, off Highway 441). After you've gone about a mile or so on 197, look for the Bethlehem Baptist Church on the the right. Turn left across the road from the church. Go about 2 miles and look for Stone Pile Baptist Church. Take a right turn there (Stone Pile Road) and after you've driven another mile, you'll see the vineyards on the right.

Clarkesville

Clarkesville is a very pleasant country town with several antique shops, a picture gallery, an up-to-date bookstore, several restaurants, and for travelers who may need their services, a hair dresser, pharmacy, food market, and flower shop.

The center of town, laid out around a square, has in the past 15 years undergone remodeling and renovation aimed at restoring its turn-of-the-century look. There is plenty of parking space on both sides of the square, making it convenient for travelers to stop, browse, and dine.

There are, in addition, numerous historical sites, some dating back to the 1830s. But, before going on, let us look back at some of the town's interesting history.

Historical

Habersham County was established in 1819, carved out of Indian territory and in 1823, Clarkesville was designated as its county seat, which it remains today. The county was named after Joseph Habersham, a statesman from Savannah who had made his summer home on the outskirts of Clarkesville. The town was named after General Elijah Clarke, a Revolutionary War hero.

At the time that the town and county were being organized, much of the area was still inhabited by Indians. In an early account, a native resident said, "I have heard my mother say that when she came to Clarkesville, a bride, in 1838, there were United States troops there for the purpose of removing the Indians. The young lieutenant in charge of the troops was J. B. Magruder, afterwards the famous Confederate general."

As early as the 1830s and for many decades afterwards, Clarkesville was a resort catering to visitors from coastal Savannah, Charleston, and Augusta, fleeing the unbearable summer heat and the scourges of fever.

In a brochure dated 1908, the Clarkesville Board of Trade wrote:

> The entire section has long been the favorite resort during the summer of citizens of Georgia and adjoining states. Great crowds annually visited it even before the railroad was built (the latter part of the 19th century) and travel was by the old mountain coach or the open buckboard. Even with all these drawbacks, the health seekers were continually coming each summer to enjoy the magnificent scenery and health giving air which the region afforded ...

According to accounts recorded at the turn of the century, the Clarkesville city square was much like the typical town squares pictures in movies with a turn-of-the-century setting–a large park-like area with grassy lawns, a band stand in the center and winding paths leading from the outer borders to the center.

Mary L. Church, a Clarkesville resident, wrote:

> ... in Clarkesville, the City Square has always been the center of civic life. In the old days, when Clarkesville was only a village, the men gathered here to discuss politics and business of all kinds. For years, the fourth of July celebration was a big event in Clarkesville. As early as 1894 we have a record of a celebration being held here. People from miles around came dressed in their best. The Clarkesville Band was on hand to provide music.
>
> There have been May Day celebrations also. I remember taking part in such a celebration when I was a small child. A huge May Pole stood in the center of the square and the children danced the May dance with dresses the color of ribbons which draped the May Pole.

Sometime around 1900-1910, a street car line was laid down in Clarkesville, its purpose being to carry passengers between town and the railroad station depot located about a mile west of town. The trolley car was powered by a two-cylinder automobile engine. By the early 1920s, the automobile had made the trolley obsolete, and the trolley rails gave way to a paved road. Today, the definitions of the town square are very much what they were then.

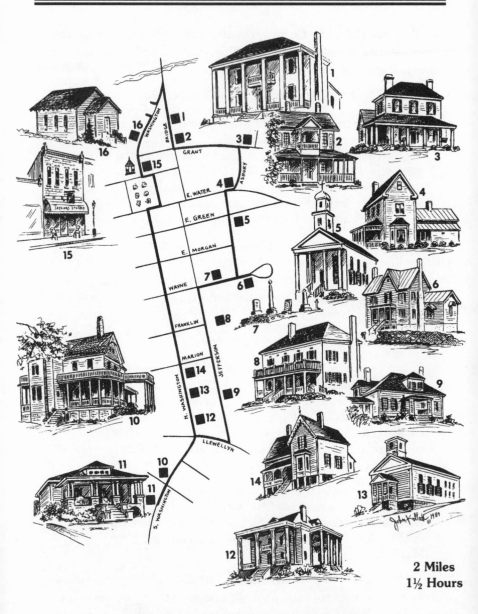

Walking Tour of Historic Clarkesville

At the northwest corner of the square, you will see the Habersham Bank building with the date 1907 (the date it was built) in the cornice. The three buildings alongside were also built at the same time. The exterior of these buildings remains virtually unaltered.

A Walking Tour of Historic Places

We are indebted to the City of Clarkesville for permission to incorporate in this guide the entire contents, with some adaptations, of their brochure "A Walking Tour of Historic Homes and Places." We express our appreciation also to John Kollock, the well-known local artist, whose fine drawings illustrate the brochure, and to Joyce D. Hammond, a local resident and businesswoman, who put this walking tour together. Three of the sites listed in the guide (the Burns-Sutton House, the Charm House, and the Taylor's Trolley Restaurant) are covered separately in this chapter and so will only be referred to by name and number in this section.

Several of the homes described in this tour were built by Jarvis Van Buren, cousin of President Van Buren. Mr. Van Buren came to Clarkesville sometime in the 1820s to start an iron works. However, he soon turned to building homes and public buildings as well as furniture. Jarvis Van Buren and his wife Eliza are buried in the old Methodist cemetery described further on in this walking tour. (Most of the homes in this tour are private residences and the town of Clarkesville requests that this privacy be respected.)

1. Porter-York House, 210 Bridge Street. Mid-19th century, two-story, wood-framed, Greek Revival style house. Historically significant as only major Greek Revival style house in Clarkesville; as the mid-19th century home of John Porter, architect-builder; and as early 20th-century home of M. C. York, owner of a dry goods store and founder of the local Standard Telephone Company (which originally consisted of a single line run between this residence and his dry goods store on the square).

2. Griggs-Erwin-Dixon Residence, Bridge Street. Mid-19th century, Plantation Plain type structure with modest Greek Revival details and a Victorian era front porch. Significant as an evolved work of architecture, and as the home of William S. Erwin, a Civil War captain and a Clarkesville lawyer.

3. Furr-Lambert-Lunsford Residence, 223 Grant Street. Two-story, wood-framed, Queen Anne–style house. Historically significant as a work of local builder-developer John Lambert and master carpenter Rusk Church. Built about 1905 for Ben Furr. John Lambert himself later lived here. Property also significant for its turn-of-the-century use as the Furr farmstead, its siting, and formally laid-out grounds.

4. Asbury-Royal-Swain-Taylor Residence, 211 East Water Street. Two-story, wood-framed, turn-of-the-century Plantation Plain type residence with Victorian ornamentation. Significant as a very late example of Plantation Plain type dwelling, decorated with appropriate period details, and as a work of local master carpenter Rusk Church. Surrounded by formally landscaped grounds containing a Delco generator powerhouse, the first in Clarkesville.

5. Grace Calvary Episcopal Church. In 1838, a group of summer residents from Savannah and Charleston purchased a lot in Clarkesville and began the construction of the Grace Calvary Episcopal Church. In 1840, the first Bishop of Georgia, The Right Reverend Stephen Elliot, was elected at a convention in Clarkesville. In 1842, the church was completed and the Bishop returned to consecrate it. The small frame building stands there today at Greene and Wilson streets, restored and renovated in 1975, but otherwise unaltered. It is the oldest unaltered Episcopal Church in Georgia and is listed in the National Register of Historic Places. It was built by Jarvis Van Buren and is a simple building, a beautiful example of Greek Revival architecture–white frame, topped by a steeple and a simple wooden cross.

There are six huge, multipaned windows–three on either side–and most of the panes are of the original handblown glass. Inside, one is struck by these windows, the smooth-worn, reddish-brown boxed pews and rails, the plain unadorned altar, the unmistakable scent of old, old wood, and the original organ situated in what was then the slave gallery.

The organ has been in continuous use since 1848, except for the brief period of its repair and restoration for the Church's 150th anniversary in 1988. It was built to specification by the Erben Organ Factory in New York and shipped from there, in sections, by steamer to Augusta and from there, brought by wagon to Clarkesville where it was assembled and installed. When it was being repaired and restored in 1988, the workmen found that squirrels had stored nuts in the works, and had gnawed away at the wood and the lead pipes. Today, it is in perfect condition, "as good as new."

6. Gloaming Cottage, 202 Wayne Street. Built by Jarvis Van Buren as his personal residence in 1840. It was originally one story, the second story being added in 1870. The "church" style windows are original. Significant for its Gothic Revival design, a mid-19th century architectural style relatively rare in Georgia. Also significant as the home of Jarvis Van Buren.

7. Old Methodist Cemetery. At Wayne and Jefferson Streets just a short distance from the Grace Calvary Episcopal Church, you will find the old Methodist cemetery occupying a large, square plot. This cemetery dates back to 1831. The old Methodist Church stood in the center of this plot and remained there until 1881. There are many ancient tombstones there marking the graves of soldiers and officers who fought in the Revolutionary War, the War of 1812, and the War Between the States. Several members of the Habersham family are buried there.

You will also find there the well-marked graves of Jarvis Van Buren and his wife Eliza, enclosed by a black wrought iron railing.

8. Trippe-Campbell-Hill-Flesner House, Wayne and Jefferson Streets. Two-story, wood-framed, antebellum farmhouse. Historically significant for having been built by Jarvis Van Buren in the 1830s as a residence for Colonel H. Trippe. Subsequently it has been the property of several prominent people: Professor Robert Campbell, a founder of the Presbyterian Church; Reverend A. C. Ketchum, first minister of the Presbyterian Church; and Walter B. Hill, Chancellor of the University of Georgia at the turn of the century.

9. Bleckley-Stewart-Carey-Pennington House, 112 Jefferson Street. One-story, wood-framed, turn-of-the-century Georgian Revival style house. Significant as one of several fine early 20th-century Georgian Revival houses in Clarkesville and the site of former home of Robert Toombs, prominent attorney, and Judge Logan E. Bleckley. The Toombs-Bleckley home was destroyed by fire in 1902.

10. Burns-Sutton House.

11. Brewer-Hamby Residence, 214 South Washington Street. One story, wood framed, early 20th-century Bungalow style. Historically significant as a fine local example of the Craftsman Bungalow style popular from 1905 to 1930. Built by Idus and Vertie Lee Brewer in 1920. Mr. Brewer was Clerk of Court for Habersham County. He and a cousin owned Brewer's Drug Store, on the square, now occupied by the Taylor's Trolley Restaurant. Fred and Joan Hamby purchased the house from the Brewer estate and restored it in 1985.

12. The Charm House.

13. First Presbyterian Church, 112 North Washington Street. One-story, wood-framed, mid-19th-century Greek Revival style church. Historically significant as a major public work in the Greek Revival style by Jarvis Van Buren, and as a Presbyterian church, relatively rare in North Georgia. The church was organized in 1832 and built in 1848. In 1907 it was turned around to face Washington Street instead of Jefferson Street.

14. Houston-Franklin House, North Washington and Marion Streets. One and one-half story, wood framed, late 19th-century Gothic Revival style house. It was moved to its present location from Turnerville, Georgia, around 1900 and served as a boarding house. The Presbyterian Church purchased it in 1983 for use as a library, classrooms, and meeting area. It is historically significant as a fine local example of Gothic Revival style, relatively rare in Georgia, and as the home of Mitchell Franklin, early 20th-century Ordinary of Habersham County.

15. The Taylor's Trolley Restaurant.

16. Day's Chapel Methodist Church, North Washington Street. One-story, wood-framed church building Built in the late 19th century and donated to the local black Methodist congregation and moved to its present location. Significant as the only structure representing black history in the city.

Other Historic Sites

The Habersham Home. The summer home of Colonel Joseph Habersham, after whom Habersham County was named, still stands today, located on Highway 441 (left-hand side going north), 2.4 miles north of the center of Clarkesville. A two-story stone and white frame building, it is now privately owned and is not open to the public. A historical marker at the site tells us:

> This was the summer home of Joseph Habersham of Savannah 1751-1805. Georgia patriot, Revolutionary War hero, political leader. He was a member of the Continental Congress and of the Georgia convention that ratified the Constitution of 1788. Educated in Princeton, he returned to Georgia to aid in the organizing of The Liberty Boys as the Revolution approached. With other patriots he organized the Council of Safety in 1775 at Tondee's Tavern. On January 17, 1776, leading a small group, he placed under guard James Wright, British Colonial governor. Twice speaker of the General Assembly in Georgia's first legislative body in 1785. Joseph Habersham signed the first charter granted to a state university, the University of Georgia. He served as Postmaster General under Presidents Washington, Adams and Jefferson. Habersham County, created in 1818 was named for Joseph Habersham.

De Soto Historical Marker. Where Highway 441 turns right, heading out of Clarkesville north, you will see, right in front of the Cooperative Craft Store, a boulder on which is mounted a historical tablet. The tablet reads: "De Soto with 5,000 Spanish and Portuguese soldiers and 200 Cherokee Indian bearers passed here about May 1540."

This is a reminder of the valiant but futile quest for gold by the Portuguese explorer Hernando de Soto. From the meager scraps of recorded history, we are able to gather that de Soto sailed from the Spanish possession of Cuba to another Spanish possession, Florida, in 1539 with nine ships and several hundred men, searching for gold. Finding no gold there, he and the soldiers and a large party of Indians headed north, overland. Historians have been unable to agree on his exact route northward, but there is general agreement that he proceeded north through Florida, then followed a meandering path through Georgia, then north to lower North Carolina. From there, it appears, he turned west into Tennessee, down the Tennessee River to Alabama, Mississippi, and Louisiana. Still in quest of gold, presumably, but never finding it, he is said to have turned north, going as far as Oklahoma, where, it is believed, he died in 1542.

Historic Inns

The Burns-Sutton House is a bed and breakfast inn and restaurant housed in a stately, turn-of-the-century Victorian style home. It is located a very short distance east of the Clarkesville town square on Highway 441 (on the right driving south).

The Burns-Sutton House derives its name from its two earliest occupants, Dr. J. K. Burns and Judge I. H. Sutton. It was built in 1901 for Dr. Burns, who lived there until his death in 1925. The house was then occupied by his widow until their daughter, Mrs. Pauline Sutton, and her husband, Judge Sutton, moved in when their own house across the street burned. Sutton was judge of the Superior Court and at one time served as a Court of Appeals judge and as Mayor of Clarkesville.

The Burns-Sutton House is listed in the National Register of Historic Places.

The structure is a three-story white frame house with a wraparound porch, sitting a good distance back from the road, surrounded by a spacious lawn and great old trees. The interior is a picture-magazine illustration of a gracious home of that time. There are paintings, Victorian furniture and other antiques in the entry hall and lounge; a carved balustrade; gleamingly polished hardwood floors. There are seven bedrooms upstairs, some of them suites, and they too are furnished with antiques. The breakfast part of the bed and breakfast is a full, country-style meal. Rates are moderate.

What was formerly the dining room of the original home has been enlarged considerably into a restaurant. It now serves both the bed and breakfast guests, and the public.

The owners are JoAnn and John Smith. Mr. Smith, a builder and architect, designed, built and furnished the restaurant so that it would blend in with the rest of the house. The 10-foot high walls, arched windows, hardwood floor and Queen Anne-type tables and chairs provide the ambiance of a gracious dining room, rather than that of a restaurant.

A wide variety of sandwiches, soups and salads are served for lunch; steak, seafood and pasta dishes for dinner. Prices are moderate.

The restaurant is open year-round, but not for all meals, so it would be wise to call ahead. The inn is open year-round. P. O. Box 992, Clarkesville, Ga 30523; 706-754-5565.

The Charm House. Quite similar in many respects to the Burns-Sutton-House, is the Charm House, also a bed and breakfast inn. (It does not have a restaurant open to the public.) The Charm House is a white frame, two-story, mansion-type house built in the Greek Revival style. It sits atop a slope just a short distance north of the Burns-Sutton House on Highway 441 (left-hand side if traveling south). Wide verandas are shaded by ancient oaks and pines. The great room, wide hallways, parlor and six bedrooms are furnished with antiques. Each bedroom has its own fireplace.

The Charm House, too, is listed on the National Register of Historic Places. It was built in 1907 by W. R. Asbury and named "Oak Heights." According to a historical note:

> Mr. Asbury was the leading merchant in Clarkesville. He also owned the Farmers Merchant Bank and he and two brothers founded Habersham Bank. Over the years, the Charm House has served as a residence, tearoom, hospital, clothing outlet store, and bed and breakfast inn, without losing any of its elegance and charm and lives on today as a reminder of the hospitality of times gone by.

The Charm House is open all year and owner Mabel Fry will quote rates upon request. P. O. Box 392, Clarkesville, Ga 30523; 706-754-9374.

Antiques, Art, Crafts, Book Store

There are four antique shops in town offering quite a varied fare among them. On the square are the whimsically named **Once Upon a Time** antique shop and **Parker Place Antiques and Gifts.**

Once Upon a Time (on the square), owned by Wally and Dellie Wenn, specializes in antiques brought over from England. Wally visits England several times a year, combs the countryside and brings back a collection of most interesting pieces and decorative items. In addition to furniture there are china, ceramics, paintings, prints, and knick-knacks. The Wenns have also added a pleasant wrinkle–old-fashioned candies, and coffees and teas imported from exotic places. 706-754-5789.

Parker Place Antiques (on the square), owned by Janet Parker, specializes in American primitives–chests, farm implements, country furniture, spinning wheels and the like. 706-754-5057.

On East Water Street, a half-block downhill from the square, is the **Dixie Gallery Antiques,** specializing in furniture, crystal, china, silver, and paintings of the 19th century. It is open every weekend (Saturday and Sunday) except the last weekend of the month. The owners also operate an antique shop in Marietta, Georgia, outside Atlanta. Clarkesville phone: 706-754-7044; Marietta phone: 404-590-7889.

Where Highway 441 makes a sharp right turn out of the square going north, you'll see (across the road) the **Habersham Antique Shop.** This has a large and varied collection including such items as 19th-century desks, chests, bedstands, buffets, and secretaries. There are also farm implements, weather vanes, stained glass and attractive reproductions of 19th-century pieces. 706-754-5454.

The Book Cellar, right next to Parker Place Antiques, down a flight of stairs, carries a surprisingly large variety and stock of books for a little country town, reflecting the wide interests and needs of the residents of Clarkesville and surrounding communities. It also offers the special service of locating rare, hard-to-find, and out-of-print books. 706-754-2717.

The Mountain Gallery (on the square) is where you will find watercolors, lithographs and other types of engravings by a number of well-known local artist including John Kollock, Mary George Poss, Sally Middleton, and Tom Landreth. 706-754-2224.

Next door to the Habersham Antique Shop is the **Cooperative Craft Shop** with a variety of interesting items handcrafted locally. This is one of three such shops organized and run by the oldest craft cooperative in the mountains. The others are in Tallulah Falls and Rabun Gap. Open daily, 10 a.m.-5 p.m.; Mail orders accepted: Box 214, Clarkesville, Ga 30523; 706-754-2244.

Restaurants, Etc.

We have already mentioned the restaurant in the Burns-Sutton House. There is one other restaurant in town where full meals ar served. In addition, there are two others where one might stop for a sandwich or a quick bite.

Taylor's Trolley Restaurant, on the square a few doors from Once Upon a Time, was Rhode's drugstore and fountain in 1907 when the building was first put up. The decor, fixtures, fountain and some of the furnishings are still there and it is not difficult, sitting there, to imagine that you are in the original store. The "trolley" in the restaurant's name refers to the trolley that used to run along Washington Street in front of the building around the turn of the century. The restaurant boasts "a complete line running from a fountain treat to gourmet dining specializing in steaks, prime ribs and seafood, plus a wide variety of sandwiches, soups and homemade deserts … " The hours are Monday through Saturday for lunch; Wednesday through Saturday also for dinner; Sunday brunch only. Prices are moderate. Wine is serve.d 706-754-5566.

On the corner where Highway 441 takes a sharp right turn toward Clayton, is **The Quick Turn Subs and Pizza,** a deli, which, besides these named specialties, also offers burritos, gyros, and sandwiches of various sorts.

On the square next to Parker Place Antiques is the **Yogurt Shop.** Besides various kinds of frozen yogurt, there are also soups, sandwiches, chili and desserts. It is a pleasant place, nicely kept, with a homey atmosphere.

Fairs and Festivals

Clarkesville boasts four events of the fair/festival type, two run by the town itself on the town square, and two operated by private enterprises at the Fair Grounds (recently named the Les Smith Memorial Fair Grounds) on Route 115 outside of town.

The Mountain Laurel Festival takes place on the square every year on the Saturday of the Memorial Day weekend. There is a parade with floats and bands, arts and crafts exhibits and sales, clogging and square dancing

performances by clogging and square dance clubs from all over northeast
Georgia, a "food court" with all the local fare–fried chicken, ribs, barbecue, etc. At 7 p.m., there is street dancing with a live band from the
vicinity.

The Fall Festival takes place on the square on the third Saturday of
October. This offers just about the same as the Mountain Laurel Festival,
except that there is an additional feature, "the country store," where local
farmers and fruit growers bring in their produce and homemakers bring in
their jams, jellies, pickles, honey, baked goods, etc., all for sale.

The Chattahoochee Mountain Fair, held at the Fair Grounds, is always
held Tuesday through Saturday, the third week in September. The hours
are Tuesday through Friday, 6 to 10 p.m.; Saturday; noon to 10 p.m.

This event offers what the Mountain Laurel and Fall Festivals present,
except on a much larger scale together with two important additional features–professional-level country music played by regional county music
bands on stage in a pavilion, and a carnival with the whole range of carnival rides and games.

The Northeast Georgia Antique Car Meet is held at the Clarkesville
Fair Grounds the third weekend in August (Saturday and Sunday). This is
where antique car enthusiasts from everywhere come with their antique
cars to compete for trophies. Formerly this event was held in Cornelia but
had to be moved when it outgrew the available space. The event draws
about 300 entries and 10,000 spectators each year. There are more than
52 classes which a competitor may enter, including conventional as well
as "hot rod." The idea, we were informed by the organizer, James Kinney
(as he pulled himself from under a 1957 fin-tail Cadillac he was working
on), is to present in each class an antique car nearest to the original
mint condition.

The addition to the car meet, there is also a large flea market, together
with the customary array of arts and crafts and foods and country music.
Inquiries about the car meet should be directed to James Kinney.
706-778-6667, or Steve Seabolt, 706-754-3937.

Region Three

Sautee and Nacoochee Valleys
Helen
Dahlonega
Amicalola Falls State Park

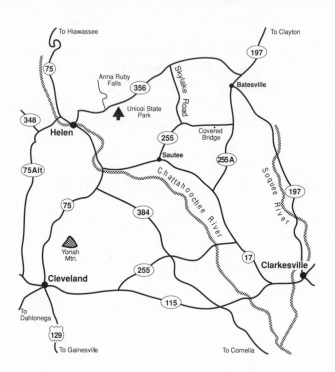

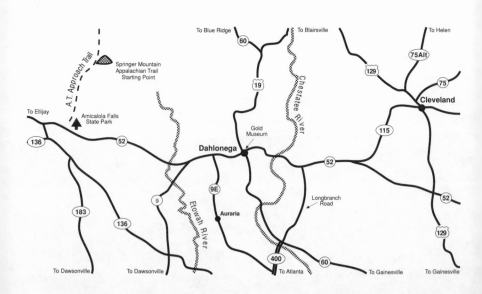

The Sautee and Nacoochee Valleys

If you will look at your map in the area of Clarkesville, you'll pick up, a short distance out of town, Route 17 going west to Helen. This road runs right through the center of the Nacoochee Valley (nah-COO-chee). Then, on Route 17, pick up Route 255 going north to the intersection with Route 197. That road runs through the Sautee Valley (SAW-tee). These valleys have the historical significance that they were the abode of Cherokee Indians up to the time of their forced removal in 1838, fertile lands where the Indians peaceably farmed, fished, and hunted. Early journals describe the Nacoochee Valley as being the site of the Indian Village of Little Chota (CHO-tah), a settlement that was wiped out in 1776 by a band of Georgia volunteers, soldiers of the U.S. Revolutionary forces fighting the British.

These two valleys were also the crossroads where two old trails intersected, the Unicoi Trail (U-nuh-coy) running east and west, the Coosa Trail (COO-suh) running north and south, these being two major routes for travel and commerce for the Indians and for the colonial settlers.

According to a preservation study conducted in the early 1980s:

> On March 1st and 2nd, 1822, two wagon trains which included 62 families left Burke and Rutherford Counties, North Carolina, and arrived in the valleys on March 10th. A settlement pattern followed which saw families with money and slaves generally securing the rich bottomlands along the Chattahoochee, Sautee and Dukes Creeks, while others found land in the mountain foothills.

> Many families who were descendants from this early group of settlers remain in this valley area today. Among others are such names as Williams, Richardson, Alley, Sosebee, Stovall, West, Abernathy, Vandiver, Henderson, Logan, Merrit, Edwards, Brown, Trammel, York and Cantrell.

An event that would eventually bring about dramatic changes in the Valley area occurred in 1828 when gold was discovered by the new settlers.

At first, the mining was undertaken by individual miners on a small scale in the creeks using primitive methods such as panning and washing of the creek bottom gravel. But then came the mining companies, sinking increasingly deeper mine shafts into the hills, attracting investors and operators from as far away as Boston, New York, Ottawa, and London, ravaging and devastating the land.

But those days are long gone, and now, the scars of mining long covered over, this is a peaceful, lovely farming countryside, giving way, only very, very slowly, to increased habitation.

Since there is no population center around which places of interest are clustered, we will take them as they come up on the route from Clarkesville west to the intersection with Route 75 on the way to Helen.

The Habersham Plantation Market

A short distance out of Clarkesville on Route 115, you'll see signs leading to the **Habersham Plantation Market Place.** Actually, this is a commercial operation, but it is so attractive that it is worth a stop, and you may find some items there you might want to buy.

When you drive onto the grounds, you'll think you've actually come upon an old plantation, with the long, low-lying, barnlike building, and two grey and weatherworn residences up on the slope. Actually, the buildings have only been there since 1976, built to the specifications of the Eddy family, who carefully modeled them after colonial homes in New England.

The Market Place, the building you come to as you come to the end of the driveway, is actually the showroom and salesroom for the reproductions of 18th-century American colonial furniture produced by the Eddys in two area workshops. The Toccoa plant produces in fairly large quantities for furniture outlets throughout the country under the Habersham line insignia. But it also sells retail, through the Market Place. The smaller workshop, in Clarkesville, produces one-of-a-kind, custom-made pieces, either from original designs, or as adaptations of the Habersham line pieces.

Every piece, in both operations, Craig Eddy assures us, is handcrafted by skilled workmen using only the basic wood-working tools and machinery. There is no mass production, nor any assembly-line work.

Items produced include tables, hutches, chairs, dressers, pie safes, bed-steads, secretaries, desks, highboys, and wardrobes. All the pieces are made of solid wood (pine, oak, maple) and finished with lacquer to give a hand-rubbed surface.

As you stroll through the Market Place, you will find room after room—each enclosed as though it were a room in a home—fully furnished and decorated in exquisite fashion. There are bedrooms, parlors, dining rooms. Even though you may not be planning to buy, you'll get some fine decorating ideas. And upstairs there's a whole roomful of baskets, woven rugs, quilts, and whatnot.

During the winter holiday season, the Market Place is decorated in traditional colonial holiday fashion.

And just think! The entire, multi-million-dollar operation with national reputation was born in 1972 when Mrs. Joyce Eddy and her two sons, Craig and Matthew, opened a small craft shop in Clarkesville, making and selling small wooden and leather items.

The Market Place is open Monday through Saturday, 10 a.m. to 5 p.m. P. O. Box 786, Clarkesville, Ga 30523; toll-free phone number in Georgia, 1-800-241-5232; other states, 1-800-221-3483.

The Dogwood Antique Shop

Our next stop of major interest is the Old Sautee Store, but on the way there from Clarkesville, you'll come to the **Dogwood Antique Shop.** (Or if you're coming from Helen, it is two miles beyond the Old Sautee Store.)

The Dogwood Antique Shop has a wide variety of American, Oriental, and European antiques. The owner, Mrs. Edith Huiet, makes frequent trips abroad buying up large lots to replenish the stock of furniture, china,

paintings, and other antiques. Unfortunately, the Dogwood Antique Shop
is not open all the time. And Mrs. Huiet told us on our last visit the business is "getting too much" for her, and she is thinking of giving it up. We
hope she doesn't. The shop is open Saturdays, 12:30 to 4:30 p.m.; Monday
through Friday "by chance" or by appointment. You might want to call
ahead, or just take your chances and stop. 706-754-9545.

The Old Sautee Store

The Old Sautee Store is located at the intersection of Route 17 and
Route 255, north. (To avoid confusion, please note there are two branches
of Route 255 heading north off Route 17. If you are coming from
Clarkesville, ignore the first of these, which is Alternate 255. If you are
coming from Helen, you'll have no problem locating the intersection and
the store.)

The Old Sautee Store is a most interesting combination of memorabilia
and a store selling a wide variety of imports from several Scandinavian
countries, but primarily Norway, which is the country of origin of Mrs.
Astrid Fried, who, with her husband, Mervin, is the proprietor.

As you enter the store, by way of the porch, you are in the "museum,"
which is essentially a collection of items gathered by Mr. Fried from lofts,
attics, and stores in the surrounding countryside. There's an old piano-
roll-type nickelodeon, ancient cash registers, butter churns, coffee
grinders, medicine bottles, an Edison phonograph, Lydia Pinkham and
Dutch Cleanser posters, bottles and containers, boxes and cannisters of
long-defunct brands of cocoa, biscuits and other groceries, a huge blacksmith's bellows, men's hats and women's bonnets of the 19th century, and
too much else to mention.

The museum is housed in what used to be (starting in 1874 and for many
decades thereafter) an old store and post office. In 1962, the Frieds bought
the building, renovated and restored it, adding a section many times larger
to serve as a store. But the rustic last-century look has been maintained
throughout the interior and exterior.

In the front part of the store there are displays of Scandinavian crystal and
dinnerware, Norwegian pewter, hand-wrought sterling, gold, and enamel

Old Sautee Store

jewelry, embroideries, books and gourmet goods from abroad, and on the topmost shelves, a most intriguing assortment of hand-carved trolls. In the rear is the imported-woolens shop, with sweaters and other items of knitted clothing from Norway.

Adjacent to the store is the **Christmas Shop** ("Jul Log" in Norwegian), selling various domestic and imported Christmas items. The little building is a hut that the Frieds shipped here from Norway and then had rebuilt on the spot, adding a sod roof to conform to the original. During the winter months, the store is closed Mondays and Tuesdays, but open Wednesday through Saturday, 9:30 a.m. to 5:30 p.m. and Sunday 1-6 p.m. The rest of the year it is open all week, except on Thanksgiving, Christmas, New Year's Day, and Easter. 706-878-2281.

The Sautee Inn

The Sautee Inn, designated by its owners John and Emily Anthony as a "country gourmet restaurant," is just a few hundred feet west of the Old Sautee Store on Route 17 (on the right). The inn is situated in what was once a gracious summer hotel built in 1898 by the Alley family and operated by that family until the 1930s when the depression brought about its demise. A subsequent owner demolished half of the original building, including the double-decker porch that went around the house. In 1972, the Anthonys bought it and turned it into a restaurant on the first floor and a home for themselves on the upper story. The antiques that decorate the hallways and corridors come from the Anthony family, dating back several generations. Although it is called an "inn," there are no rooms for lodgers.

The meals, lunch and dinner, are served buffet style. For dinner there is a choice of three meats, several vegetables, salad bar, coffee or tea. Prices are inexpensive. You may have the same for lunch, same price, or a more basic lunch for less. The Anthonys do all the cooking and baking and boast that instead of the standard country fare served in that area, they prepare their meals from "gourmet style recipes in whatever interesting place we can find them"—magazines, cookbooks, suggestions from friends abroad, etc.

Thanksgiving to mid-December, and during March and April, the Sautee Inn is open weekends only. It is closed completely January and February and the Christmas–New Year week. It is open all week, May through mid-December. 706-878-2940.

Grampa's Room

Grampa's Room is a bed and breakfast place with a gift shop, owned by Libby and Mack Tucker. It is located about 300 feet beyond the Sautee Inn, going west, on the same side of the road. The home in which it is located belonged originally (1872) to James Glen, Mrs. Tucker's great-grandfather and, in its day, housed summer boarders. It has remained in the family since then. Eventually, Mrs. Tucker inherited the home and in time restored it to its present use, retaining most of the original structural and decorative features, as well as the antique furniture. The gift shop is situated in what was formerly the room belonging to Mrs. Tucker's grandfather.

There are four rooms for overnight (or longer) stays. One is a large room with private bath and large canopied bed. Three other rooms, each with two double beds share a bathroom in the hallway. A full country breakfast is included with all rooms. Rates are moderate. Grampa's Room is open year-round 706-878-2364).

The Stovall Inn

The Stovall Inn is a country inn and restaurant. To get there, drive about 1.5 miles north on Route 255, from where Route 255 and Route 17 intersect at the Old Sautee Country Store. It is on the right.

The house was 150 years old in 1987. It was built in 1837 by Moses Harshaw, who obtained the land (about 300 acres) in the land lottery of 1832. It was sold after he died in the middle 1800s, and went through many owners until 1893, when William Stovall acquired it. His family and their descendants lived in the house until the middle 1940s. The Stovalls contributed significantly to the development of the area, and many of the Stovall line still live in White, Habersham, and Rabun Counties.

After the Stovalls sold the house, it went through many hands until 1981, when Ham Schwartz and his wife Kathy bought it and opened a bed-and-breakfast inn, expanding a few years later by adding a restaurant. Ham, who is from Pennsylvania, brought along many family antiques and paintings to the Stovall House.

Room rates are moderate, with special rates for children and multiple-night stays; continental breakfast included. The restaurant serves à la carte and is open evenings for dinners, and for Sunday brunch only. Entrees feature such dishes as fettucine, poached trout, stuffed chicken, phyllo pastry, pork chops, and grilled steaks. Prices are moderate.

The inn is open all year. The restaurant is, too, but with certain limitations. In the spring, summer, and fall, the restaurant is open for dinner seven nights a week. In the winter it is open for dinner Thursday, Friday, and Saturday nights only. 706-878-3355.

The Stovall Covered Bridge

Just about 1.5 miles beyond the Stovall House, is the **Stovall Covered Bridge,** on the right. Built in 1895, it was named after Fred Stovall, Sr., the miller who operated the grist and saw mill, which stood there for many years, powered by water from the Chickamauga Creek. The water-driven turbine and all the rest of the mill are gone, but some remains of the dam are still evident. The Stovall Covered Bridge is one of 17 still in existence in Georgia.

Gourdcraft Originals

Back in 1976, Priscilla Wilson and Janice Lymburner bought a few gourds at a roadside stand, dried them, and began experimenting with the different kinds of objects they might create out of these gourds. Since then, their imagination and creativity have produced many varieties of fanciful handcrafted and hand-painted objects, which they sell to a most receptive trade. These include decorative containers, natural utensils, planters, woven gourds, rolling toys, puzzles, mobiles, and just plain comical objects.

In addition to their retail store they have a museum in which they exhibit many unusual and interesting gourds, as well as gourds from other countries. For do-it-yourselfers, they have materials and printed information.

"Gourdcraft Originals," which is the name of their shop, is located on Route 384 about halfway between the intersections of that route with Route 255 South and Route 75. (This is a new location since the spring of 1991.) They are open all week May through December; weekends only and by appointment January through April. 706-865-4048.

Other Points of Interest

A few miles beyond Grandpa's Room, Route 17 joins with Route 75, making a sharp right turn toward Helen. Within a very short distance of this intersection, in both directions there are eight points of interest. For the sake of convenience, we will make our starting point a historical marker on the left side of the road just 0.7 mile before you get to the intersection.

This historic marker reads:

> At this point just north of the safest ford in the Chattahoochee River, the first white settlers in this area built their campfires in 1822. A trading post was soon established on the site and the Indians traded gold nuggets and gold dust to the settlers for merchandise. The first Nacoochee post office was established at the trading post with Charles Williams, son of one of the first settlers serving as postmaster for more than 30 years. To this same site, in 1838, soldiers gathered the Indians from the surrounding valleys and highlands to begin their Trail of Tears to the West.

Across from this marker, up on a slope, is an old building, part frame, part brick, with a metal roof. It is said to incorporate within its structure the Trading Post mentioned in the marker. The building is now privately owned and occupied as a home and is not open to the public.

Four-tenths of a mile beyond that, on the right is the **Crescent Hill Church,** built in 1871 as a Presbyterian House of worship by well-to-do summer residents from the coast. It later became a Baptist church. This little white frame building with its columned portico, arches, arched windows, and slim spire is a delight to the eye and to the spirit. It stands today almost exactly in the same form in which it was erected. By all means drive into the driveway, park your car, and spend some time in the peaceful interior with its unadorned altar and pews. Note while you are there, the balcony in the rear of the church. Although we have found no specific reference to it in the historical notes, we may assume that was the gallery for black house servants and farm hands.

About 0.3 mile beyond the Crescent Hill Church, just before you come to the intersection, on the right is the **Hardman House,** built in the 1870s. It may be difficult to see it through the trees, but there is a short driveway there. It is blocked off by a gate to prevent further entry, but there is no

Cresent Hill Church

reason why you cannot drive up, park, and sit there to admire the gracious beauty of an elegant home of days gone by. There is the main building, with its broad front porch, a breezeway leading to another smaller struc- ture, and another outbuilding to the right. All are freshly painted in white set off by red roofs, and the home is topped by a square turretlike structure which, one may imagine, served as a hideout for the children of the many generations that inhabited the dwelling. It has, no doubt, been restored several times, but it retains its basic structure. Around the turn of the century, it was purchased by Lamartine G. Hardman, who later became governor of Georgia (1927-31).

Nacoochee Indian Mound

Across the road from the Hardman House, in a large field, is a massive mound, topped by a gazebo-like structure. This is the **Nacoochee Mound.** Yonah Mountain looms in the distance.

There are all sorts of stories and legends about this mound, handed down word-of-mouth from the days of the early white settlers. The most popular one (and as much as we regret to say this, nothing more than a fanciful legend made up by some romantic soul) has it that Nacoochee, the beautiful 16-year-old daughter of a Cherokee chief, falls in love with Sautee, the handsome son of a Chickasaw chief, a tribe despised by the Cherokees, at a chance meeting during a period of truce. The lovers are warned that if Wahoo, Nacoochee's father, were to learn of this liaison, the two would be doomed. But this does not daunt them, since they believe that through their alliance, they will bring peace between the two tribes. So, they escape to nearby Yonah Mountain, and in a secret cave, spend several rapturous days.

Meanwhile, Wahoo has learned about his daughter's deceit, sends his warriors to seize the two, and orders Sautee thrown from a high cliff on Yonah Mountain, with Nacoochee forced to look on. Nacoochee tears away from her father's restraining hands, leaps from the cliff and joins her lover in death. Overcome with remorse, Wahoo buries the two in a huge burial mound, to commemorate his folly and their love.

In actuality, historians are uncertain about the origin of this mound, and of several others in Georgia. Some believe them to be common burial mounds of the Cherokee. Others think they once had some ceremonial function for the Cherokee. Still others believe these mounds were made by an aboriginal people predating the Cherokee.

Regardless of their origin, they are a fascinating artifact and a visible reminder of the Indian civilization that flourished throughout northeast Georgia.

Across the road on Route 75, just about where Route 17 joins it, is the Unicoi Trail historical marker. It reads as follows:

> Unicoi Turnpike [with arrows pointing east and west]. This is the old Unicoi Turnpike, the first vehicular road to link western Tennessee, western North Carolina and north Georgia with the head of navigation on the Savannah River system. Beginning on the Tugalo River to the east of Toccoa, the road led through Unicoi Gap, via Murphy, North Carolina to Nine Mile Creek in Maryville, Tennessee. Permission to open the way as a toll road was given by the Cherokees in 1830 to a company of Indians and white men. Georgia and Tennessee granted charters to the company.

Continuing now on Route 17/75 on the way to Helen, you will come soon to **Nora Mill.** In researching the history of Nora Mill, we came across a reference to it in a regional book titled *Somethin's Cooking in the Mountains*, and we are taking the liberty of reprinting it in its entirety:

> Nora Mill is one of those rare historic locations that is still functioning with its original purpose. Since 1876 there has been a mill on this location on the Chattahoochee River on Ga. 75, just north of the intersection of Ga. 17.

John Martin, an Englishman who had come to north Georgia as a miner had the mill built using the best heart pine and blue poplar. Over the years, the overshot wheel ground not only corn and wheat but rice grown on the Hardman Farm ... The mill was purchased by Dr. Lamartine G. Hardman in 1905. Some years later he named the mill Nora in memory of one of his sisters. The mill has been converted into a turbine operation and the dam has been replaced a number of times. Nora Mill had its most dramatic moment in the summer of 1950 when it was used as the site of the "drowning scene" in the movie *I'd Climb the Highest Mountain.*

The mill still grinds every variety of grain daily, and anyone can purchase bags of the different meal and flour–grits, cornmeal, whole wheat, rye, buckwheat, and pancake flour. The current miller is Grandpa Fain, in his 93rd year at the time of this writing. He was born in nearby Robertstown.

Right next to the mill is an old-fashioned country store also operated by Grandpa Fain. It had been operated by Grandma Fain until her death in 1990. This building, too, dates from 1876. In the store you can purchase country-cured hams and bacon, cider, honey, sorghum syrup, jams, jellies, pickles, old-fashioned hard candy, old-fashioned kitchen utensils and whatnot.

Across the road from Nora Mill is a large frame house, the **Martin House.** It was constructed in 1876 by John Martin, the man who built Nora Mill. There was considerable gold mining still going on in the vicinity at the time, and this house was built as a headquarters for the mining operations and as a rooming house for the miners. Currently it houses a number of antique shops.

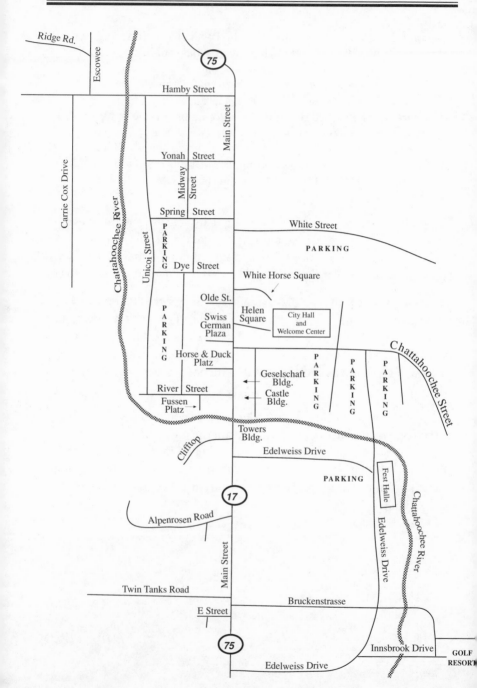

Helen

Who could imagine, looking at "Alpine Helen" today, that some 80 years ago there was nothing there but farmland and virgin forest. "Today's Helen," a local historian relates, "was the site of several pioneer houses and cultivated fields, mainly of corn, until 1911, when it was selected a the site of a tremendous sawmill. Virgin timber, especially pine and poplar, up to seven feet in diameter, covered the mountains."

With the sawmill came a railroad, and with both came hundreds of new families to the area. The following few paragraphs tell us what the town was like at that time.

> Helen, in 1913 was booming. Fred Pass opened the first drug store. John E. Mitchell, as president established the bank of Helen with J. Williams as cashier. Williams became the first Mayor, Solomon Maloof with his younger brother Charlie (immigrants from Lebanon) opened a general merchandise store. Burt Matthews operated the commissary along with Bill White. The inventory included silk, thread, ribbons, clothing, overalls, shirts and meat.

> G. A. Vandiver was receiving 16 ½ cents a pound for slaughtered cattle. The severe winter of 1917 permitted the cutting of block ice from a pond and the ice was stored in a specially constructed ice house for use during the following summer.

> The town was served by three telephones: at the bank, mill office and drug store where youths were paid five cents to run messages. A public water well was dug on Main Street. R. J. Davidson established a weekly newspaper in 1914, *The Herald*. Bub Black, a 12-year-old native, helped with the area's only mechanical typesetter. George Slaton is remembered as the man who maintained his own supply of beer and liquor after the county went dry by stashing it in a hole in the mountains. Folks thought nothing of walking 15 miles to see their local baseball

team play. The Maloofs were the first in town to sell gasoline. It was hauled from Cornelia in two 50-gallon barrels on a two-horse wagon. Dandy G. A. Vandiver had, in 1916, the first car, a Model T.

There were dances at the homes with music from guitars, banjos and fiddles. Sunday school and church revivals, corn shuckings, cake walks, and sorghum candy pulls provided recreation and socializing. The Mayor prohibited the wearing of bathing suits on the city streets.

With lumbering as the mainstay, the town grew and prospered–until 1930. Then came the depression, and with it, the depletion of the forests that had been all but denuded by the operators of the lumber industry. Following that, the town all but died.

Between the 1930s and the 1960s, there was little that went on in Helen and the surrounding area that local historians considered worth talking about.

Then in 1968, a new Helen was conceived. Here is how Carroll Proctor Scruggs relates it.

In the spring of 1968 three Helen businessmen, Jim Wilkins and Bob Fowler of the Orbit Manufacturing Co., and Pete Hodkinson III, who were daily lunch companions at Paul Westmoreland Jr.'s Steak House (now Paul's Steak House and Lounge) gazed through the large plate glass window overlooking the Chattahoochee River and the business community. What they saw was depressing. A ragbag of dilapidated store fronts being continually bypassed by a stream of tourists headed for the mountains and lakes of the north. The luncheon trio remarked that something, almost anything, had to be done to rejuvenate the town. But at that point the confabulation ended.

Again, in the fall of that year, the conversation returned to the same topic. Mr. Hodkinson allowed as how he knew an artist who might help–John Kollock.

The historian then continues with quotations from an article written by John Kollock himself.

I was going to a meeting of the Georgia Mountain Association in Robertstown. Driving up the road at dusk, I saw the fading sunset dropping behind the mountains had left the bowl of the valley in a sea of rising mist. I stopped the car to study the scene for a possible painting.

The only sounds were the rushing waters of the Chattahoochee and distant church bells lost off somewhere in the fog. The buildings of the town were invisible and I felt suddenly as if I were back in one of the villages in Bavaria where I had spent a year in the service. The fog had a dreamlike quality that helped my woolgathering ...

That was in 1965. Three years later, in December of 1968, Kollock was approached by Hodkinson for any suggestions that might help brighten up the face of the town. Kollock said he would give it some thought. Back home, he mulled over the problem for several days. And then the idea hit him. What would it be like to transform Helen, in appearance at least, into a picturesque Bavarian village.

For the next several days, Kollock walked through the town, taking photographs of the stores and other buildings.

Eventually, I had pictures of every building–from every angle–in the business section ... back in the studio. I spread out the photographs and then dug back in my files for snapshots along with every postcard and book I collected ... A week later, I took a folder of drawings matched up with the views of the buildings as they existed, and journeyed back to Helen. The most I expected was a polite 'thank you' and regrets that it was too expensive and too impossible to attempt. The reaction was instantaneous and enthusiastic.

And thus began the transformation of Helen, a small, quiet, drab gray mountain town, into an alive, exciting, colorful "Alpine Village," with spires and turrets, gables and balconies in the brightest colors of the rainbow. The news got over to Germany, somehow, and several German businessmen and restaurateurs came over to set up their businesses in Helen, bringing with them German food, German customs, German fetes, German music, German gemutlichkeit, all of which became interwoven with the fabric of Helen. "House" became "haus," "place" became "platz," and German dishes–wursts, schnitzel, rouladen, schinken, ripchen,

Downtown Helen

became a part of the menus of virtually every restaurant in town. Restaurants, motels, and inns were established bearing such names as Edelweiss, Alt Heidelberg, Hofbrau Haus, Helendorf, and Alpenhof. Stores came into being selling imported German, Austrian, and Swiss goods of various kinds. One shopping area became Marketplatz, another Fussen Platz. The pre-Lenten celebration–Fasching–was imported from Germany and Austria and it, too became an annual celebration in Helen. So did the Oktoberfest with its beer-hall style celebration, beerdrinking, wursts, oompah bands, yodeling, dancing, and singing. Quaint little alleyways came into being with fanciful names.

But while the German motif became pervasive, it did not, by any means, overshadow the American and Southern "country" features that continued to dominate in many of the stores, restaurants, lodgings.

Aside from the restaurants, motels, and inns, Helen today is a town of shops–dozens of them; shops selling hand-carved wooden items; art; leather goods; jewelry; antiques; figurines; dolls; miniature villages and houses; unique music boxes; Christmas goods; sculptured candles; fudge and other homemade candies; imported costumes and woolens and porcelain and figurines and records and tapes from Germany, Austria, Switzerland, Holland, Ireland, and the Scandinavian countries; rocks; cuckoo clocks; etched glassware; spun glassware; and countless other gifts and collectibles. One can spend a couple of days going through these shops and never come to the end of them.

So this is Helen that attracts millions of people each year, from all over the United States and abroad, to come and visit and browse, and shop and shop, and dine and enjoy all the beauties and recreational features of the surrounding north Georgia mountains.

In alphabetical order below are the restaurants, motels and stores in Helen and some of the cabin groups nearby.

Restaurants

Alt (old) Heidelberg Restaurant and Lounge. Typical German restaurant in menu and decor. Menu consists of several varieties of wurst, sandwiches, and platters, as well as German entrées (schnitzel, sauerbraten, ripchen, etc.). Also serves a variety of American-type sandwiches; wines, beers, and cocktails. A strolling accordionist entertains during dining hours, and on weekends The Old Heidelberg band plays German and American music for listening or dancing. The restaurant is open for lunch year-round. From November through March, dinner is served on weekends only. During the season, dinner is served every night. Prices are moderate. White Horse Square. 706-878-2986.

Cafe International. An attractive and pleasant outdoor restaurant, set on a covered chalet-type deck overlooking the Chattahoochee River. There is also an indoor dining room immediately adjacent. Open for lunch and dinner, the "international" aspect of this restaurant comes from its having some German, some Italian, some American, some Greek, and some Scandinavian dishes. A variety of interesting salads and sandwiches for lunch. Ditto for dinner, plus several German and Italian dishes, plus chicken and prime rib. Beer and wine served. Prices are moderate. Located on Main Street, at the river, across the road from Paul's. 706-878-3102.

Chef Hans. Specializing in German dishes, but also serving seafood and steaks. The luncheon menu consists of a variety of American sandwiches and German platters. Wine, beer, and cocktails are served. The owner, Hans Raab, does the cooking himself. He is from Heidelberg, Germany. Lunch and dinner are served year-round (closed Tuesday). Breakfast is served April through December. Prices are moderate. Main street between Dye and Spring Streets, a very short distance beyond the shopping center. 706-878-231.

Courtyard Restaurant and Lounge. An outdoor cafe (umbrella-shaded tables) on a patio alongside the Chattahoochee; also an inside dining room in the Castle Inn building, a few steps up. Inside is also a full bar and lounge and a small theatre where, on scheduled evenings, you may be entertained while dining by professional comedy or dance and vocal groups from Atlanta. (Or you may pay admission and attend without ordering dinner.) Luncheon menu includes sandwiches, salads, and various wurst platters. Dinner menu includes chicken dishes, steaks, seafood, pastas. Also Sunday brunch. Prices are moderate. Located in and alongside the Castle Inn Building on Main Street, across the river from the Cafe International. 706-878-3117.

Edelweiss Restaurant and Lounge. Serves a wide variety of genuine German dishes for lunch and dinner. The owner, Egon Beyer, is from Heidelberg. The lunch menu features mainly various German wursts in sandwiches and platters, plus American-type deli sandwiches, salads, and platters. The dinner menu features various schnitzels, sauerbraten, goulash, etc., plus wurst platters. In addition for dinner there are steaks and seafood. Prices are moderate. Wine, beers and cocktails are served. The interior is nicely decorated in the German style. Live entertainment while dining Tuesday through Saturday. Dancing (German and American numbers) Saturday night. Located in the Horse and Ducky Platz. 706-878-3466.

Edelweiss Deli, Bake and Sausage Shop. Right across from the Edelweiss Restaurant. Serves, over the counter, sausages and other deli items; strudels and other home-baked goods.

Garden Cafe. Semi-outdoor "garden-type" restaurant, breakfast and lunch only (closes at 3 p.m.). Specialties are Belgian waffles, overstuffed sandwiches, three-egg omelettes, stuffed potatoes. Also sandwiches, salads, soups, chicken, steaks, and seafood. Prices are moderate. Wine and beer served. Hours vary with day of week and season. Off season, they are open for lunch (no breakfast) on Monday, Wednesday, Thursday, and Friday; weekends they serve breakfast and lunch. In season breakfast and lunch are served all week. Closed Tuesdays, year-round. Edelweiss Drive 706-878-3472.

Gathering Place. Breakfast, lunch, and dinner. Breakfast, standard variety; lunch: American and Italian sandwiches. Dinner: Italian dishes and steaks. Prices are inexpensive. Pleasant, spacious, pine-paneled interior. Located on Main Street across from the Days Inn. 706-878-107.

Gesellschaft Haus Restaurant and Lounge. Large, attractive dining room and cocktail lounge. On the lunch menu are a variety of sandwiches and salads. The dinner menu includes chicken, seafood, steaks, German dishes. Prices are mostly moderate. Open for lunch only during the winter months; lunch and dinner in season. Dancing to a rock-and-roll band, Wednesday through Saturday evenings. Located on Main Street, between the river and Chattahoochee Street. 706-878-2136.

Hofbrauhaus Restaurant and Lounge. The building entrance is on Main Street but the restaurant overlooks the Chattahoochee River. (This is part of the Hofbrauhaus Inn and Restaurant. There is a separate item on the inn under "Motels.") The dining room and lounge are both attractively furnished and decorated and both have views of the river. The lounge (with piano bar) is open at 3 p.m., the restaurant (serves dinner only) at 5 p.m. The restaurant serves a variety of genuine German entrées, steaks, and a few Italian/French dishes. Prices are mostly moderate. Wine, beer, and cocktails. Proprietor Chris Hammersen. Located on Main Street, north of Hamby Street, on the north edge of town. One Main Street, Helen, Ga 30545; 706-878-2248.

Mamie's Kitchen. A real "country Southern" type restaurant that was operating years before Helen's conversion into an "Alpine Village," changing only its exterior decor to conform with the Alpine look. Breakfast, lunch, and dinner. "Full breakfast" served until 2:30 p.m. For lunch and dinner, one meat (choice of several) and two vegetables. Also, a buffet including biscuits, chicken, bacon, sausages, country ham, steak, pork tenderloin, etc. Prices are inexpensive. Main Street adjacent to the Alpine Village Outlet Shops. 706-878-3438.

Mountain Valley Kitchen. Serves breakfast, lunch, and dinner. Breakfast is served buffet style with a wide array of choices: eggs, grits, bacon, sausage, biscuits, muffins, etc., and various fresh fruits in season. Lunch and dinner offer steak, chicken ham, trout, catfish, plus a wide variety of specials, including one meat and three vegetables (e.g., beef stew, country fried steak, chicken livers, fried chicken, etc.). Prices are inexpensive. Wine and beer are served. Very cozy, pleasant atmosphere. "Tiffany"-type lamps. Live fireplace in winter. Located on Chattahoochee Street, a few doors down from the Welcome Center. 706-878-2508.

Paul's Steak House and Lounge. This is an establishment in Helen–the oldest, largest and probably the most popular restaurant in town. It consists of two large rooms, one the restaurant, the other the lounge with dance floor and full bar. Both rooms have an all-window wall overlooking the Chattahoochee. The lounge also has a balcony. There is live music and dancing Wednesday through Saturday nights. Thursday, there is a Blue Grass band; the other three nights another band plays country and rock. The lounge opens at 3 p.m; the restaurant opens at 5 p.m. for dinner. The restaurant serves chicken, seafood, steaks, and a few German dishes. Prices range from moderate to somewhat expensive. 706-878-2468.

River's Edge Restaurant. Combines scenic on-the-river location and "Alpine" construction with stylish interior in restaurant and cocktail lounge. Lunch: a variety of sandwiches, soups, salads and platters; dinner: appetizers, chicken, steaks, and seafood. Prices are moderate. Edelweiss Drive, right next to the Bavarian Lodge Condos. 706-878-1030.

Wurst Haus Restaurant and Beer Garden. Serves indoors as well as at the outdoor sidewalk beer garden. Menu consists of every variety of German wursts. Also American-type sandwiches and a wide variety of domestic and imported beers; also wines and cocktails. Friday nights and Saturday afternoon and evenings during the summer there is live entertainment. Prices are inexpensive. Located in front of White Horse Square on Main Street. 706-878-2647.

Wendy's Restaurant (Chain). Across the road from the Helendorf Inn as you turn into Edelweiss Drive from Main Street on the way to the Festhalle.

Motels

Alpenhof Motel North. Two levels, 35 units, TV, air/heat, phones. Two large double beds. Nonsmoking rooms available. Complimentary coffee. Conference rooms for meetings or parties. Outdoor swimming pool. No pets. Rates are moderate and vary with day of week and season. Located beyond Betty's Country Store on Yonah Street. 1-800-535-8678.

Alpenhof Motel South. Two-level, 28 units. TV, air/heat, phones. Complimentary coffee. Two large double beds. Non-smoking rooms available. A good sized heated indoor pool. No pets. Rates are moderate and vary with the season and day of week. Located on Main Street past the Alpine Village Outlet Stores (driving north). 1-800-535-1251.

The Castle Inn. This motel is located in the "Castle Inn" building, which also houses the Courtyard Cafe and the Museum of the Hills. In fact the entrance to the museum is the entrance to the motel. All the rooms are up one flight of stairs from the museum level. There are 11 rooms, some with private balconies overlooking the river. Cable TV, air/heat. Parking is behind the Castle Inn building, approach through Chattahoochee Street. Rates are moderate and vary with the season. P. O. Box 258, Helen, Ga 30545; 706-878-3140.

Chalet Kristy Motel. Located in an attractive setting right on the Chattahoochee. This is a two-story motel, all rooms approached by exterior walkway. TV, phones, air/heat, complimentary coffee. Two king-size beds in each room. Rates are moderate and vary with day of week and season. No pets. There is also a conference room for meetings or parties. This motel has a Christian gift shop and book store; there is, however, no other religious connection. All are welcome. Located on River Road which dead-ends at the Chalet Kristy Motel. P. O. Box 456, Helen, Ga 30545; 706-878-2155.

Bavarian Lodge and River's Edge Condominiums. There are two physically distinct sections to this complex, the lodge (motel rooms) on one side of the road (Edelweiss Drive) and the "condos" or suites on the river side. The lodge (motel) has 24 rooms, some in standard motel decor, others in "rustic cabin" style. These all have TV, air/heat, but no room phones. Some have efficiency kitchens and fireplaces. There is also a pool. The building across the road, housing the "condos" surely looks like a fanciful storybook version of a Swiss Alpine lodge, its three sections actually having Germanic names painted on their outside wall–Annaliese, Brigitta, and Cristl. This section (the "condos") are right on the Chattahoochee River and many of the rooms have private balconies and river views. The others face the road.

The condos have kitchens and fireplaces and may be rented as one-bedroom, two-bedroom or three-bedroom suites. Some have whirlpools. The rates vary with the different arrangements, also with the season, and are inexpensive to moderate. Edelweiss Drive. 1-800-422-6355 or 706-878-2840.

Chattahoochee River Front Motel. Fronts on Main Street; backs up to the Chattahoochee River. Shaded by great old trees. Twenty-four units, including singles and doubles. The riverfront rooms, on two levels, are all doubles, with patio or balcony. TV, air/heat, phones. There is also a swimming pool. Rates are inexpensive to moderate and vary with the day of week and season. Located on Main Street at the corner of Hamby. P. O. Box 1134, Helen, Ga 30545; 706-878-2184.

Comfort Inn. Standard as advertised. Built in 1990. Very attractive building and grounds, nicely landscaped. Nice lounge-type lobby. Two levels, 60 units. TV, air/heat, phones, built-in hair dryers. Complimentary Continental breakfast. Accessible rooms for handicapped. Nonsmoking rooms available. Rates are moderate off-season, but increase considerably during Oktoberfest. Located on Edelweiss Drive, the very first road on the right as you enter town driving north. P. O. Box 1178, Helen, Ga 30545; 1-800-221-2222.

Days Inn. Standard as advertised, but constructed (1989) to conform with "Alpine" style. Fifty-four units on two levels. TV, phones, air/heat, complimentary Continental breakfast. Rates are moderate and vary with the season. Located on Main Street a short distance from the Alpine Village Outlet Mall. 706-878-4079.

Derdenhof Inn Motel. Two levels, 28 rooms, two double beds in each. TV, phones, air/heat. Located on Bruckenstrasse (the second street you come to, on the right as you enter town driving north, just a half block in from the highway.) Rates are seasonal and moderate. No pets. P. O. Box 405, Helen, Ga 30545; 706-878-2141.

Heidi Motel. Sits atop a slope a short distance north of the center of town, opposite Betty's Country Store. Picturesque Alpine construction. Large rooms with hand-painted furniture. Two story, Alpine units, one of which is a two-room suite with fireplace. All rooms have TV, air/heat, phones. There is a swimming pool. Rates are moderate and vary with the season. No pets. P. O. Box 507, Helen, Ga 30545; 706-878-2689.

Helendorf Inn. This was one of the first establishments to be built in the "rebirth" of Helen as an Alpine village, and this is reflected in the very "Alpine" look of the motel in its entirety. There are 82 rooms on two levels, arranged around an inside parking court. One section of the motel overlooks the Chattahoochee. Some of these river rooms have kitchens; all river rooms have balconies above the river. Many are furnished and decorated "in the Bavarian style." There are, in addition, two spacious, nicely decorated suites with fireplaces, complete kitchen-bars and river-view balconies. All rooms have TV, air/heat, phones, two double beds. Next to the entry lobby is a cozy sitting room with fireplace. Room rates are moderate and vary with the season; suites are $135 and $150. Located on Edelweiss Drive, as you turn in from Main Street, just before coming to the river. P. O. Box 305, Helen, Ga 30545; 706-878-2271; reservations only: 1-800-445-2271.

Hofbrauhaus Inn. The building entrance is off Main Street but the inn and restaurant overlook the Chattahoochee. The three "European-style" guest rooms are upstairs. The restaurant and lounge are on ground level. Each room has a queen-size bed, TV, phone, air/heat. Two rooms have a private balcony overlooking the river. Listed in the AAA Travel Guide; recommended by the Georgia Hospitality and Travelers' Association. Rates moderate, vary with season. Located on Main Street north of Hamby Street, on the north edge of town. Owner Chris Hammersen. One Main Street, Helen, Ga 30545; 706-878-2248.

Cabins and Lodges

Chattahoochee Ridge Lodge. Situated atop Chattahoochee Ridge, high above Helen offering seclusion in a lovely mountain setting. There are three individual rooms and two two-room efficiency suites, all within the lodge and all with separate entrances. The efficiency suites each have a kitchen and a fireplace; they each sleep up to six. All have TV, air/heat. There is also a hot-tub "spa" in a self-contained unit outside. The Lodge boasts double insulation (a plus in the mountains) and a solar hot-water backup. The rates, which are moderate, vary with the season and the number of occupants. No pets. To get to the Lodge, turn in on Hamby Street (at the Chattahoochee River Front Motel), cross the bridge, and turn right (Escowee Drive), go about a block and take the left fork up the hill (Ridge Road). Go about 0.5 mile. The Lodge is on the right. Bob and Mary Swift. P. O. Box 175, Helen, Ga 30545; 1-800-476-8331 or 706-878-3144.

Cherokee Ridge Cabins. Four cabins in a wooded setting. A comfortable living-dining area with Scandinavian-type fireplace, kitchen, one bed-room, full bath. TV, air/heat. Deck and grill. Two cabins have one large double bed; two have two large double beds in the same room. Rates on inquiry. Located on Route 356, about 2.5 miles beyond Unicoi State Park. Route 1, Box 1405, Sautee, Ga 30571; 706-878-2380.

Mountain Madness Cabins. An adult resort. These are handsome, beauti-fully constructed, very attractive inside and out and most livable. They were built by John Koenig, very well known in this region for his timber-frame construction. The interior walls are all pine paneling, and the beams are visible in the two-story-high vaulted ceilings. The living/dining areas are spacious, comfortable, and nicely furnished; ditto for the bed-rooms. There are eleven cabins: one-bedroom cabins sleeping two and two-bedroom cabins sleeping four. All have kitchens, fireplace, full bath-room, air/heat. All have decks with grills, some have whirlpool tubs. No phones, and only one has TV. No pets and no children under 18 except with permission. All cabins are well separated from each other on wooded slopes. Rates are mostly moderate. Located on Route 356 about 1.5 miles beyond Unicoi State Park. P. O. Box 308, Helen, Ga 30545; 706-878-2851.

Skyridge Cabins. Five cabins in scenically beautiful and secluded moun-tain location. As you enter the grounds, there is a gazebo alongside a small pond. The road winds uphill, and as you come to each of the cabins along the way, you are impressed that they look more like homes than cabins. The road and surroundings are very nicely kept, and when you reach the office at the top (which is also the home of the manager) you are atop the ridge with the view of the surrounding mountains. Some of the cabins sleep two to six persons; the larger ones sleep two to ten. All have a "greatroom" with fireplace, fully equipped kitchens, air/heat, TV, decks, grills, etc. The larger cabins have 1 ½ or 2 baths and dishwasher. All are comfortably furnished, with homelike atmosphere. The rates are moderate and vary by season and day. No pets.

They will also arrange weddings (in the gazebo) providing minister, flowers, etc., for honeymoon occupants, with receptions in the cabin. Can be reached from Helen or from Old Sautee Store on Route 17. From Helen, drive north on 17/75 to Unicoi State Park turnoff (Route 356). When you come to the 6-mile marker, look for Sky Lake Road on the right just a few hundred feet ahead. Turn right and drive about 2.5 miles to Skyridge entrance. Sky Lake will be on the right. From Old Sautee Store, take Route 255 north about 2.2 miles to Skyridge sign, turn left and drive about 0.5 miles to Skyridge entrance. Route 1, Box 1286, Sautee, Ga 30571; 706-878-3244.

Tanglewood Resort Cabins. Thirty-two comfortable cabins in a 33-acre wooded area. Typical cabin consists of a tidy living/dining area and kitchen, fireplace, TV, air/heat, deck and grill. One-, two-, three- or four-bedrooms, each with a large double bed. There is also a restaurant serving three meals. During the winter months, the restaurant is open only for dinner weekdays; three meals on weekends. In season, open seven days for three meals. The menus for all three meals are basic and moderately priced. Cabin rates are moderate. Located on Route 356, 1.5 miles beyond (north of) Unicoi State Park. P. O. Box 435, Helen, Ga 30545; 706-878-3286.

Timberloft Cottages. Six compact, cozy cabins; nicely constructed, attractive. All are identical and consist of the following: combination living/dining/bedroom area and sleeping loft. Woodburning fireplace, TV, air/heat. Kitchenette, full bathroom. Also a swimming pool. No pets. Rates are inexpensive and vary with season. Located on Route 356 about 2 miles beyond (north of) Unicoi State Park. P. O. Box 341, Helen, Ga 30545; 706-878-2950.

Specialty Shops

Bavarian Glass Blowers. A most unique and creative assortment of hand-blown and hand-spun glass items such as little animals, unicorns, peacocks, bells, clowns, stagecoaches, sailing ships, sewing machines, Christmas decorations, wedding cake tops, etc. Prices range from $4 for the smallest, simplest items to $60 for the largest and most complex. Weekends only during the winter; all week in season. Located on the street level of Geselschaft Haus building on Main Street. Main Street, Helen, Ga 30545; 706-878-3156.

Bavarian Haus of Gifts. A variety of interesting collectibles. Features the "heraldry" line, with 375 names and the family crest that goes with each. These are imprinted on cups, steins, bells, and wall plaques. Also, Bosson's wall masks; Hummel figurines; complete line of limited-edition Emmett Kelly items; member of the Bradford plate exchange; Black Forest clocks from Germany; Gone with the Wind figurines, others. Located in Helen Square. Thom Dupree, owner. P. O. Box 1087, Helen, Ga 30545; 706-878-3164.

Becky's Small Wonders. A very nice collection of miniatures. These are Becky Fiero's "small wonders." Among the collection are Lilliput Lane cottages of England, Scotland, Germany, and USA; Pendelfin Rabbits from England; Spangler's Realm dragons; Alex Haley's (Roots) collection of black figurines; History of Santa–a depiction of various versions of Santa throughout the world and ages; Precious Memories (little teardrop children); Hummel miniature figurines; Davis's farm life series; Jan Hegera porcelain dolls; Snow Village, Dickens Village, Alpine Village, North Pole (Santa) Village, and others. Located on Main Street across from White Horse Square. P. O. Box 575, Helen, Ga 30545; 706-878-3108.

Betty's Country Store. As much a place to see as it is a place to buy every variety of food, usual and unusual, that you can think of. Here's what we encountered on our visit (this is just part of it). Out front, stalls of attractive fruits and vegetables. Inside, jars of old-time candies, cheeses of all kinds; homemade pickles, jams, jellies–hundreds of jars; country hams, grain milled at Nora Mill; old-timey soft drinks; all sorts of cook books; difficult-to-find varieties of corn, rice, and beans; barrels of different varieties of coffee; crocks and vases; lots of deli and baked items; fresh meat, ham, sausages; cannisters, posters, and other memorabilia. Located on Main Street, corner of Yonah. 706-878-2943.

Candles by Anita. Beautifully fashioned and colored candles that look nothing like candles, but rather like artistically creative sculptures and statuettes. You can come in and see them being made. Located on Main Street, across the road from White House Square. 1-800-358-4130 or 706-865-6131.

Christmas Shop. A two-story shop displaying and selling a large, varied, and interesting collection of Christmas items. In addition to all sorts of Christmas ornaments and lights, there are dolls (Madame Alexander), Snow Villages, Dickens Villages, toys, decorations, creches, and other Christmas sets and figurines. Many items are imported from Finland, Germany, Austria, and Switzerland. Located in White Horse Square. P. O. Box 521, Helen, Ga 30545; 706-878-2540.

Damron's Glass Engraving. A very large collection of glassware which Bob Damron engraves, by hand, with a variety of artistic designs (about 300 of them)–bowls, glasses, dishes, decanters, pitchers, candy dishes, stemware, barware. He has been doing this for 40 years, and his father, before him, for 60 years. Open all year. Located on Main Street, lower level of the Geselschaft Haus, opposite the Bavarian Glass Blowers P. O. Box 909, Helen, Ga 30545; 706-878-2087.

Das Ist Leather. As the name implies, this is a shop that specializes in a wide variety of leather items (U.S.-made): purses, wallets, belts, vests, jackets, moccasins, skirts, pants, saddlebags; sheepskin slippers and jackets; and deerskin halters. Also hat bands, hat pins, knives; Western hats; etc. Located on Main Street (near Geselschaft Haus) a short distance before you get to Chattahoochee Street, walking North. P. O. Box 685, Helen, Ga 30545; 706-878-3534.

The Dulcimer Shop. Handmade dulcimers and other folk, musical instruments, many of them made in this shop. Also, tapes, records, and books on folk music; also music instrument accessories. Located at the old Nacoochee Post Office building, at the junction of Routes 17 and 75. P. O. Box 570, Helen, Ga 30545; 706-878-3149.

Fain's Antiques. Specializes in old doors, windows and fixtures that have come out of old homes; also beds, chairs, tables, hutches and art of the Victorian era. The owner, Rob Fain, is the son of Grandpa Fain, owner and operator of Nora Mill, and descendant of one of the oldest families in this region. Located across the road from Alpine Village Factory Outlets. 706-878-2927.

Hansel and Gretl Candy Kitchen. Made-on-the-premises fudges, chocolate bark, pecan turtles, peanut brittle, artistically fashioned candies, and various other confections. There are two locations. One is on the corner of Fussen Platz on River Street. The other is on the corner of Main Street and Olde Street. P. O. Box 327, Helen, Ga 30545; 706-878-2443.

Harris of Helen, Inc. A most interesting, unique, and wide-ranging collection of wares for the selective buyer. There are imported Irish handwoven and handknit stoles, shawls, sweaters, hats, and scarves. There is a collection of Beatrix Potter (Peter Rabbit and Friends) items, one of the largest such collections in the U.S., according to the owner, Jim Harris. There are figurines by Royal Dalton and Wedgwood; collector dolls by Madame Alexander, Robin Wood, Jan Hagara and others; handcrafted wooden toys by Warren; ponchos, shawls, stoles, scarves etc. by Churchill Weavers; handwrought silver and copper jewelry by Stuart Nye; stuffed animals, music boxes, lamps. It is all "quality," Mr. Harris says, but also affordable. Located on Main Street, right next to the Geselschaft Haus. P. O. Box 179, Helen, Ga 30545; 706-878-2599.

Holly House. A very attractive and interesting collection of dolls. Specializes in porcelain "artist dolls"; Maude Humphrey Bogart (mother of Humphrey Bogart) figurines of children in period costumes. Also, the Maurice Midman cottages, representing the American collection of the John Hine studios–typical American homes, covered bridges, train stations, river boats, etc; Miss Noah Originals (plush Animals); June McKenna Santas; Ron Lee and Jan Hegera dolls, etc. Located on Main Street, just outside White Horse Plaza, up one flight of stairs. P. O. Box 836, Helen, Ga 30545; 706-878-3131.

House of Tyrol. A large collection of Swiss, German, and Austrian imports: mugs, steins, glassware, crystal, porcelain, drinking sets with decanters, tea sets, lederhosen, dirndls, Tyrolean hats, lace curtains, tapes and records from Germany and Austria, Hummel figurines. They have catalogs from which one may order these and a variety of other imports. Located on Main Street across the road from Chattahoochee Street intersection. 706-865-2951.

Jewelry Trend. Wholesale and retail sales of imported jewelry–gold, silver, rings, watches, chains. Features vermeil gold by Qualita Italiana and Black Hill gold watches. Located in White Horse Square. 706-878-3080.

Jolly's Toys. Hand-made wooden toys: name trains, animal trains, trucks, automobiles, "Old Folks" toys, puzzles, airplanes, rifles, crayon holders, pedal-wheel boats, etc. Located on River Street at entrance to Fussen Platz. P. O. Box 75, Helen, Ga 30545; 706-878-2262.

Kennedy's Irish Cottage. Irish imports. Woolen items such as sweaters, socks, scarves; Irish food items; linen; Irish records, tapes, books; glassware; china, etc. Located at the corner of Main and Olde Streets 706-878-2489.

Master Works of Helen. They carry the Austin line of foundry-cast reproductions of sculptures by famed artists. Also Elfin of Wildewood (spirits, elves, dragons). Also handcrafted earrings by 140 artists (American and European) including Mark Ehrmann designs. Located at the corner of Main and River Streets. P. O. Box 31, Helen, Ga 30545; 706-878-2352.

Mathena's Handmade Woodcrafts. Made out of hardwood (walnut, cherry, maple, cedar). Such handcrafted items as bowls, candlesticks, magazine racks, baskets, kitchen box holders, tissue box holders, door harps, trivet baskets, birds, etc. P. O. Box 356, Helen, Ga 30545; 706-878-3305.

Music Box Plus. An interesting and unique collection of music boxes in every shape and form: teacups and teapots, key rings, children's banks, Christmas objects, birds, figurines, Disney collection, Beatrix Potter collection, Gone with the Wind collection, carousels, churches, etc. Located on Main Street, across from White Horse Square. P. O. Box 923, Helen, Ga 30545; 706-878-3428.

Old Norway. This is a branch of the Old Sautee Store featuring imported Scandinavian sweaters and other knit goods, trolls, figurines, toys, jewelry, glassware. Located on Olde Street. 706-878-2475.

Opa's Chalet Imports. A wide variety of imports from Austria, Germany, and Switzerland. Tyrolean attire, dirndls and lederhosen, personalized beer steins, stuffed animals from Germany, Austrian wood carvings, music boxes of various kinds, Alpine wall treatments, Kolf linens from Austria, and David Winter cottages. Located in the little square called Bavarian Village, adjacent to the International Cafe, Main Street, just before you cross the river going north. 706-878-2090.

Rocks to Riches. In addition to a collection of imported jewelry items, this shop also sells various specimens of exotically colored and shaped (also hand-carved) decorative rocks, minerals, gemstones. There is also a museum displaying many rare specimens and Indian artifacts that are not for sale. Located in White Horse Square, upstairs from Jewelry Trends. P. O. Box 633, Helen, Ga 30545; 706-878-3415.

Shop Antiques. An attractive and interesting little antique shop specializing in 19th-century American furniture and accessories. They also carry antique china, crystal, lamps, art. Located on Main Street, between Dye and Spring Streets. 706-878-2359.

Tekakwitha Indian Shop. A unique collection of genuine Indian goods, crafts, and relics: silver jewelry; leather; pottery; beaded belts and other beaded items; moccasins; antique Indian costumes and clothing; arrowheads and tomahawks. You will recognize the shop by the large area in front of the store decorated with Indian symbols. The shop is named after a Mohawk Indian woman, Kateri Tekakwitha, the first Mohawk Indian to be converted to Christianity. The owner of the store, Ruth Lammers is part Shawnee. Once a year, generally the second week in June, Ms. Lammers organizes "Indian Days" in Helen. Indians from many different tribes come to display and sell their crafts, do tribal dances, and perform tribal ceremonies. Proceeds go to Christian Indian missions throughout the United States. This Indian store is located on Main Street, opposite the Alpine Village Factory Outlet mall. 706-878-2938.

Tobak Haus. Pipes, pipe tobacco, imported and domestic cigarettes, smokers' accessories. Corner of Chattahoochee and Main Streets. 706-878-2956.

Weaver Leather Works. Handcrafted, custom-designed leather belts and buckles. The belts may be decorated with various hand-tooled designs.

Buckles may be decorated with designs of purchaser's choice, such as sports, fishing, hunting, flags, military insignia, and organizational insignia, etc. Dress belts, hats, and other leather goods also. Located at the end of Horse and Duck Plaza. P. O. Box 578, Helen, Ga 30545; 1-800-327-7533 or 706-878-2837.

Windmill. An extensive line of Delft and other Dutch ceramic imports, all beautifully decorated: dishes, pitchers, vases, clocks, lamps, tea sets, candelabra, and candlesticks, etc. Plus Dutch dolls, wooden shoes, jewelry. Owners Mary and Peter De Groot. Located on White Horse Square. P. O. Box 226, Helen, Ga 30545; 706-878-3444.

Alpine Village Factory Outlets

This is a typical discount outlet mall with a wide variety of shops in the "affordable" range. The mall is divided into two main sections. They are located next to each other on the right just as you enter town, driving north.

These are the shops in the first section:

Kids Port U.S.A. Playwear and dresswear for children of all ages.

Prestige Fragrance and Cosmetics. A wide variety of name brand perfumes and toilet waters, cosmetics.

Bannister Shoe. Dress, casual, athletic.

Manhattan. Shirts, sportswear, etc.

Aileen. Ladies' casual wear.

Corning Revere. Kitchenware. Corning, Visions, Pyrex, Revere.

Fashion Flair. Men's and women's wear. Izod, La Coste, Monet.

Hanes Activewear. Men's and women's "sweats," knit tops, socks, etc.

Orbit. Miss and women's sportswear.

Van Heusen. Fashion apparel for men and women.

Clothesworks. Variety of men's and women's clothing.

L'eggs, Hanes, Bali. Hosiery, undergarments, lingerie, activewear, etc.

In this section there is a "quick bite" eatery: **The Yogurt Shop,** serving frozen yogurt and toppings, plus a variety of sandwiches.

These are the shops in the second section:

Old Mill. Ladies sportswear.

Toy Liquidators. Mattel, Hasbro, Tonka, others.

Clothes Ltd. Popular brands of ladies' clothing and accessories.

Bass. Wide range of dress, casual, and sports shoes.

Leather Loft Stores Inc. Handbags, brief cases, wallets, belts, accessories, etc.

Cape Isle Knitters. Sweaters and knits, men and women.

Habersham Winery. Wine tasting and sales of Habersham wines.

Ribbon Outlet. Ribbons and trims; bulk, precut, or by the yard.

Callaway Gardens. Baskets, lamps, pottery, dried flowers, stuffed animals, jams and jellies.

Totes/Sunglass World. Totes umbrellas, raincoats, rain hats, luggage. Brand name sunglasses.

Kitchen Collection. Wearever, Proctor-Silex.

American Tourister. Luggage.

Little Red Shoe House. Name-brand dress, casual, and athletic footwear for the family.

Gitano. Casual and active sportswear, junior, misses, maternity, and men's.

Huckleberry Patch. Moccasins, Western boots, shoes, and leather goods.

Amusement and Recreation

Innsbruck Golf Course. Established mainly as a membership club, this golf course is open on a daily basis to visitors and to occupants of Innsbruck villas, which are rentable on a daily or weekly basis. Tennis courts and swimming pool are open only to members and to occupants of villas. The course is a beautiful 18-hole tournament-level course, surrounded by scenic hills. The clubhouse is built like a Swiss Chalet, offering such amenities as seasoned golfers would be looking for. A bar and grill are open year-round. A restaurant offering a variety of steaks, seafood, and specialties is open weekends, May through October. To get to the Innsbruck, turn right at the very first street you come to (Edelweiss Drive) on the right, entering town on 17/75 driving north. If you miss that, the second street (Bruckenstrasse) will take you there, too. P. O. Box 580, Helen, Ga 30545; 706-878-2100.

Museum of the Hills. One of the most imaginative, evocative, and true-to-life replications of the past we have ever seen, plus a venture into storyland, equally creative. The first part of this adventure is a journey into the past. You walk in a darkened corridor and peer through glass windows into a series of tableaux with lifelike wax figures, dressed in turn-of-the-century clothing engaged in various home and farm settings. Here is a sampling of the scenes: family kitchen with a mother and two children; a country preacher marrying a young couple; a barber shop, the barber cutting a child's hair; an ice cream parlor, children being served sodas; a general store with pot bellied stove and all sorts of general store goods; a blacksmith shop, coals glowing. The last tableau is that of the children asleep in bed drifting off to dreamland, and you enter dreamland with them as they dream about Goldilocks, Little Red Riding Hood, Hansel and Gretl, Alice in Wonderland and others. As you move from scene to scene, you hear music appropriate to the scene. Then the children wake up to the bright morning sunlight and look over beautiful farms and country scenes. Children and adults alike will be charmed by the experience. The museum and tableaux were designed by John Kollock, famed local artist who also designed the Alpine Village of Helen. The wax figures are said to have come from a private collection owned by the great-granddaughter of Madame Tussaud of the famed London wax museum. Admission prices are inexpensive and vary by age. Located on Main Street in the Castle Inn Building. P. O. Box 258, Helen, Ga 30545; 706-878-3140.

Festivals

The major festival events in Helen are the **Fasching** (January and February), **Mayfest** (May), **Hot Air Balloon Race** (June), **Oktoberfest** (September and October), and the **Christmas Market** (November and December).

Fasching is an Austrian and German carnival held between Epiphany and Shrove Tuesday, similar to the Mardi Gras carnival of New Orleans, Paris and other cities. In Helen it starts the weekend after Epiphany and continues every weekend thereafter, winding up on Shrove Tuesday. There are masked costume parades, singing and dancing outdoors and in the restaurants and on the town square–Market Platz, with many other local imaginative variations. Throughout there is joyfulness and revelry.

Mayfest is a one-day event (5 p.m. to midnight) celebrating "May Day," held in the Festhalle (the huge, enclosed auditorium), where many of Helen's major events take place. There is a Maypole around which May Day dances and ceremonies are performed. Then from late afternoon to midnight, there is musical entertainment (vocal and band) and dancing to the music of an "oompah" band. The participants are seated at beerhall-type plank tables, singing, conversing, jesting, eating and drinking. German-style dishes and beer and wine are available, and everyone attests a good time is had by all.

Hot Air Balloon Race. In 1973, local businessman Pete Hodkinson and Lanier Chambers bought a hot air balloon and sponsored a balloon race as a promotion for Helen. Malcolm Forbes was one of the contestants. Since then, the balloon race has become an annual event, attracting some 15,000 people. The race balloons take off at 7 a.m. the Thursday morning preceding the first weekend in June. Balloonists from all over the country come to participate. The race starts in the field alongside the Festhalle and ends on the Atlantic coast–anywhere from Maine to Florida that the prevailing wind currents may take the balloons. Then, on Thursday, and during the weekend, balloon rides, both tethered and free-sailing, are offered.

Tarp Head, a local businessman and balloon enthusiast who organizes the annual event assures us that careful prior study of atmospheric conditions and wind currents makes balloon sailing a safe activity. For more information on this event, call the Convention and Visitors' Bureau. 706-878-2181.

Oktoberfest. This is the granddaddy of them all. The Oktoberfest originates in Germany and is said to date back to Munich in 1810, when King Ludwig I married Princess Therese. However, in more recent years, in Germany and by imitation elsewhere, it has come more to be associated with the celebration of beer and beer-drinking, and all the singing and dancing and revelry that goes with it. The Oktoberfest in Helen is all of that and much more. It is held in the Festhalle. On stage, there is continuous entertainment from 5 p.m. to closing time–midnight. The festivities and entertainment are led by a master of ceremonies, or mistress of ceremonies (or both) of German or Austrian origin, who sing, banter, and lead the hundreds (sometimes it seems more like thousands) of participants in singing or in German toasts and familiar songs. Throughout the night there is dancing–polkas, waltzes, and other German types, as well as some American numbers. A half-dozen different bands alternate throughout the festival, several of them having come over from Germany and Austria. The audience is mostly from Georgia and nearby states, many even from up North. But during Oktoberfest, everybody is German, and it is not at all unusual to see people decked out in dirndls, lederhosen, Alpine socks and boots, and Tyrolean hats, and you would swear they were German or Austrian or Swiss until you heard them speak and you recognized the familiar "y'all." There is, however, one distinctly southern touch in the entertainment and that is the performance, throughout Oktoberfest, of the Alpine Village Cloggers, an assemblage of 20 or more young ladies from Helen and environs performing dazzlingly intricate clogging numbers. Also, at least once each night, the band plays "Dixie," and suddenly, everybody is a "sure 'nuff" southerner–even the people from Yankeeland. There's plenty of German-style food, beer and wine available, served cafeteria style and consumed beer-hall style.

Oktoberfest runs all of September and October. During September, it is held on Friday and Saturday nights only; during October, every night except Sunday.

Christmas Market. Christmas festivities with a German flavor begin the weekend after Thanksgiving and continue right up to Christmas. Every weekend the Christmas Market is set up in Market Platz (town square), with tents and stalls of Christmas wares, gifts, crafts, home-baked cakes, and other food for Christmas. There is, of course, Christmas music and caroling. The restaurants also feature special Christmas entertainment and celebrations.

Unicoi State Park and Anna Ruby Falls

Unicoi State Park must be the realization of some park planner's fond dream. In a magnificent setting, it combines comfortable, convenient, modern lodging accommodations in a 100-room lodge and several groups of cottages with most everything one could want in outdoor, country recreation: swimming, fishing, canoeing on a 50-acre lake; hiking trails; picnicking; RV camping; and just plain enjoyment of scenic beauty.

The grounds consist of 30 acres of landscaped park land in the midst of a 2,000-acre forest preserve situated in the foothills of the mountains. The focus of the park is the Lodge and Conference Center complex, modern and commodious in every respect, spacious and bright. Roadways from this building lead to discreetly hidden parking areas, groups of cottages, tent and trailer areas, beach areas at the lake and hiking trails.

An attractive dining room, situated in the Lodge/Conference Center complex offers three ample meals a day, country cuisine, at incredibly low prices. It is open, also, to the public. The conference center, catering to small and large groups, has several spacious meeting rooms.

The complex also contains a large arts and crafts shop, and there is a daily schedule of activities centered around country living and the ways and beauties of nature. Reservations and information: 706-878-2824.

Unicoi State Park is located just north of Helen. To get there, go through town on Route 17/75, and continue for another mile to the intersection (on the right) with Route 356. Turn onto 356 and continue for another 1.5 miles, until you come to the entrance to the park entrance on the right.

Within just a few minutes' drive, there is the road leading to **Anna Ruby Falls,** one of the most beautiful in the state. To get there from the Lodge/ Conference Center, drive to the Park exit and turn left on Route 356 toward Helen. You'll come to a bridge and as you cross, you'll see on the right a lovely, picturesque small lake. This is **Unicoi Lake,** part of the state park, and it is where you do your swimming, fishing, and canoeing.

After you've crossed the bridge, you can, if you want to, pull in, park, rest, picnic and explore the lakeshore and surroundings or continue right on to the falls. Just a few hundred feet beyond the bridge, on the right, is the road to Anna Ruby Falls. It is so marked.

The winding drive uphill–about 2.5 miles–ends in a parking area. The **Heritage Book Store** is next to the parking area. Park your car there and then you have a four-tenths-mile hike up to the falls. The path follows the course of Smith Creek, the stream leading away from the falls. It is rugged and scenic. The uphill hike is strenuous, but there are places you can rest. As you trod slowly and laboriously uphill, you see on your left the creek cascading downhill, swiftly and furiously over the stone-strewn creek bed. Each turn of the road presents a more beautiful scene than the one before. You find yourself wanting to stop at each turn to absorb and commit to memory the beauty of the scene, the sound of the rushing creek, the smell of the water and the woods.

As you plod upwards, you meet people coming down from the falls, grinning with pleasure and encouraging you with "It's just a few hundred feet more." And then you make the last turn, and there before you are the falls–actually twin falls–plunging to the creek bed in a spectacular display. One of the two falls originates in Curtis Creek and drops 153 feet. The other right beside it originates from York Creek and drops 50 feet. At the base they form Smith Creek, which, after its winding, downhill course, empties into Unicoi Lake.

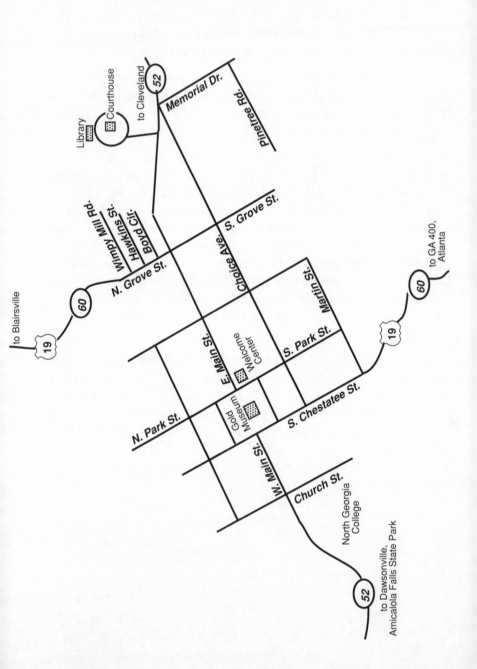

Dahlonega

"I was deer hunting one day when I kicked up something that caught my eye. I examined it and decided it was gold. It seemed, within a few days, as if the whole world must have heard of it ... They came afoot, on horseback and in wagons – acting more like crazy men than anything else ... "

— Benjamin Parks
in an 1894 interview with
the *Atlanta Constitution*

Less than an hour from Atlanta in the shadow of the beautiful Blue Ridge Mountains is a charming little town with a 19th century look. Dahlonega (da-LON-uh-ga), located in Lumpkin County, Georgia, is best known as the site of North America's first major gold rush, in 1828. When word got out that gold had been discovered here, prospectors came by the thousands, drawn by the promise of quick and easy fortunes.

Everywhere in the town are reminders of the community's historic past. Dominating the skyline is the golden steeple atop Price Memorial Hall on the campus of North Georgia College. The steeple – like the dome of the state capitol building in Atlanta – is covered in real Dahlonega gold. Price Memorial sits on the foundation of a former United States Mint where gold coins were minted prior to the outbreak of the Civil War. Today, visitors to Dahlonega can still pan for gold, right on the public square or at nearby Crisson Mine.

In the town, too, are many nostalgic shops overflowing with Appalachian crafts, pottery, and gold jewelry. Names of a number of area businesses incorporate words like gold, golden, mint and nugget, reflecting the town's history as a gold mining community.

On the public square, where many of the most interesting shops are located, old buildings have been restored to authentic 19th century

Georgia, complete with lawns, trees, and brick walks. Some buildings, including the Greek Revival- style Lumpkin County Courthouse, built in 1836, are on the list of National Historic Sites. Today, the old courthouse houses the Dahlonega Gold Museum.

Dahlonega also serves up some really fine home cookin'. The most notable example is the Smith House, just off the square. The quality of delicious meats and fresh vegetables here has become legendary.

This, too, is a town of festivals that are fun for all. Each year in April is Dahlonega's Birthday Celebration. In May is the Wildflower Festival of the Arts, which combines visual and performing arts with nature. The Dahlonega Blue Grass Festival is always the last week in June. On July Fourth is the Family Days Celebration. Huge crowds attend Gold Rush Days, when "world championship gold panning" competition is held in October. For the holiday season, there's an Old Fashioned Christmas cele-bration and parade in early December.

Near Dahlonega are beautiful drives and places to hike, camp, raft down a river, and ride horses. Amicalola State Park and its magnificent waterfall and campsites is just 14 miles from the center of town. The Chattahoo-chee National Forest, which surrounds much of the Dahlonega area, makes for a lush, green environmental setting.

When you're headed for the North Georgia mountains, Dahlonega is an intriguing and historic first stop along your way. Traveling north from the Atlanta area, take Highway 400. Continue for about 40 minutes to where the highway ends at Georgia 19. From here, follow the signs to Dahlonega.

Gold Fever!

Gold was thought to have been first discovered in Lumpkin County by Benjamin Parks early in the year 1828. Though gold also was found in the early 1800s in neighboring counties and states, Lumpkin County has long been proclaimed the center of America's first major gold rush. Thousands of people came to the county during the 20 years following the first gold discovery. Much of the ore found here produced a higher percentage of gold than did the later California mines.

The first settlement in the county by gold immigrants was the town of Auraria, located on a ridge between the Chestatee and Etowah Rivers. An early mine owner here was John C. Calhoun, a vice president of the United States and later a South Carolina senator. Calhoun favored a name for the gold mining community that pertained to gold. Auraria, the name selected, is from the Latin word meaning gold mine.

The town grew, and at one time, there were about 100 homes, 4 or 5 taverns and 18 to 20 businesses, as well as several doctors and lawyers, all serving the mining community. But Auraria was not destined to last. A settlement 5 miles north was the choice for the permanent county government.

The new county seat, called Talonaga, which means precious yellow or gold, was chosen from the Cherokee language. A Cherokee Indian recommended that the name should be correctly spelled "Dahlohnega." Ultimately, the second "h" was dropped, giving the town the name of Dahlonega.

There were once several mines here, including the Dahlonega Consolidated Gold Mine, at that time the largest east of the Mississippi River. In the early days, gold was found in the streams and stream beds. Later, using a technique called hydraulic mining, it was found in veins in the earth. Dynamite was used in the process of creating elaborate tunnels which were used to reach the gold.

From 1828 to 1837, $1.8 million in Georgia gold reached the Philadelphia mint. In 1835, the U.S. Congress authorized the nation's first branch mints at New Orleans, Charlotte, and Dahlonega. Three years later, the Dahlonega Branch Mint opened. Over the next 23 years of its operation, the mint coined 1.3 million coins worth about $6 milllion. Only gold coins were minted in Dahlonega. The coins were in denominations of $1.00, $2.50, $3.00 and $5.00.

After the outbreak of the Civil War, the Dahlonega Mint closed. The Confederacy used the building before Union cavalrymen took control of it. For several years, until 1869, the basement housed a small military prison. In 1871, the building and 10 acres were donated to the trustees of the newly created North Georgia Agricultural College. Seven years later, in 1878, the mint building burned. Today, Price Memorial Hall, the

Dahlonega Mint

administration building of North Georgia College, stands above the basement foundation of the old Dahlonega Mint.

Many Dahlonega miners went westward after 1849. Green Russell, an Auraria gold miner, returned from mining in California and later, with his two brothers, led a gold party to the Kansas Territory. This group started the "Pike's Peak or Bust" stampede that gave birth to Colorado.

Mining continued to some extent in Dahlonega until World War II, when equipment used to run the mines was sold for scrap to help the war effort. In the 1970s, when gold rose in price, interest again revived in gold mining.

Many who continued to mine or pan for gold here into the 20th century were third and fourth generation gold miners. Said one old-timer, "Gold mining means heartaches and disappointments. My mom and dad would sometimes live high on the hog, sometimes not. You have to stick with it. On many days, you don't get any gold."

Another member of an old Dahlonega mining family reminisced, "A lot of the time, we didn't have enough money for food. Mom could sometimes dig in our yard and find enough gold to buy groceries for a week!"

Trying Your Hand at Gold Panning

Today, the most interesting place to pan for gold is probably the **Crisson Mine**, which opened in 1847. While the mine has not operated commercially for a number of years, it has been open to the public for gold panning for the past 21 years. During the summer and fall, the mine has as many as 200 visitors a day.

To get there from Dahlonega's Public Square, turn onto Highway 19 north at the town's only traffic light. Turn right, almost immediately, onto Wimpy Mill Road. The mine, panning area, gift shop and Crisson family home are located on the right about 2 ½ miles after you turn onto Wimpy Mill Rd.

At Crisson Mine, managers Tammy and Tony Ray will show you around the gift shop and give you a lesson in gold panning. The mine itself is closed to the public. You can try your luck by buying dirt from the mine for $1.50 a pan. If you're really enthusiastic, purchase a small bucket of dirt for $5.25 or a large bucket for $8.00.

During our gold panning experience here, we talked with John Faulk, a Texas native who has found enough gold at Crisson Mine to pay for his automobile. John purchased a pan of dirt and showed us how to place the pan in the large pool of water, swirling it around until all the pebbles in the pan were washed clean. After discarding all the pebbles larger than a small pea, Faulk swirled the pan with a gentle motion. Lightweight minerals in the pan, he said, are picked up by the moving water. You can wash these over the side of the pan by tilting it while swirling. The heavy minerals, including gold, settle to the bottom.

Faulk showed us the difference between gold flakes and gold nuggets. And, lo and behold, from the bottom of his pan, he lifted a shiny gold nugget. "I'd say that's worth about $40," he said with a smile.

In the gift shop you'll find 10K and 14K gold rings, bracelets, earrings, necklaces and other items. You can also buy jewelry and gift items made of pyrite (fool's gold).

The Crisson Mine gift shop and panning area are open every day. Weekday hours June through August are 10:00 a.m. to 5:00 p.m. During other months, weekday hours are 10:00 a.m. to 6:00 p.m. On Saturdays and

Sundays, hours are 10:00 a.m. to 6:00 p.m. For more information, call 706-864-6363.

Other places to pan for gold include the front yard of the Smith House, one block off the square, and Gold Miner's Camp on Highway 60 about 2 miles south of town.

Where to Shop, What to Do and See

Dahlonega Courthouse Gold Museum. Regardless of which road leads you to Dahlonega, you'll find yourself circling the public square in the center of town. The most prominent feature here is the Dahlonega Court-house Gold Museum, located on a beautiful tree-shaded lot in the middle of the square. The museum, operated by the Parks, Recreation and Historic Sites Division of the Georgia Department of Natural Resources, is a logical first stop.

The staff of the Gold Museum is quite informed about the history of gold mining in the area. On display on the ground floor are a variety of gold

Dahlonega Courthouse

coins and other objects made of gold. On the walls are photos showing mining operations and many of the politicians, miners and others who played an important role in Dahlonega's history during the period of active mining and minting of gold coins. Available too are references on gold mining in the vicinity. Upstairs in the building are more exhibits and a small auditorium where visitors can see a 30-minute film called *Gold Fever,* the story of gold mining in Dahlonega. For more information, call the Gold Museum at 404-864-2257.

The Chamber of Commerce Welcome Center is across the street from the Gold Museum. Here, you'll find a friendly staff and a host of brochures and other information about area restaurants, lodging, festivals, and recreation. For more information, call 706-864-3711 or write Dahlonega Welcome Center, P. O. Box 2037, Dahlonega, Ga 30533.

The shops along the square offer a variety of antiques and reproductions as well as artwork and crafts by area artists. All are within walking distance of one other. Store hours of operation seem to vary with the owners and the time of year.

Brad Walker, Original Pottery is located on the square at N. Park Street. "I've been a potter since 1966 and in business for 13 years," says Walker, a friendly, burly mountain man. "All the work in my shop is original, and all the clays and glazes are made from my own formula." Walker's creations range from coffee cups with funny faces to bowls with beautiful, colorful glazes. All the glazes are leadless and dishwasher and microwave safe.

Timber and Treasures, in the same block of shops with Walker's Pottery, offers quilts, watercolors, and collectible items in wood and brass. A specialty here is Tom Clark gnomes. 706-864-6703.

Hummingbird Lane is a shop where the theme is "Friend of nature." Here, shopkeepers Camerone Malloy and Connie Hampton will show you reproductions, cards, calendars, local wood crafts, nature photography, and original art, all pertaining to wildlife. Other items include handmade kaleidoscopes, tapes, and furniture. The shop is located upstars in Hall's Block Building on the square. 706-864-5991.

The Little Country Store, in the Fred Jones Building on the square, has homemade quilts and pillows by area craftsmen as well as custom-built, handcrafted furniture. 706-864-7557.

The History Store is operated by local historian Bill Kinsland. Stop in and chat with him about Dahlonega's rich history, and browse through his inventory of maps, history books, and hiking and travel guides. Among the maps available are relief maps, lake and river guides, Indian maps, geologic and mineral maps, and historic and antique maps. Book topics include American Indian history, the Civil War, Georgia history, Appalachian and other trails, nature guides, gardening, the Foxfire series, and children's books. The History Store also carries unique postcards, historic American flags, and a variety of music on tape including American Indian flute, Civil War songs, and bluegrass, classical, and new age music. The store is on N. Park Street, just off the square. 706-864-7225.

Antiques and Gifts of Dahlonega, on N. Park Street, is a shop really worth your time if you are interested in antiques, jewelry, crafts, memorabilia and decorative accessories. 706-864-3637.

Conner House. Several interesting shops carrying antiques, crafts, and Christmas decorations are located in the Conner House, an old two-story structure on the public square. These shops seem to change with the seasons, so we will not list all of them. On a recent visit, two of the shops were **Flossie's Antiques 'n Stuff,** 706-265-7177, and **Queen Ann's Lace,** 706-265-7177, which carries antiques, art, flowers, and lace.

The campus of **North Georgia College,** just west of town, is worth strolling through. The second oldest institution in the University System of Georgia, the college was founded in 1873. Today, about 2,500 students are pursuing 40 major areas of study, including business administration, premed, nursing, education, criminal justice, and computer science. A primary point of interest on the campus, as mentioned earlier, is Price Memorial Hall with its steeple coated in Georgia gold.

North Georgia College Gallery. Inside the Student Center (across from the Great Room on the theater level) is the North Georgia College Gallery, which provides exhibition space for high quality art shows. Here are the works of the school's fine arts department faculty and students as well as outstanding local and regional artists. Adjacent to the gallery are display cases of the North Georgia College Museum which contain a history of the college through memorabilia. The gallery is open from 8:00 a.m. to 5:00 p.m. Monday through Friday, and from 1:00 p.m. to 3:00 p.m. Saturday and Sunday.

Consolidated Gold Mines offers a 40 minute guided tour, with an actual miner, back into the history of gold mining. The miner guides you past the famous "Glory Hole" and deep into the largest gold mine operation ever established east of the Mississippi River. Trying your hand at panning for gold is part of the tour. Open everyday, 10 a.m. to 5 p.m. 125 Consolidated Gold Mine Road. 706-864-8473.

Dining in Dahlonega

There are several good dining choices, right on the square or within walking distance.

Caruso's Italian Restaurant on Main Street, just off the square, is a favorite of locals. At this very casual establishment, patrons choose from a variety of tasty salads and soups as well as homemade pastas and veal, chicken, and shrimp dishes. Pizza also is on the menu. Espresso coffee and homemade desserts are available. You can choose from several domestic and imported beers and a few wines. Entrees are inexpensive. Lunch is served Monday through Saturday from 11:00 a.m. to 2:00 p.m. Dinner is 4:00 to 9:30 p.m. Sunday hours are 12:00 to 8:00 p.m. Hours vary in winter. 113 E. Main Street. 706-864-4664.

The Front Porch. This is an excellent place to sit, enjoy lunch, and do some people-watching on the public square below. Located outdoors on the upper level of the Sargent Building on the corner of the square and N. Park Street, The Front Porch provides its patrons a cool, shady seat overlooking the square and the town. Two old sycamore trees stand tall over the brick sidewalk. Specialties include Italian sausage sandwiches, hot dogs (including knackwurst or Polish sausage with sauerkraut) and, in summer, fresh corn on the cob. Other menu items include a barbecue plate and a chicken sandwich. Lunch only. Closed in winter. 706-864-4020.

The Little Red Hen occupies two rooms inside a small, white two-story house with red trim. The decor of this restaurant is billed as "a touch of Williamsburg." The Hen's hallmark is baked goods. Owner Millie Liggin is known for miles around for her muffins, home-baked bread, and desserts. Salads served with meals are cold and crisp. A lunch specialty is chicken salad atop pineapple or inside a tomato and homemade soups are. Another specialty is spinach or crab quiche. Lunch is 11:00 a.m. to 2:00 p.m. daily except Sundays. Dinner choices include prime rib or apple glazed cornish hen served with two vegetables, a house salad, and homemade bread. Inexpensively priced. Dinner hours are 5:00 to 9:00 p.m. Fridays and Saturdays. No wine license here yet, but you can brown-bag. Just off the square at 201 Chestatee Street. 706-864-8047.

The Mint Cafe and Sandwich Shoppe, on Main Street between the old theater and the college, offers a comfortable and casual dining atmosphere. The motif is country/western – wooden floors, plaid tablecloths, and an antique piano. Specialties include made-to-order sandwiches like reubens, clubs, subs, gyros, and steak. Salads, soups, and chili are also regular fare. Dinner entrees include ribeyes and chicken and shrimp dishes. Beer and wine are available. To go orders are welcome. Lunch served Monday through Saturday. Dinner is Monday, Thursday and Friday, closing at 8:00 p.m. 706-864-4488.

Nature's Cellar is a little place where you'll find a variety of all natural vegetarian sandwiches, salads, and other natural food items. Located at North Park Street on the square. 706-864-6829.

Park Place Family Restaurant, just down the hill from the Dahlonega Welcome Center on the square, is a simple, casual place for good food during the daytime hours. Park Place has a buffet style food bar with meats, vegetables, biscuits, rolls, cornbread, soup and salad. If you prefer, you can order steaks, sandwiches, and other items from the menu. Side orders include baked potato and French fries. Special children's menu prices. The buffet (Monday through Friday) is inexpensive. Meals served 11:00 a.m. to 5:00 p.m. 105 S. Park Street. 706-864-4625.

The Smith House is easily the most famous restaurant in all of Lumpkin County. For more than 50 years, this family style restaurant has been serving platters of delicious fried chicken, beef stew, corn, beans, ham, dump-

The Smith House

lings, okra, candied yams, and so on. Some Smith House recipes date back 100 years.

The two-story house which houses the restaurant and several hotel rooms are built on a vein of Dahlonega gold. The site was once planned for a mining operation, but the city fathers refused to allow such an operation just one block from the public square.

At the Smith House, you eat dinner "family style" at long tables in large rooms with huge fireplaces. As platters brimming with food are passed around, you'll get to know those sitting next to you. At lunch, there is a buffet line for making food selections. All patrons are welcome to have all they care to eat. A great conclusion to the dining experience is fruit cobbler or strawberry shortcake.

Reservations are not required, except for parties of 30 or more. Meals are served 11:30 a.m. to 3:00 p.m. Tuesday through Thursday. On Friday, Saturday, and Sunday, serving hours are 11:30 a.m. to 3:00 p.m. and from 4:00 to 7:30 p.m. Hours vary slightly during different times of the year. Lunch and dinner are moderately priced. 202 S. Chestatee Street, one block from the square. 706-864-3566.

The Fudge Factory, on the square across from the Gold Museum, sells a large variety of made-on-the-premises sweets including 12 types of home-made fudge and caramel turtles. 706-864-2256.

Where to Stay

Cavender Castle Winery, which sits atop Gold Hill, is open during the summer and fall months. From a vantage point 2 miles from the town square, visitors enjoy panoramic views of Mount Yonah, Three Sisters Mountain, and Black Mountain. Guests are invited to stay overnight, taste and purchase wine in the tasting room, picnic on beautiful rolling vineyards, and sit on the deck and sip a glass of Dahlonega-made wine. Billed as Georgia's first bed and breakfast winery, Cavender Castle offers lodging, breakfast, winery tours, tastings, outside dining for lunch, RV hookups, campsites, and gold panning. From the square, take Hihgway 60 to Georgia 19N. Follow this road one-fourth mile to Wimpy Mill Road. Turn right on Wimpy Mill and continue for 2 $1/2$ miles to Cavender Castle. 706-577-1111.

Dahlonega Inn offers a panoramic mountain view from its vantage point high on a knoll just one-half mile south of the square on Georgia 60. This 62-unit modern motel has a pool, direct dial phones and color cable TV with free Showtime. Rooms are inexpensive. For reservations, call 706-864-4343.

Days Inn, on Hwy. 60 just south of Dahlonega Inn, has 40 units. Rates are inexpensive. 706-864-2338.

Forrest Hills Mountain Resort is perfect for those who want a remote, peaceful, romantic retreat, bordered by the Chattahoochee National Forest. This resort, 12 miles from town square, features 25 cottages, including 11 honeymoon cottages with whirlpools in the rooms. Each cabin is situated in a private wooded area and is furnished with "country charm." Cabins are oversized and have fully equipped kitchens, canopy beds, stereo systems, fireplaces, TVs, VCRs, and swings on the back porches. Southern-style meals are served in the "Candlelit Dining Room" Friday through Wednesday. Guests can also enjoy tennis, horseback riding, hiking, and a swimming pool. Facilities are available for group business meetings. Rates are expensive per night (double occupancy) including a buffet breakfast and dinner. Open all year.

From Dahlonega, take Highway 52 West toward Ellijay and Amicalola Falls. After traveling 12 miles on this road, turn right on Wesley Chapel Road and follow the signs to the Forrest Hills office. 706-864-6456.

Golden Inn, on North Grove Street (Highway 19) a mile north of the square is a 40-unit, four-story inn with an elevator. The modern rooms have phones, cable color TV with free Showtime, king-size beds, and water beds. There is an outdoor pool and camper hook-ups on the property. Major credit cards accepted. Moderately priced. Special rates for Senior Citizens (AARP). 706-864-6191.

Gold Dust Lodge is nestled in a secluded, wooded setting about 4¹/₂ miles from town on old State Road 9E, also known as Auraria Road. About a mile from the lodge, gold was found in 1828. The all-adult lodge has lovely rooms and suites with private baths and color TV. Hidden in the woods is a pool, waterfall, and spa pavilion. Guests can pan for gold, discover a hiking trail, or enjoy the recreation room with exercise equipment, pool table, cards, and chess. Free continental breakfast. Inexpensive rates. From Dahlonega, travel south on Highway 9S (52 W) for two miles. Cross the bridge, then turn left. Continue 2 ¹/₂ miles to the lodge. 706-864-6848.

Mountain Top Lodge is a friendly, relaxed, country style bed and breakfast lodge with 13 units and a spectacular 360-degree view of the North Georgia mountains. Guests have private baths and rooms furnished with pine furniture, mountain crafts, antiques, and unusual flea market finds. Some rooms have queen-size beds, fireplaces and in-bath jacuzzi tubs. Suites have sitting rooms and private decks. The lodge's cathedral-ceiling great room offers a nice place for conversation, reading, and indoor games. Each morning, a generous country breakfast is provided, including ham, sausage, eggs, fruit, grits and homemade biscuits. On weekends, rates are upper moderate, per night for two adults. Deluxe rooms with a fireplace and refrigerator are available.

Groups and conferences can be accommodated. No pets. Open year round. The lodge is about 5 miles from the public square. From town, take Highway 52 W to Siloam Road. Turn right. Make another right turn onto

Old Ellijay Road at the Siloam Baptist Church. The road ends at the lodge. 706-864-5257.

Scott's Place is a recently opened bed and breakfast located inside a charming, newly decorated Victorian home on W. Main Street. Prices are moderate based on double occupancy, including a hearty country breakfast.

The Smith House, one block off the square, has 16 rooms in its **Carriage House Inn.** The inn is housed inside two quaint wooden, two-story buildings built in 1922. Rooms are simply furnished with Southern antique reproductions. Right in the front yard, you can pan for gold! Room rates are moderate. Open year- round. 202 S. Chestatee Street. 706-864-3566 or 1-800-852-9577.

Vanderhoff's Royal Guard Inn, a bed and breakfast in Scandinavian style, is within one-half block of Dahlonega's public square. The inn is housed inside a restored historic home sheltered by huge Magnolia trees. The large rooms are elegantly decorated with a European flair. Guests enjoy a complimentary wine and cheese tray upon arrival. Breakfast, served Scandinavian style in the dining room or on the porch, includes coffee or tea, juice, fruit, eggs, sausage casserole, muffins, Danish pastries, and more. Rates are moderate. No pets. VISA and MasterCard accepted. 203 S. Park Streeet. 706-864-1713.

Worley Homestead, a charming and stately two-story homestead built in 1845, sits on W. Main Street across from North Georgia College. For many years, the house was owned by Captain William Jasper Worley, the great grandfather of the present owner, Mitzi Francis. Captain Worley, who died in 1913, was an officer in the Confederate Army during the Civil War and was one of Dahlonega's best known early community leaders.

The seven antique-filled rooms are named after Worley and his seven children. Three have fireplaces and some have claw-foot tubs. Guests may sit a spell in the parlor, warming themselves by the fireplace or on one of many comfortable chairs on the front porches.

Breakfast, the only meal served, may include cheese-egg casserole, cheese grits, fresh croissants, apple crepes, sausage, and a special beverage made with orange juice, fresh pineapple, and banana.

Rates are moderate. Special rates for groups. Well behaved children welcome. No pets. Major credit cards and personal checks accepted. 410 W. Main Street. 706-864-7002.

Activities to Enjoy
in the Dahlonega Vicinity

As mentioned earlier, Dahlonega is a town of many festivals. In fact there is one for every season.

Gold Rush Days, the best known of these, draws more than 150,000 people during the third weekend in October. This festival has been voted one of the top 20 events in the Southeast by the Southeast Tourism Society. During Gold Rush Days, the town square becomes an open-air stage for events like buck dancing, greased pig chasing, a beard growing contest, and a pioneer parade. Typically, there are more than 200 arts and crafts exhibitors. Other typical events are a children's treasure hunt, a fashion show, a coronation, and the Gold Rush Dance. And, of couse, there is the "world championship" gold panning competition. For information, call the Chamber of Commerce at 706-864-3711.

The Dahlonega Blue Grass Festival is held during the last week of June at Mountain Music Park, just south of town. This four-day festival offers as many as 14 blue grass bands, an open flea market, camping , and plenty of good things to eat. 706-864-3721.

The July Fourth Family Day Celebration features a spectacular fireworks display that illuminates the skies over Dahlonega. This extravaganza also offers free watermelon, music, and other entertainment, barbecue, buck dancing, various contests, and arts and crafts exhibitors on the public square.

The Wildflower Festival of the Arts comes to Dahlonega on the third weekend in May. During this festival, Dahlonega abounds with visual and performing arts and interesting exhibitions and programs about regional wildflowers. In an art-for-children area, kids can create their own works of art from a variety of media.

Old-Fashioned Christmas Celebration. When the holidays draw near, during the first weekend in December, Dahlonega hosts its annual Old-Fashioned Christmas Celebration. The town square is beautifully decorated, and shopkeepers serve hot-spiced punch and other treats while Christmas carolers, Santa Claus, bands, and choruses delight the young and old.

For more information about any of the festivals, call the Chamber of Commerce: 706-864-3711.

The **Appalachian Trail** is accessible at two points, both about 15 miles from Dahlonega. In fact, the southern terminus of the trail is at nearby Springer Mountain. One entrance to the trail is located at Woody Gap on Georgia 60, north of town. Incidentally, the winding, 15-mile drive here has spectacular overlooks. Along the route are boiled peanut stands, trout ponds, and picnic areas. Amicalola Falls State Park, on Georgia 52, 15 miles west of Dahlonega, has an approach trail to the Appalachian Trail. For more information, write the Georgia Appalachian Trail Club, Inc., P. O. Box 654, Atlanta, Georgia 30301.

Blackburn Park, a few miles south of Dahlonega, has 100 campsites acccessible to water and electrical hookups. The campground has hot showers, picnic areas, a pavilion, an athletic field, a beach for swimming, a concession stand, and an area for fishing. Call the park office at 706-864-4050 for campsite reservations and for information about gold panning, canoe trips or horseback riding.

Just bring your tent, sleeping bag and personal gear, and get ready for an enjoyable outdoor experience which includes a complimentary country breakfast. To reach Blackburn Park, take Highway 400 north from Atlanta and follow the signs to Auraria. The park is seven minutes from Dahlonega on Old Highway 9E.

Appalachian Outfitters is a canoe outpost one mile south of Dahlonega on Highway 60 (not far off Hwy. 400). Your canoe trip will carry you down the Chestatee or Etowah rivers through lush forests past riverbanks covered in azaleas, mountain laurel and an array of wildflowers. The outpost is open for put-ins Wednesday through Sunday, April through September. Trips include all necessary equipment, basic instruction, and a return shuttle. Canoeing equipment and canoe trailers are available for daily rental. 706-864-7117 or 864-3982.

Babyland General Hospital, in nearby Cleveland, is just a few minutes from Dahlonega. The hospital is the home of the original Cabbage Patch Kid dolls. A visit to Babyland will, no doubt, prove to be one of life's most unique experiences. Located in a charming building originally built in 1919 to serve as White County's only medical clinic, the building today is filled with the cuddly, collectible Cabbage Patch dolls. Doctors and nurses scurry around, rushing to attend to Cabbage Patch deliveries. If your timing is right, you may be able to watch the procedure as the baby is delivered and placed in the delivery room window. Since many babies are delivered every day at Babyland, you'll find there are hundreds of unique kids from which to select. One you've found the perect baby, you'll take the Oath of Adoption, receive an official birth certificate and adoption papers and become a real, live Cabbage Patch parent!

Hours are Monday -Saturday, 9:00 a.m. to 5:00 p.m. and Sunday 1:00 to 5:00 p.m. No admission fee. Parking for buses. Handicapped access. From Atlanta, take I-85 north to exit I-985/365. Continue to exit 6. Go north on Route 129 to Cleveland. 706-865-5505.

Amicalola Falls State Park

Every one of the state parks we have visited has its own distinctive character. At **Amicalola** (am-i-cah-LO-la) **Falls State Park,** the central and
most impressive feature is the lodge, built in 1989. This is a handsome
four-story structure of contemporary architecture adapted to a mountain
setting. You enter a spacious, sitting-room-type lobby with its massive fireplace. You are in the main hall, a three-story atrium with a top-to-bottom
glass wall. Branching off from this hall are corridors leading to 57 guest
rooms, each with a beautiful view of the lofty mountains that surround the
area. All rooms have TV, air/heat, and telephones. Three junior suites
have their own private porches. An executive suite has a separate bedroom, kitchenette, dining room, and private porch.

There is an attractive restaurant in the lodge–the **Maple
Restaurant**–open to guests and the public. A long bank of windows offer a
striking mountain view. The restaurant serves breakfast, lunch, and dinner. Weekends, lunch and dinner are served buffet style with choices of
meats, several vegetables, salad bar, and a variety of cobblers and pies.
Weekdays, lunch and dinner are served à la carte with sandwiches,
seafood, steak, chicken, etc. Prices are inexpensive. Adjacent to the
restaurant is an attractive, resort-type gift shop.

On the first floor (the one below the entrance lobby) is the conference center, with a comfortably furnished lobby and a veranda with patio chairs and
tables, looking out on a broad grass lawn and facing the mountains. The
main conference room can accommodate 200; there are also several smaller
meeting rooms. The audiovisual equipment is "state-of-the-art." The management will cater for conference groups, banquets, and receptions.

In addition, there are 14 rental cottages, all in wooded settings, with
decks and wood-burning fireplaces. Also 17 tent and trailer sites, numerous picnic sites, 5 picnic shelters, and several playgrounds.

The Amicalola Falls, once the "main attraction" at this park, have been,
to an extent, overshadowed by the lodge. But they still continue to provide an exciting natural spectacle. Amicalola means "tumbling waters" in
Cherokee, and these falls do indeed tumble down the 728 feet of steep,
many-shelved stone cliff. They are the highest falls in Georgia. The falls
should be viewed both from the top and from the bottom. At the top, they

are approached by a wooden walkway to a platform overlook from which you may peer out into the distant landscape or watch the water as it spills over the cliff. At the bottom, you have a clear view of the falls (obscured in some places by foliage) as they spill down over the cliff to the bottom.

From this state park, there is an 8-mile approach trail to Springer Mountain, the southern end of the Appalachian Trail.

On the drawing board for the near future is a 7,000-square-foot, rustic walk-in lodge, approachable only by means of a four-and-a-half-mile hike through the forest. Sleeping accommodations will be in bunks (in separate rooms). Guests will have to bring their own palettes. Food will be available in a restaurant.

Amicalola Falls State Park is 15 miles northwest of Dawsonville. From Dawsonville, take Highway 53 west, then Highway 183 north, to Highway 52 east. From Dahlonega, take Highway 52 west. Star Route, Box 215, Dawsonville, Ga 30534; lodge and cottage reservations, information: 706-265-8888; camping reservations, park information: 706-265-2885.

Region Four

Hiawassee
Young Harris
Blairsville

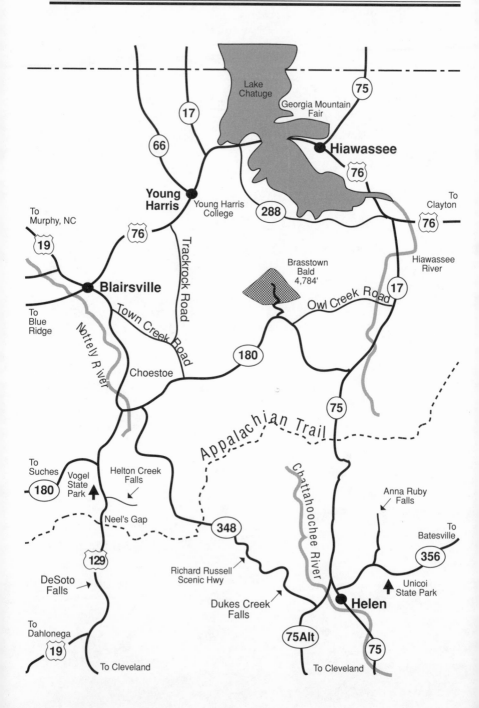

Lake Chatuge

Georgia Mountain Fair

75

Hiawassee

17

66

76

Young Harris

Young Harris College

288

76

To Clayton

76

To Murphy, NC

19

76

Trackrock Road

Brasstown Bald 4,784'

Hiawassee River

Blairsville

Town Creek Road

Owl Creek Road

17

To Blue Ridge

Nottely River

Choestoe

180

Appalachian Trail

75

To Suches

180

Vogel State Park

Helton Creek Falls

Chattahoochee River

Anna Ruby Falls

To Batesville

Neel's Gap

348

356

129

DeSoto Falls

Richard Russell Scenic Hwy

Unicoi State Park

To Dahlonega

Dukes Creek Falls

Helen

19

75Alt

75

To Cleveland

To Cleveland

Hiawassee

Hiawassee lies in a valley surrounded by mountains astride the lower reaches of Lake Chatuge, a 7,500-acre reservoir which dams the waters of the Hiawassee River back into North Carolina. The approach to Hiawassee from any direction takes you through beautiful country–scenic mountains alternating with pastoral farmland.

The town itself is a little community with a few modest motels and restaurants, but the area offers some fine opportunities for recreation on the lake as well as the enjoyment of authentic country, bluegrass and mountain music and Appalachian lore.

The major attractions in the vicinity of Hiawassee are the Georgia Mountain Fair and the presentation of the play *The Reach of Song* in the music hall at the fairgrounds.

The Georgia Mountain Fair

The Georgia Mountain Fairgrounds are located about a mile out of Hiawassee going west on U.S. 76.

The name "Georgia Mountain Fair" is used to mean several different things. It identifies the fairgrounds–the site. It is also used to refer, overall, to the numerous activities and events taking place there during the entire season. And, it is also used to designate specifically the main event of the season–a 12-day fair that takes place annually, beginning the first Wednesday in August and ending on a Sunday, 11 days later. So, when we refer to this specific event, we'll refer to it as the **August Georgia Mountain Fair.**

The Mountain Fair season starts with the **Spring Country Music Festival,** a two-day event in May (the dates vary from year to year) concentrating on country music and clogging. For the rest, it is a condensed version of the August event (described below), featuring The Pioneer Village, the crafts exhibits and the old-home-and-farm activities demonstrations.

The second big event of the season is the **August Georgia Mountain Fair.** Here's what you get to see, hear, and do during the 12-day program:

> The Pioneer Village, an authentically reproduced mountain village of the past with its log cabin, one-room schoolhouse, barn, corn crib, and smokehouse.

> Demonstrations by mountain folk, whose families have lived here for generations, of the way they used to mill corn, make soap and hominy, do quilting, make cider, work at a smithy, and operate a moonshine still.

> Mountain crafts exhibits with dozens of native craftsmen showing their skills at woodworking, woodcarving, jewelry making, leather working, pottery, tole painting, and others.

> Two shows daily (except Sunday) of country music, by nationally-known entertainers; and on Sunday, gospel singing.

> Clogging, daily, along with the country music; and on the first Saturday, an all-day Cloggers Convention, with cloggers of all ages performing.

> The Georgia Mountain Fair Heritage Parade, at noon, on the first Saturday, featuring horse-drawn and mule-drawn old-time farm wagons, ancient horse-and-buggies, antique cars, floats, and marching bands.

Then, in October, generally the third and fourth weekends, the **Fall Harvest Festival** is celebrated. On the first of these two weekends, there is a two-day country music competition. People come in from the surrounding counties and nearby states (Tennessee, North Carolina, South Carolina, Alabama) to compete. There are vocalists, solo instrumentalists and country bands. On Sunday, that weekend, Gospel singers compete.

The second of these two weekends is devoted to the **Fiddlers Convention,** a two-day elimination contest of fiddlers and pickers (guitar, banjo, mandolin).

Both weekend contests are open invitation to amateur local talent. But let no one be fooled by the word "amateur." We were lucky enough to be on hand for one of these Fall Harvest Festivals, and we can assure you that the display of talent is dazzling, and ever so much more exciting because it is "country-authentic" and natural.

In addition to all this are the "superstar" concerts. Throughout the season, once (sometimes twice) a month, nationally known entertainers come in to perform at evening concerts. Among the best known of these who have performed at the Festival, are Roy Clark, Randy Travis, the Gatlin Brothers, George Jones, Conway Twitty, Barbara Mandrell, and Loretta Lynn.

All music and dance performances are given in the Fair's Anderson Music Hall, a large, covered amphitheater.

On the fairgrounds there is a five-acre garden with 2,000 rhododendron and azalea plants. Shaded walks meander through the garden. The blooms are at their peak in May and June, but even at other times, a sojourn through the garden can make for a very pleasant, relaxing hour. This garden–the plantings and upkeep–are a gift from Fred Hamilton, a retired airline man with a love for gardening.

On the fairgrounds and in the **Towns County Park** across the highway, together, there are 200 RV and tenting sites, all with water and electricity, some with sewer facilities. These are available April through October. All facilities are closed November through March. Reservations are necessary. For reservations or any other information about the Georgia Mountain Fair, call 706-896-4191.

The Reach of Song
An Appalachian Drama

For the past several years, the auditorium of the Georgia Mountain Fair has been the setting for the presentation of a new play–**The Reach of Song**–written by Tom DeTitta. While this production is not actually a part of the program of the Georgia Mountain Fair, it fits in beautifully with the fair's spirit and substance.

The play is described as follows:

> *The Reach of Song* is an epic celebration of the song, dance and heritage of the north Georgia mountains as seen through the life

and works of native poet Byron Herbert Reece. Created through the memories of the living and legacies from the past, *The Reach of Song* is the story of the Southern Appalachian Mountains.

There is fiddlin' and pickin' and dancin' and singin' and talkin' and quiltin' and whittlin' and healin' and storytellin' all weaving the fabric of the Appalachian lore.

Anyone who comes to these mountains cannot help but be charmed and enchanted by the Appalachian lore and moved by a desire to preserve it as part of one's own deep feelings, memories, inner self. Since images and impressions fade with time, we must rely on the artists to put these in a form to which we can refer over and over again. Eliot Wigginton and his students have done this with their Foxfire publications. John Kollock has done this with his paintings and books. And Tom DeTitta has done it for us, too, with *The Reach of Song*.

A writer who came wandering into these mountains and stayed to write a play, DeTitta drew his inspiration from the mountains and the people themselves. But behind these was a ghost, a mountaineer poet and bal-ladeer, a tragic figure, dead since 1958 by his own hand: Byron Herbert Reece.

This is what a commentator says about Reece:

> From the furrow of a rocky farm in the mountains of north Georgia, there began to emerge several decades ago poetry so exquisite, so perfect in form it began almost immediately to attract national attention, and wide publication ... a poet of surpassing genius whom Ralph McGill called one of the really great poets of our time.

In his biography of Reece, author Raymond A. Cook tells us that Reece "was born in a one-room, hand-hewn log cabin in a meadow adjoining Wolf Creek ... The meadow is now covered by the waters of Vogel Lake." (Vogel Lake, now called Lake Trahlyta, is part of Vogel State Park, some 11 miles south of Blairsville.)

The old home cabin is gone, but the home and farm buildings in which Reece and his parents lived and worked at another location later on are still there. And so are the people–kinfolks and friends of Reece–and out of what these people told him, not just about Reece, but about the folkways of the time, DeTitta fashioned his play. Reece himself comes back in the play as a living presence and voice.

Judging from the great success this play has had in its first few years, it should continue running for a long time. It is given for a period of about two months each summer. The exact dates are set at the beginning of each season and inquiries should be made at these phone numbers: 706-896-3388 or 1-800-262-SONG.

Lakeside Accommodations

In a class by itself, three miles west of Hiawassee on U.S. 76, is the **Fieldstone Inn,** a lakeside lodging that comes as near to meeting the description "elegant" as one could hope for outside a large city.

As constructed originally, the inn was designed to accommodate not only individual guests and families, but also small groups–up to about 40– requiring meeting and conference accommodations. It has since added a conference center that includes an auditorium and conference rooms.

In addition, adjacent to the inn on the same grounds is a marina with 80 slips for motorcraft and sailboats. Some of the people docking their craft here are year-round residents in the mountains; others own summer homes in the area. Others live at distances from the mountains but dock their boats here year-round and come up to use them, as suits them, and stay at the inn. There is also a fishing pier.

A few hundred feet from the main inn building there is the **Fieldstone Restaurant,** which operates independently of the inn but is available to guests of the inn, as well as to the public.

The inn is handsomely constructed. The interior is even more attractive, featuring a 24-foot-wide, two-story-high fieldstone fireplace wall with cozy sitting areas around the fireplaces on both sides of the wall and on two levels. In addition, the two-story atrium construction of the lobby features a 70-foot curved glass wall, two stories high, with splendid views of the lake and the mountains.

The inn has 62 guest rooms and four executive suites all attractively fur- nished in traditional style. All rooms open onto balconies, half with a view of the lake, half with a view of the mountains. The rates vary with the season, the view, and the amenities. A little on the expensive side, they are certainly a very good value for fine accommodations. For reservations: The Fieldstone Inn, P. O. Box 670, Hiawassee, Ga 30546. 706-896-2622.

Boundary Waters Resort and Marina. For those interested in boating and fishing, as well as a "getaway" experience on a lake and in scenic surrounding, Boundary Waters Resort and Marina offers that combination. The "resort" accommodations consist of lakefront one-bedroom condominiums with sleep sofas, accommodating three to four people; a three-bedroom lake house accommodating up to six people; also two-bedroom mountain houses accommodating up to six people. All accommodations are fully equipped for housekeeping.

The marina sells all sorts of boating accessories, water sports equipment, bait, gasoline for power boats, snacks, gifts, etc.

Since there are so many different rates for the various lodging arrangements, depending on the number of days for which they are rented, and for the pontoons and fishing craft and canoes depending on the number of hours for which they are rented, it will be necessary for you to telephone. The marina is open year-round, but the lodgings are closed from the second week in November through March. Boundary Resort and Marina is located on Route 288 (off Route 76 about two miles west of Hiawassee). Turn in on Route 288 and drive about one mile to the Boundary Waters Resort and Marina. 706-896-2530.

Lazy Acre Cottages. Sixteen simple, old-fashioned cottages along Lake Chatuge, some on the lake, some a few feet away, all set in a wooded area. The cabins are fully equipped for housekeeping and sleep two to six persons. There is a 260-foot boat dock and an area for swimming; picnic tables and grills and a play area for children. Rates are inexpensive. Lazy Acre Cottages are located about 2.5 miles west of Hiawassee off Route 76. No pets. Closed November to March. 706-896-3759.

Shady Rest Cabins. There are eight rustic cabins, nicely situated lakeside, fully equipped for housekeeping; with cable TV. There is a boat dock, launching ramp, boat and pontoon boat rentals; also a country store. Rates are inexpensive. These cabins are located one-half mile west of

Hiawassee on Route 76. John and Joan Rand, Route 4, Box 312, Hiawassee, Ga 30546; 706-896-2240.

Salale Lodge. This is not really a lodge, in the traditional sense, but rather a four-unit, motel-type arrangement (two up and two down), housed in a recently constructed, nicely painted and nicely kept frame building. The rooms are very large, and outfitted with the latest motel-type conveniences: TV, air-conditioning, heating, spacious bathroom and dressing area, etc.

The lodge is set up on a slope along the shore of Lake Chatuge. All rooms have individual porches and face the lake, with a good view of lake and mountains. There is swimming in the lake and a boat dock.

Approaching the location, one is likely to be put off by the gasoline station and a country store. There are also some older cabins alongside, but these are not related to the lodge. Salale Lodge is located about three-quarters of a mile east of the Hiawassee city limits (on the left driving west); the first commercial building on the left after you pass the intersection of Routes 17/75 and 76. Open all year. Rates are inexpensive and vary with day of the week and the season. Well behaved pets accepted. Route 1, Box 36, Hiawassee, Ga 30546; 706-896-3943.

Cabins and Motels

Swallows Creek Cabins. This is a group of six cabins of semi-contemporary-type exterior construction, attractive in the woodsy, hilly setting. They were built in 1984 and are in fine condition. Some are one-level, others two-level. All are fully equipped for housekeeping; five sleep up to four, one sleeps up to eight; air-conditioning; color TV, electric heat and fireplaces. Rates are moderate and vary with size of cabin and length of stay. The Swallows Creek Cabins are located 4 miles east of Hiawassee off Route 76. Traveling west, turn left on Swallows Creek Road, and go about a mile until you see the entrance sign on the left. Open May through November. P. O. Box 538, Hiawassee, Ga 30546; 706-896-4707.

Hiawassee Motel, located on Main Street just east of the center of town, is a basic, no-frills, clean, comfortable motel. It has 12 rooms; rates are inexpensive. Pets are allowed. 706-896-4121.

Mull's Motel, also located on Main Street, is very similar in basic particulars to the Hiawassee Motel. It has 13 rooms; rates are inexpensive. 706-896-4195.

Restaurants

The Fieldstone Restaurant is located on the spacious and attractive grounds of the Fieldstone Inn, 3 miles west of Hiawassee on Route 76. It is the first building you come to after you enter between the two stone pillars. In style, variety of menu, and quality of cooking, the Fieldstone Restaurant, too, stands in a class by itself in the Hiawassee area. It has a spacious, attractive dining room, with a view of the lake from most seats.

The breakfast menu is typically "country Southern." For lunch there is a wide variety of sandwiches and salads, plus a number of "hot plates." There is an "all-you-can-eat" lunch bar.

Dinner, says owner Bob Bryant, goes from "beans and taters to prime ribs and fine seafood." There is also an evening buffet and Sunday brunch. The restaurant has its own bake shop offering a variety of breads and pastries; it also has its own smokehouse. Prices are moderate. The restaurant is open year-round. 706-896-4141.

Ann's Place Restaurant. Ann Dennison, who owns and operates Ann's Place Restaurant, says she learned to cook "the way people like it" on Ocmulgee Creek in the vicinity of Macon, Georgia. While the menu is basically chicken, steaks, and seafood, they are done with Ann's personal touch, and steaks are cut by Ann personally at the time they are ordered. Prices are inexpensive. Ann's Place is housed in a chalet-type attractive, frame building, window-enclosed on three sides. The two-story-high chalet ceiling and the glass enclosure provide a pleasant feeling of spaciousness. To get there, pick up Route 288, about 2 miles west of Hiawassee off Route 76. (On the left driving west.) Drive in on 288 about a mile until you see a little white church on the right. Immediately after the church (don't cross the bridge), turn right on Hog Creek Road and go about 0.4 miles. Open Thursday, Friday, and Saturday evenings for dinner, Sunday through Wednesday for private parties. Route 1, Box 618, Hog Creek Road, Hiawassee, Ga 30546; 706-896-2667.

The Georgia Mountain Restaurant. In many places in the north Georgia mountains, there are restaurants where, for $4 to $5, you can get a lunch or dinner consisting of one meat (from choice of three), three vegetables (from choice of four or five) and tea or coffee. One such is the Georgia Mountain Restaurant located on Main Street, Hiawassee. Besides this menu, there are several other choices, including a salad bar. During summer weekends there is also a breakfast bar. This is a large restaurant and it seats about 100, but it is very busy most of the time, and when the Georgia Mountain Fair (just a short distance down the road) is open, you may have to wait in line; but the line moves quickly. Don't expect frills; what you get is down-to-earth, basic country cooking at a down-to-earth price. This restaurant is located about three-quarters of a mile west of Hiawassee town center, on Route 76. 706-896-3410.

There are also several "quick bite" places in town: **Papa's Pizza** (a chain), on Route 76 west of town; **Hardee's** (chain) on Main Street and **O.K.'s Barbecue,** on Main Street.

Recreational Areas

Just a short distance out of town, going west, there are two recreation areas, the Towns County Park and the Chatuge Recreation Area.

Towns County Park. About a mile out of town going west on Route 76. It is directly opposite the fair grounds of the Georgia Mountain Fair. There's ample parking adjacent to the recreation area. Atop a tree-shaded knoll there's a lovely picnic grove with tables and benches and a playground for the children. The knoll descends gradually to the lake shore. A wide, sandy beach is ideal for swimming. There is a launching ramp for boats, also some tennis courts. And, in the distance, a thrilling view of the mountains.

Lake Chatuge Recreation Area. About a mile further on (about 2 miles out of town going west), look for the intersection of Route 288 on the left and a sign that says Lake Chatuge Recreation Area. Turn onto 288, go about 0.9 mile, and on the left you'll see a sign for Chattahoochee Mountain Forest Campground. Turn in. This is mainly a campground for tents and trailers in a nice, wooded spot. The campground is situated along the lake shore but the campsites are not directly on the lake. However, if you have fishing in mind you can make your way down to the lake shore on foot by a not-too-difficult descent. There is also a ramp for boats just inside the entrance to the campgrounds.

Book Store

The Book Place was recently opened by Elizabeth Sligh and specializes in books about local history and by local authors. The store also stocks a full range of children's classics, and has a section of used books and some gift items. Located in the Little Place Shops, Highway 76, 706-896-1571.

Young Harris

This little town is known mainly for its college of the same name; also for being both the birthplace and home of Georgia's governor, Zell Miller. The town and the college are named after Judge Young L. G. Harris of Athens because of his magnanimous contributions to the financial needs of The McTyre Institute, an educational institution for mountain people of that area. In 1886, the name of the institute was changed to Young Harris, and it changed its focus to higher education. Shortly thereafter, the town took on the judge's name, too.

While passing through town, a worthwhile stop would be a visit to the campus of Young Harris College. The college hosts a number of cultural events throughout the year, and one of these might well be on the schedule when you are staying in or passing through the area.

Another school of interest in the locality is the **John C. Campbell Folk School,** located in Brasstown, NC, about a 20- to 30-minute drive from Young Harris. The school is open year-round and gives courses in a wide variety of crafts, such as basketry, spinning, weaving, rug braiding, knitting and dyeing, quilting, calligraphy, glass etching, photography, woodcarving, woodworking, wood turning, and jewelry making. There are also classes in folk dancing and music, focusing on traditional mountain musical instruments and music.

There are a few points of interest, as well as motel and restaurant in Young Harris. Since there are not enough of these to list by category, we will just list them serially.

Birdie Miller's Rock Home. Located on Main Street (on the right driving west) you will see a sprawling one-level stone house. This is the home where Governor Zell Miller and his sister Jane were raised by their mother, Birdie Miller. She is no longer alive, but the home continues to be maintained by the family and is open to the public once a year during a

"tour of homes" before Christmas. The story of this home is given, as follows, in a local annotation during a recent tour of homes:

> When Birdie Bryan moved from South Carolina in 1919 to
> teach art at Young Harris College, she fell in love with the
> mountains as well as a man named Grady Miller, her future hus-
> band. But tragedy occurred in 1932 and Mr. Miller died leaving
> Birdie with two small children and not much money.
>
> During the eleven years the Millers were married, they had
> never owned a home and Birdie wanted to build a monument
> that would last forever. From a creek that flows from the foot of
> Double Knob, Birdie would wade in the cold water selecting
> rocks of brown, gold and amber colors polished by the swift
> moving water. She had $700 to build the home which lasted
> long enough to get the rocks laid, a roof on, the windows in and
> one room finished.
>
> In 1942, the family moved to Atlanta to work. When the war
> ended, Birdie and her son, Zell, moved back to the mountains.
> Birdie decided to dig a basement which she did on her hands
> and knees. Many years later, when Birdie was in her 70's, she
> decided to cement the basement, and her handprints can be
> seen on the basement walls today.
>
> On the side porch of the house, there are handprints of Zell
> and his sister Jane, and written into the cement with a nail
> by Birdie, "Built in honor of Stephen Grady Miller, for Jane
> and Zell."

Miss Lydia's Guest House. This is a stately two-story brick structure,
fronted by typical antebellum white pillars. The home was, in fact, built
before the Civil War and except for decorative elements, has undergone
few structural changes. It stands right next to Birdie's Stone House on
Main Street.

The guest house is named after Mrs. Lydia Corn, the mother of the present owner, Mrs. Cecile Corn Kelley.

You enter the house from the rear through a "garden room" nicely furnished with wicker and wrought iron pieces. Beyond, there is the "family
room," the parlor, a dining room and a guest room on the ground floor.
Upstairs there are three more guest rooms. All rooms are very attractively

furnished with a melange of cherry and walnut furniture, many pieces dating back several generations. One most rare heirloom is a pre-Civil War sewing machine. In the front yard there stands a maple tree planted before the house was built.

Mrs. Kelley stresses that this is not a bed-and-breakfast arrangement. Guests have breakfast "by invitation." Reservations and rates: Mrs. Cecile C. Kelley, Route 1, Box 1028, Young Harris, Ga 30582; 706-379-3496.

Appalachian Studio Gallery. Established in 1975 by David Sellers after returning from Paris where he taught print making and studied with renowned artists. In addition to his own works, Sellers also exhibits the works of other artists from the southern Appalachian region, including etchings, watercolors, oil paintings, and sculpture. Other artists have their studios there, too, and visitors can see the artists at work. Located adjacent to Young Harris College tennis courts. 706-379-3807 and 3870.

Young Harris Motel. Located on Main Street. There are 25 rooms laid out on a spacious, attractive area with swimming pools; gives a "modern, kept-up" appearance. Cable TV, heat, air-conditioning. Full tub and shower bathrooms. Rates are inexpensive. No pets. 706-379-3136.

Coat-of-Arms Restaurant. Adjacent to the Young Harris Motel on Main Street. This is a traditional small-town family restaurant, serving a wide variety of breakfast dishes, luncheon sandwiches and salads, and "chicken, steak and seafood" type dinner entrées. All at inexpensive prices. 706-379-1276.

Blairsville

Blairsville is the county seat of Union County and the accepted story has it that when the county was founded during the Civil War one of the founders asked, "What shall we call the county?" and another founder replied, "Let us call it Union County, for none but loyal Union men live here."

The town itself was founded in the late 1800s. The only significant remaining establishment of that era still stands on the town square–the old county courthouse, built in 1899. This, several other places of scenic and historic interest, plus numerous hiking trails and several waterfalls make this a very attractive area to visit and stay.

Scenic Drives

Blairsville is the gateway to some of the most scenically beautiful country in the eastern part of the north Georgia mountains. A leisurely drive along Georgia Routes 129/19, 180, 17/75 and 356 (you can locate these on your map) south and southeast of Blairsville will take you through lofty mountain passes and unspoiled wilderness alternating with valleys of farm-land dotted with generations-old farmhouses and cabins. It is not difficult, through stretches of this drive, to imagine what the countryside here looked like a hundred years ago when there were no automobiles or high-ways–only wagon roads and horse trails in the valleys and Indian trails over the mountain passes and through the forests.

But best of all is the **Richard Russell Scenic Highway** (Route 348). Cutting through the Chattahoochee National Forest, it, and the entire area that surrounds it, are pristinely free of habitation or any other evidence of human presence. The road winds through the mountains, ascending and descending, offering spectacular panoramic vistas from frequent scenic overlooks and even from the road itself, with a new and more striking view as you round each curve. It is equally as beautiful on the return trip, presenting new and different views in all directions.

Places of Interest

The Old County Courthouse. Today, the old brick courthouse no longer serves a civic function. It has been turned into a museum.

The Union County Historical Society has undertaken to renovate the old building as closely as possible to its original state. This task has been going on for several years. The restored area now houses a cultural collection depicting the life of Union County from the 1880s. There is also there a special collection featuring the life and works of native poet Byron Herbert Reece. The restored section of the building is open to the public, but only from June through October and only a few days a week. Union County Historical Society: 706-745-5493.

The Book Nook. Patricia Kay is usually on hand to help find the latest best seller or books about the area. Georgia authors are well represented. P. O. Box 1239, Blairsville, Ga 30512; 706-745-7076.

Duncan's Saddle Shop. About three-tenths of a mile south of the town square, on Route 129/19, there is a little cabinlike structure that houses this most interesting shop. To locate it, look for the Circle K Convenience Store. The shop sits right next to it. Inside the shop you will find an array of saddles, halters, bridles, stirrups, horseshoes, and nails, and all the other accoutrements of horseback riding, plus a collection of leather belts and western hats. But the prize item is a decorative metal saddle (said to be of silver) that looks very much like the kind with which the knights of old used to saddle their horses. Mrs. Ruth Duncan, who was tending the store when we visited, tells us that this saddle is reputed to have been used by Lash LaRue, famed Western movie star of the late 1930s and early 1940s. There are photographs of the late Harlan Duncan, former Union County sheriff, and Tom Duncan current county sheriff and son of Mr. and Mrs. Harlan Duncan, riding horses with this saddle. The Duncan Saddle Shop is said to be more than 60 years old (and probably much older).

Brasstown Bald

Brasstown Bald, at an altitude of 4,784 feet above sea level, is Georgia's highest mountain. The "bald" refers to a naked three-quarter acre area at the top. According to an information brochure from the U.S. Forest Service, "The name Brasstown comes from a confusion of the Cherokee work *itse-yi* meaning 'new green place,' with the word *untsiayi* meaning brass."

The term "breathtaking" has become commonplace in describing scenic beauty in this area, but if there is any place where it truly does apply, it is the views from the top of Brasstown Bald, a view that reaches to the horizon in every direction and extends into four states: Tennessee, North Carolina, South Carolina, and Georgia. They say that on a clear, sunny, day, you can actually see as far as Atlanta, more than 100 miles away. But it is not so much the distance that is striking as it is the beauty of the views–mountain ranges in successive tiers in every direction, bathed in the bluish haze of the Blue Ridge Mountains. We need to add the explanation that, while the surrounding mountains are between 3,500 and 4,800 feet in altitude, they rise from an elevated plateau that is itself about 2,500 feet above sea level. Therefore, one does not get the dramatic effect of steep mountain and lofty peaks, but rather that of towering waves in a sea of mountains. There is an elevated 360-degree circular walkway at the top of Brasstown Bald to enable the spectator to enjoy every bit of the surrounding scenery.

While the view from Brasstown Bald would in itself be worth a visit, there are also an exhibition hall and theatre there with a great deal to enjoy and to learn. The **Heritage Book Store** is next to the parking area.

A free "Man and the Mountain" exhibit traces the history of the mountains back to it geological origin, 250 million years ago. Then in text and illustrations it depicts the life of the Indians in these mountains, the Gold Rush of 1828, the land lottery in which the Indians lost their land, and the sad story of the Trail of Tears. It also maps the route Hernando de Soto was supposed to have traveled through Georgia in his quest for gold.

There is in addition an exciting slide presentation in the Mountain Top Theatre, showing what Brasstown Bald and the surrounding area looks like through the seasons—the snow-locked winter, the flowering spring, the verdant summer, the blazing color display of fall. There is also a 50-foot-high lookout tower there, but that is for the rangers only and not open to the public.

For serious hikers, there is an additional attraction at Brasstown Bald. Backpackers will find there a convergence of two rugged trails. One is the 4.5-mile Jack's Knob trail, which crosses Route 189 at Jack's Gap and intersects the Appalachian Trail. The other is the 5.5-mile Araquah Trail. Both are National Recreation Trails, and both, we are warned, have sections that are extremely steep.

To get to Brasstown Bald, take Route 180 (from either direction) to the Brasstown Bald turnoff. When you come to the end of the spur near the top of the mountain, you will have to park your car and take a "jitney bus" to the top for the view, the exhibition hall, and the slide show. There are restrooms at the parking lot and at the top.

Brasstown Bald is open daily from Memorial Day through October and on weekends in early spring (depending on the weather). For more information call the visitor information center at 706-896-2556.

Byron Herbert Reece's Homeplace. In our discussion of the play *The Reach of Song* (Georgia Mountain Fair, Hiawassee), we made brief mention of the poet Byron Herbert Reece. In the Blairsville area, however, and even throughout the state, this poet is a legend, and so we will spend a little more time talking about him here.

Reece (he was called "Hub"), as we have noted, was born in a one-room, hand-hewn log cabin in a meadow adjoining Wolf Creek, which flows down from Frogtown Gap or "Walasi-Yi" (Place of the Frogs), as the Cherokee called it. The area in which Reece was born is still called Choestoe (cho-e-STO-e), an Indian name that translates to "The Place of the Dancing Rabbits."

In 1921, when Hub was four, his family (father Juan, his mother Emma, and several children) moved into the home where Byron's mother had been raised. Built by Emma Reece's grandparents before the Cherokee removal, it was located between Blood Mountain and Slaughter Mountain, so named because of the battles fought there with the Indians over fishing rights in Wolf Creek and the Nottely River.

Many years later, when Hub was grown, he built a new house for himself and his parents. That is where Hub himself spent much of his adult life farming and writing. That home–the Reece homeplace–still stands, as do his studio, a barn, and a corn crib. Situated there also is the house in which one of his sisters used to live.

The homeplace buildings are being restored, but they are not now open to the public. They are located about 9 miles south of Blairsville between the Sunrise Grocery and the Goose Creek Cabins, on the right (going south) down an incline. One needs to be driving slowly to see them.

In our earlier reference to Reece (see "Hiawassee"), we said that the poet had died by his own hand. According to his biographer Raymond A. Cook, Reece shot himself through the lung, the significance of that being, according to Cook, that it was the lung that had been wasted by tuberculosis, an illness that, had made the poet's life "a living hell," draining his energy, confining him to a sanitarium, for long periods to bed, and causing him endless misery.

His entire life as boy and man were filled with the arduous tasks of farming to keep himself and his parents alive. He was never free to devote himself entirely to writing. Despite this, he wrote prodigiously, and his poems and ballads were published in several books and magazines. However, they brought him only a pittance–this despite the fact that they had garnered him many prestigious literary awards. He had even been offered a post as writer-in-residence at Emory University in Atlanta, but had been unable to accept it, except for a few months, because of his illness. Even to his last days, he lived in humble circumstances.

We are moved to quote the closing paragraph in the poet's biography:

> All we have of him are the two novels and the slim volumes
> that contain some lyrics and biblical ballads whose musical
> purity have been unsurpassed in this country. The subdued lyricism of Reece is drowned by the din of an artificial strident and
> discordant age. But whenever men retreat to the quiet vales of
> the mind to seek a lifting of the heart in friendship, a warm
> joy in simple things, and a catching of the breath in supernal
> beauty, there the lonely, questing spirit of Byron Herbert Reece
> will have found a haven, and his haunting, flutelike music will
> be heard.

The biography is titled *Mountain Singer–The Life and Legacy of Byron Herbert Reece,* by Raymond A. Cook (Cherokee Publishing Company, Atlanta). This publishing company (the publisher of this guide book) has also reprinted six books of Reece's poetry and ballads.

Walasi-Yi Center (wala-SEE-ye), located about 14 miles south of Blairsville on Route 129/19, is a mecca for hikers, known to backpackers and day hikers throughout the Southeast and especially to devotees of the Appalachian Trail. Hiking enthusiasts have been coming here for several decades to purchase equipment and supplies, to get directions and pick up their mail, to spend an hour or two swapping stories and information with the trailwise owners (currently Dorothy and Jeff Hansen). Appalachian Trail hikers pursuing the trail in this region have had to come here because the trail passes right under the Center's roof. Today, the Walasi-Yi Center is still serving hikers in all these ways, and, for those who need it, will arrange for shuttle service (to pick up hikers who make long hikes and do not wish to make the long trek back). The center also stocks a goodly supply of hard-to-find regional maps and books, as well as a variety of local mountain crafts.

An additional inducement is the view through Neel's Gap and the surrounding heights.

Before 1930, there was nothing here but wilderness, and the location was called Frogtown Gap. Then, in 1930, the state put through a paved road (now 129/19). The engineer was a man by the name of Neel, and as part of a political debt to someone or other, Frogtown Gap was renamed Neel's Gap, much to the consternation of the natives, including Byron Herbert Reece, who had this to say in a letter to a friend:

> I have always been angry about the name Neel's Gap. Before the highway came the gap bore the name of Frogtown, or more properly Walasiyi which is Cherokee for 'place of the frogs.' Neel was merely the engineer who selected the route for the highway. I have never been able to see why we should have sacrificed a perfectly good name for a mere man.

In 1933, the Civilian Conservation Corps (C.C.C.) began the construction of the building in which the Walasi-Yi Center is now housed. It was intended originally as a lodge for the C.C.C. workers, but after its completion in 1937, it was converted into an inn and restaurant. Several years later, it was converted once more, this time into a gathering place and supply depot for hikers, its function today.

It is a beautiful stone building, large and spacious, and hardly changed on the outside from its original state. There have been several structural changes in the interior, but the walls and beams of chestnut and pine have not been touched and the original fixtures are still there. The atmosphere inside is that of a spacious, comfortable, homey country store, where one would like to come and stop and "set awhile." Walasi-Yi Center, Route 1, Box 1240, Blairsville, Ga 30512; 706-745-6095.

Vogel State Park, the oldest in Georgia, is located some eleven miles south of Blairsville on Route 129/19. It is nestled in a picturesque hollow, its 250 acres blending in with the beautiful mountains behind it.

Whereas some of the other state parks emphasize modern construction with architecturally designed landscaping, this park maintains its basic, original theme of rusticity. This does not, by any means, mean that the facilities and cottages are primitive. On the contrary, they are most up-to-date so far as convenience and comfort are concerned. All of the park's 36 cottages are fully furnished and equipped for housekeeping (as are all cottages in the State Park system). All are heated; some are air conditioned.

It is the wooded settings in which the cottages are situated, and their design (differing from cottage to cottage) that gives this park the distinctive feel of being a rustic, camplike hideaway. Adding to this feeling is lovely Wolf's Creek, which runs through the park, emptying into the sylvan 20-acre Lake Trahlyta (trah-LITE-uh) in which one may swim, fish, or pedal-boat. Scattered unobtrusively around the grounds are several playgrounds and primitive camping sites (no power or water). In addition there are 100 tent and trailer sites and a family group shelter. There are several hiking trails leading out of Vogel State Park. Three are shorter than a mile in length and are more for walks than hikes. For the more serious hiker, there is a 4-mile "loop" trail–Bear Hair Gap Trail–described as "moderate." There is also the 12.7-mile Coosa Backcountry Trail designated as "moderate to strenuous."

The cottages are of varying sizes–one, two and three-bedrooms with various arrangements for expanded sleeping quarters. The rental prices for these vary according to size and day of the week. Reservations (as in all state parks) may be made in person or by phone or mail. Vogel State Park, Route #1, Box 1230, Blairsville, Ga 30512; 706-745-2628.

Waterfalls

Helton Creek Falls. The road leading to these falls starts on Route 129/19, midway between Vogel State Park and Walasi-Yi Center. It is the first road on the left, south of Vogel State Park. The sign to the entrance road is small and inconspicuous so you will have to watch for it carefully. Turn in there, and continue driving. The road and surroundings are uninteresting, but do not let that dissuade you. When you've driven 2.3 to 2.4 miles, you will find a pullover on the right. (There are two or three pullovers before this, but ignore them.) Park your car and walk back about 75 feet and there, on your left, you'll pick up the trail going downhill. The distance to the falls is about one-tenth of a mile. It is a narrow, rough trail through dark forest. Watch for rocks and roots on the trail to keep from tripping. Almost at the end of the trail there are two separate paths, one to the lower falls and one to the upper falls.

Go left to the lower falls first, down some steps. The waterfall–or rather waterslide–cascades over a broad, flat rock surface about 40 feet in height, into a pleasant pool. To the left of the pool there is a broad, flat rock shelf, where you can picnic or just sit and enjoy the sight and sound of the waterfall.

Then, retrace your path up the stairs and continue on to the upper falls, a very short walk. Again you come to a broad rock shelf and a pool. The falls originate at a height of about 60 feet, cascade down a broad rock shelf, and then, midway down, split into two separate falls and pour down into the pool.

One can get mundane describing a waterfall in terms of height and rocks and pools. Actually, the sight and sound of these natural phenomena fill the soul and the spirit as you stand there, drink in their beauty, and wonder on the immensity and awesomeness of nature.

De Soto Falls. These falls, so the legend goes, obtained their name from the fact that early settlers found a piece of Spanish armor in the vicinity and believed it was left there by Hernando de Soto and his soldiers on their way through Georgia in quest of gold.

There are three falls here–a lower, a middle, and an upper. All are fed by small streams and hence do not present the spectacular display that some of Georgia's other waterfalls do, except after a period of substantial rainfall.

The site of the falls is also the site of the **De Soto Falls Scenic and Recreational Area.**

Access to the falls is through the recreation area, off Route 129/19. The entrance is about 7 miles south of Vogel State Park (on the right driving south) and is very clearly marked. You take a sharp right turn and after a very short drive you come to the recreation and camping area and parking lot. The grounds are lovely, scenic, wooded, ideal for hiking, picnicking, or camping. There are several camping and tenting sites. There are also several hiking trails, including the ones that lead to the falls.

The trail to the falls begins across a bridge over Frogtown Creek. A sign with arrows and distances to the three falls marks the path. The distance from the beginning of the trail down to the lower falls, back to the middle and upper falls, and back to the beginning of the trail is a total of 3.7 miles.

The path to and from the lower falls is rather easy and moderate, but the path to the middle and upper falls is more difficult and strenuous, especially from the middle to the upper falls.

The lower falls splash down a 30-foot rock face into a pool. The middle falls drop in four stages for a total fall of about 90 feet. The upper falls are more spectacular, sliding at a 45-degree angle over a distance of more than 150 feet.

There are observation decks at the lower and middle falls, and a railed observation area at the upper falls.

Dukes Creek Falls. The access to these falls is from the Dukes Creek Recreation Area located about 1.7 miles north of the southern terminus of the Richard Russell Scenic Highway. If you are traveling south, the entrance will be on your right.

About an eighth of a mile after you turn in (the entrance is clearly marked), you'll come to the parking lot. Look for the trail leading to the falls. The path is downhill, but in a very gradual descent. It is about eight-tenths of a mile in length, snaking down in long loops that fold back and forth over and over again. The path has been graveled, but constant walking has worn down the gravel and protruding roots and stones can cause you to trip if you're not careful. However, with that caution, it is a pleasant walk through lovely woods, taking between 30 and 45 minutes. It may seem like a lot longer, but it is surely worth the effort. As you descend, you can hear the muted but powerful sound of the falls; then you lose it and then pick it up again, lose it and pick it up again.

Finally, the sound of the falls remains constant and you know you are nearly there. The trail ends in a clearing, and there they are, right opposite you, smashing down a rocky course from a height of about 250 feet, and breaking, not too far from the top into two separate falls. The falls actually originate from Davis Creek, but at the bottom, they plunge into Duke's Creek, which then cascades down the mountain in a powerful, surging stream.

If you're concerned about the hike back uphill after you've seen the falls, don't worry. The distance is, of course, the same, and the trail is uphill. However, it is, in fact, much easier than the downhill course because you have a better foothold going up. It took us 30 minutes to make the return trip, and we weren't winded a bit.

Also, we found that the drive north toward Blairsville on the Richard Russell Scenic Highway was even more scenic and exciting than the drive south.

The Sorghum Festival

Blairsville is the site of the now-famous **Sorghum Festival,** taking place each year the last three weekends in October, and now in its third decade. The main event each day is the crushing of the locally grown sugar cane and the cooking of the juice into sorghum syrup. This is followed by the biscuit-and-sopping contest, which speaks for itself. In addition, there are numerous booths displaying and selling arts and crafts; pickles, jams, jellies, and honey; and home-baked cakes and cookies. Plus country music, square dancing and clogging. And contests: "'baccer spittin'," pole climbing, rock throwing, log sawing, etc. The event is sponsored by the local Jaycees, with proceeds going to local charities. Information: Blairsville Jaycees, P. O. Box 701, Blairsville, Ga 30512; 706-745-4745.

Cabins, Cottages, Motels

Blood Mountain Cabins, just around the curve, going south, from Walasi-Yi Center on Route 129/19, is located in the heart of some of the most scenic mountain country in all of north Georgia. There are 10 two-bedroom cabins, four of them sitting high on a ridge with a spectacular view. All cabins have fireplaces, large decks, sleeping lofts, and are fully equipped for housekeeping. They have furnace heat and air-conditioning. There is also a friendly country store selling various arts and crafts items, groceries, jams and jellies, rocks and gemstones. Rates moderate. Open all year; no pets. Blairsville, Ga 30514; 706-745-9454.

Brasstown View Estates. Don't be misled by the "estates" in the name. These are, in fact, one- and two-bedroom cottages offering privacy and seclusion in a beautiful, wooded mountainside setting with an unsurpassed view of Brasstown Bald. The cabins are fully equipped for housekeeping, nicely furnished in the country style, with large decks and lots of glass exposure offering beautiful views. A special feature are the whirlpool baths, one in each cabin. All have fireplaces and firewood is provided. These cabins are located 6.5 miles south of Blairsville, a short distance from the intersection of Route 129/19 and the Owltown Spur Road (look for sign "Brasstown View Estates" at intersection). Rates are moderate Blairsville, Ga 30512; 706-745-4007.

God's Country Farm. This is a "sure enough" 50-acre farm, with a farmhouse, barn, farm animals and the like. Lodgers are accommodated in modern log cabins overlooking the farm, and gather in the farmhouse, evenings, for sociability. The cabins, accommodating two to six, are charmingly and comfortably furnished, with fully equipped kitchens and wood-burning stoves. There is a one-acre fishing pond. Nearby Lake Nottely offers fishing and boating. These cabins are located on Route 325, about 3 miles north of the intersection with Highway 515/76. Rates provided on request: Bill and Arlene Gray, Route 4, Box 4380, Blairsville, Ga 30512; 706-745-1560.

Misty Mountain Cabins. A cut above the rustic "in the woods" mountain cabin, the Misty Mountain Cabins are quite homey, furnished with various types of antique furniture of regional origin. All have fireplaces and are fully equipped for housekeeping. The setting, right in the midst of this area's most scenic country, is peaceful, soothing, pleasant, conducive to relaxation. However, there is every variety of activity–antiques shopping, boating and swimming, sightseeing, hiking, and scenic drives and overlooks–within short distances.

To get to Misty Mountain Cabins, take Route 129/19 south from Blairsville, about 3 miles to Townscreek Road, on the left. Drive about 4.5 miles on Townscreek Road. Rates on request. Phone or write: Frank and Miriam Deen, Misty Mountain Cabins, Townscreek Road, Route 7, Box 77886, Blairsville, Ga 30517; 706-745-4786.

Seven Creeks Cabins. There are five log cabins in a pleasant, meadowlike setting, looking out on a small lake, surrounded by woods and rolling hills and nestled in between two mountain ranges. All are fully equipped for housekeeping. Some have fireplaces. Some, with two bedrooms, can accommodate six. The atmosphere is one of peacefulness, relaxation and seclusion; yet it is within a short driving distance of the various scenic and

historic sites and a wide variety of "things to do" close by. Seven Creek
Cabins are located 10 miles south of Blairsville on Horseshoe Cove Road,
which is 1 mile south of Route 180. Rates available on request: Marvin
and Bobbie Hernden, Seven Creek Cabins, Route 2, Box 2647, Blairsville,
Ga 30512; 706-745-4753.

Motels and Restaurants

Season's Inn Motel, located on the town square. This is a new establishment (built in 1990), nicely furnished in "country decor." There are 26
units, a conference room, restaurant and shops. Rates are moderate.
P. O. Box 2342, Blairsville, Ga 30512; 706-745-1631.

Milton Inn, located on Route 76. There are two sections, an old and a
new, with 64 units all told. They are modern, nicely furnished, comfortable. Rates are inexpensive. 706-745-6995.

North Georgia Restaurant, located on the town square. This little restaurant serves breakfast and lunch only. The breakfast fare is country as well
as traditional. For lunch there is a variety of sandwiches plus a few "short
order" dishes (like chicken livers, barbecue, pork chops, etc.) and soups.
There is also a buffet lunch (meat and vegetables). The prices are very,
very reasonable. What this restaurant lacks in "chic" it makes up in
friendliness and substance. Open seven days a week. 706-745-5888.

Tucker's Inn Restaurant. Jack Tucker, proprietor, says folks come from as
far away as Marietta, Georgia, and Copper City, Tennessee, for his Sunday
buffet, where he carves roast beef, ham and turkey at a very reasonable
price, including tea or coffee, salad and dessert. Tuesday through Saturday
evenings, he also serves a buffet at the same reasonable price, offering a
variety of main dishes such as fried chicken, country fried steak, stuffed
green peppers, etc, plus a full salad bar and dessert, tea or coffee. There is
also a regular menu with entrées at moderate prices. Friday and Saturday a
man comes in to play "old-time tunes" on the piano. The atmosphere is
very pleasant, and Mr. Tucker stresses that families especially appreciate
it. Tucker's Restaurant is located three miles north of Blairsville on Route
129/19, on the left driving north. 706-745-6474.

Region Five

Fort Mountain State Park
Cohutta Lodge
Chief Vann House
New Echota
Barnsley Gardens
James H. Floyd State Park
Cloudland Canyon State Park
Chickamauga Battlefield

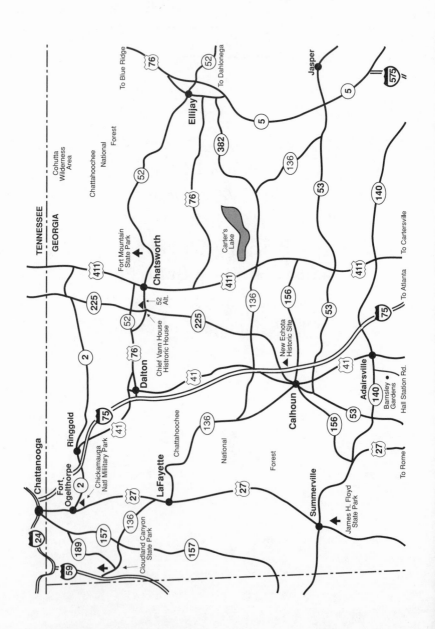

Western Mountain Region

In the northwest area of this state, there are three state parks and a number of very important points of interest including several historic sites.

The state parks are: Fort Mountain State Park, well known for the mysterious stone wall that snakes across the mountaintop; Cloudland Canyon State Park, with its spectacular, wild gorge; and James H. Floyd State Park, a popular stopover for fishermen because of its two well-stocked fishing lakes.

The points of interest are: the New Echota Historic Site, the restored capital of the Cherokee Nation; Chief Vann House, the mansion built by Cherokee Chief James Vann; the Chickamauga Battlefield and Military Park, site of the crucial military campaign that marked the beginning of the end for the armies of the Confederacy in the Civil War; and Barnsley Gardens, the restored ruins of a pre-Civil-War mansion and its fabulous gardens.

A two-day or three-day visit to this area should be most rewarding.

Fort Mountain State Park

Fort Mountain State Park is located on the summit of Fort Mountain, one of the highest peaks in the Cohutta Mountain Range. The feature for which this state park is known, aside from its very nice accommodations, lake, and scenic mountain setting, is the stone wall stretching 885 feet along the top of the west face of the mountain. The wall is 2 to 3 feet high in some places, 5 to 6 feet in others. It is interrupted at regular intervals of 29 feet by a series of circular pits built into the wall. The origin of this wall has been explored by many parties of archaeologists but none have come up with a definite answer. The most acceptable explanation offered by experts is that the wall was built by a tribe of Indians about 500 A.D.

for ceremonial purposes. No artifacts have been discovered in the vicinity of the wall to provide any clues.

The park's accommodations include 15 cottages, some two bedroom, some three-bedroom, all with fireplace, porch, picnic table, and grill. All cottages are heated and have air conditioning. No pets are allowed in the cottages or cottage areas. All of the cottages are nicely situated in wooded areas. Five of them (lower cottage area) are situated near the lake. The lake is a lovely meandering body of water surrounded by wooded hills. There is fishing from the shore and swimming from a beach. There are no canoes or boats for rent, other than pedal boats. No private boats are allowed.

Accommodations also include 75 tent and trailer campsites, all with water and electricity; primitive camping sites and a pioneer camping area for groups. There are 8.2 miles of back-country hiking trails and 12 miles of foot trails; also a backpacking trail with three overnight camps. There are seven picnic shelters; one family and group pavilion can accommodate 80 people.

The ranger warns that anywhere in the park (adjacent to the Cohutta Wilderness) camper or hikers or visitors may encounter copperheads or rattlesnakes. There have been no casualties, but the advice is "Be careful." Wildlife in the park's widespread acres include black bear, bobcat, deer, fox (and of course raccoon and opossums), and many different birds of prey. All (including the snakes) are protected.

The mysterious wall atop the mountain cannot be viewed from any panoramic peak or overlook. It is overgrown along its entire length, but in some areas, there are small exposed stretches. One may hike a trail that follows the wall, but only experienced hikers should undertake this, since the terrain is wild and rugged. For those who are not regular hikers, but would like to take a relatively short (but strenuous and uphill) hike to where one end of the wall begins ask at the park office for a map of the park and drive to the parking lot. From there you start your uphill hike. At the foot of the path is a tablet telling you about the wall; proceed from there. Where you reach the summit, you will come to a stone tower about 40 feet in height, with stairs leading to the top. This tower is not part of the wall and has no archaeological significance. It was built in 1939. From the tower there are trails to overlooks. We suggest you don't take them unless you are part mountain goat, or under 35, surefooted and in tip-top rock-scrambling shape.

Fort Mountain Park's 1,930 acres were donated to the federal government in 1929 by Ivan Allen, Sr., an Atlanta real estate magnate. In the early 1940s, the U.S. Department of the Interior turned the land over to the state of Georgia.

Fort Mountain State Park is 7 miles east of Chatsworth, via Highway 52. Take Exit 366 off I-75. Box 1K, Route 7, Chatsworth, Ga 30705; 706-695-2621.

Cohutta Lodge

Cohutta Lodge is within easy distance of Fort Mountain State Park, Amicalola Falls State Park, the Chief Vann House and the New Echota Historic Site. Situated atop Fort Mountain, it provides comfortable and attractive accommodations for an overnight stay or dining in a beautiful mountain setting. The rooms, all nicely furnished and spacious, have telephone, air/heat, and TV. Most have balconies and offer spectacular, panoramic views. Swimming pool and tennis courts. Cohutta Lodge is a Best Western affiliate. The rates are moderate, except during "leaf season," when they are a little more expensive. Small pets accepted by reservation and deposit.

The restaurant serves all three meals. Breakfast buffet. For lunch, salads and sandwiches. For dinner, steaks, pork, chicken, seafood. Prices are moderate.

Cohutta Lodge also has a convention center for conferences, receptions, and banquets. The main room accommodates up to 250; there are two smaller rooms, one accommodating up to 160, the other up to 40.

Cohutta Lodge is off Highway 52, 7 miles east of Chatsworth. 5000 Cochise Trail, Chatsworth, Ga 30705; 1-800-325-6686 or 706-695-9601.

Chief Vann House

After the white settlers moved into Cherokee territory in the 18th century and settled among them in the mountains and valleys, transcultural developments took place in both directions. Many of the Indians took on the style of life, and mode of habitation, commerce, and dress of the whites. Some of the whites intermarried and took on the style of the Cherokees, mixing it with their own. One of these was Clement Vann, a Scotch trader. He settled among the Cherokees in the late 18th century and married a Cherokee woman with whom he had many children. One of the children was James Vann, who, retaining the Indian side of his heritage, became a chief in his tribe.

Chief Vann, in the course of several years, developed and managed an immense plantation comprising 899 acres of cultivated land, 42 cabins, six barns, five smokehouses, a gristmill, a sawmill, a blacksmith shop, a trading post, and thousands of peach and apple trees.

Chief Vann House

Central to this plantation was a splendid brick mansion, combining Federal and Georgian styles of architecture, furnished with the finest furniture of that time. The construction was begun in 1804, completed in 1805.

Chief James Vann, "known to be pugnacious when drinking," was killed in a barroom brawl in 1809.

The mansion and the rest of the property passed on to his son Joseph Vann, but Joseph and his family did not retain it. In the 1830s, all Indian-owned lands (and property on these lands) was seized by the Georgia state government, divided into "lots" and given by lottery to white settlers. The Vann mansion, plantation, and all the property thereon went to a white settler, and the Joseph Vann family was evicted by force. The family made its way to Oklahoma, where Joseph built a replica of the original Vann mansion.

The Georgia mansion and plantation were poorly managed by the new owner, and after some decades the neglected property began to deteriorate. It was in ruins when, in 1959, the community purchased the house and three acres of land and gave them to the Georgia Historical Commission. The roof was gone; the dining room floor had collapsed; the brick arches over the doorway had cracked and were falling in and every windowpane had been shattered by vandals.

Over a period of several years, the Georgia Historical Commission restored the building and partially furnished it. Some of the furniture was originally in the mansion; the rest, of the same period.

We are indebted to the state agency for a description of the mansion supplementing our own observations:

> Two-story high brick walls are crowned front and rear with a classic cornice. Each facade has two-story white washed plaster pilasters and two fan-lighted doorways one above the other, framed by large painted wood panelling and opening off wide hallways onto covered porches. On each side of the two main floors are two rooms 30 feet by 20 feet with a wide hallway between. To the left of the main entrance is an elaborately carved staircase, the oldest example of cantilevered construction in Georgia ... Handcarving with the Cherokee rose predominating is an outstanding feature of the house inside and out.

We add our own notes as follows: The parlor to the right of the entrance on the first floor has a huge fireplace surmounted by a mantel reaching to the ceiling. Over the fireplace hangs a handsome portrait (of museum quality) of Joseph Vann. The dining room is furnished with elegant dining room tables and chairs and cupboards. To the left of the entrance is the parlor, furnished with a sofa, some chairs, a grandfather clock, a beautiful grand piano, and several tables.

On the second floor there are two large bedrooms furnished with canopied beds, a sleigh bed, chifforobes, chests of drawers, and tables.

On the third floor are two narrow, oblong rooms, believed to have served as sleeping quarters for the servants and children.

In the entrance hall, which also serves as a museum, there are several interesting articles, including Joseph Vann's violin, a book listing the owners of the land chosen by lottery, and of all things, a picture of Will Rogers who, the descriptive tablet explains, was a descendant of Chief James Vann. Will Rogers' father, the note says, was Clement Vann Rogers, named after the father of Chief James Vann.

In addition, there are prints of the portraits of several of the Cherokee chiefs, including Chief James Vann. If we had not read the inscriptions below the prints, we could easily have imagined we were looking at the portraits of members of the United States Cabinet, so fine and stylish was the dress of the men in the portraits.

The Chief Vann House is located on the outskirts of Chatsworth on U.S. 52 between Dalton and Chatsworth, at the intersection of Highway 52 and Highway 225. It is open year-round, Tuesday–Saturday, 9 a.m. to 5 p.m.; Sunday 2 p.m. to 5:30 p.m. Closed Mondays, Thanksgiving, and Christmas Day. Route 7, Box 7655, Chatsworth, Ga 30705; 706-695-2598.

New Echota Historic Site

Before we tell you what you will see when you visit **New Echota** (eh-CHO-tah) **historic site,** we need to tell you about its history. Without this explanation, the rest would have little meaning. The following historic information is taken from material prepared by the Georgia Department of Natural Resources.

On November 12, 1825, the legislature of the Cherokee Nation adopted a resolution providing for the establishment of a capitol called New Echota. This new seat of government became headquarters for the small, independent Indian Nation that spread across present-day northern Georgia into western North Carolina, eastern Tennessee, and northeastern Alabama.

By this time the Cherokees had discarded the traditional Indian clan system of ruling a tribe, with an indefinite number of clan chiefs and town chiefs making up the tribal council. Instead, they patterned their government after that of the United States, creating a republican form of control. The nation was divided into eight districts and a legislature established to make laws and approve treaties. Four delegates from each district were elected to the lower house, the National Council. This body chose the twelve members of the upper house, the National Committee. In turn, the National Committee selected the top level officers–Principal Chief, Assistant Principal Chief, and Treasurer.

The principal meeting place of the legislative branch of the Cherokee government in 1819 was the Council House at New Town. When New Echota was established in 1825, it centered around the New Town Council House. The name New Echota honored Chota, an old beloved town long remembered in the tribal history. Old Chota was located in present day eastern Tennessee.

A remarkable development in the Cherokee progress came in 1821, when the principal men adopted a written form of their native language. It was the invention of a mixed-blood Cherokee named Sequoyah (or George Guess, or Gist). Sequoyah succeeded in creating a syllabary for the Cherokees. The symbols in his language represent syllables. The Indians had but to memorize the characters, and they were literate. Thus, the Cherokees had a means of communication unique among American Indians of that time.

This invention was put to use at New Echota in the Print Shop. Here, the Cherokees established a national press and newspaper. While the printing office was being built at New Echota, type in both Cherokee and English languages, along with a press and other equipment, was being secured. From the New Echota print shop the first issue of the *Cherokee Phoenix* appeared on February 21, 1828, printed in Cherokee and English. The paper maintained existence until 1834.

Much of the cost of outfitting the Indian newspaper was paid for by the American Board of Commissioners for Foreign Missions in Boston. One of the ablest missionaries sent out by the American Board was the Rev. Samuel A. Worcester, who arrived in New Echota in 1827. He built a home near the capitol, which remained standing while other New Echota buildings disappeared. This house has been renovated by the Georgia Historical Commission as part of the New Echota Restoration.

One of the buildings at New Echota which Worcester used for mission purposes was the Court House, which reflects the Cherokee's legal progress. In the Court House the Cherokee Supreme Court met to hear cases appealed from Cherokee circuit and district courts. Police officers for the Nation were a marshal and a ranger in each district.

Accompanying Cherokee developments in government, law, and religion was a general adoption of the American frontier economy. This Indian nation of farmers (93% of the Cherokees, according to the Federal Removal Census of 1835, were agrarian) tilled their land and lived in houses of trimmed or unhewn logs, clapboards, or stone, depending on their individual circumstances. Some Indians owned Negro slaves. Several Indian dwellings were at New Echota, as were a number of stores.

Vann's Tavern, among the buildings in the New Echota Restoration, is a Cherokee-built structure, although it was not originally erected at the Indian capitol. It was moved to the New Echota site by the Historical Commission to prevent inundation of the house when Lake Lanier was filled. Originally built by James Vann as a "public stop" at the Chattahoochee River crossing near Oscarville, the large rough-hewn structure is representative of some of the Indian taverns which stood in this vicinity.

Thus, with a national newspaper and printing office, a legislative hall, a supreme court house, a mission station, and several dwellings and commercial establishments in its capital town, the Cherokee Nation possessed a dramatic and unusual seat of government–as compared with other Indian tribes of the past century–New Echota.

Following the westward removal of the Cherokees in 1838-39, during which time New Echota served as one of the centers of removal activity, the last capital of the Cherokee Nation in the East fell into disuse. Save for the Worcester House, the buildings were soon torn down and the public grounds converted into farm lands.

In the early 1950s, a group of Calhoun citizens initiated efforts which eventually led to the restoration of New Echota. After locating the site exactly, they purchased 200 acres of the town site and deeded it to the State of Georgia.

As you enter the visitor's center to the New Echota Historic Site, you see several historic markers that relate the establishment of New Echota as the Cherokee capital at this site, retell the tragic events of the Trail of Tears, and note that it was at this site that the treaty was signed (under duress) in which the Cherokees relinquished their land. Within the building there is a museum with historical photographs, engravings, and artifacts relating to the life of the Cherokees, their leaders, and the removal of the Cherokee nation. There are also facsimiles of pages from the *Cherokee Phoenix*, and visitors may in fact obtain a facsimile of page one of the very first issue of the *Cherokee Phoenix*, dated Thursday, February 21, 1828.

Visitors are then given an annotated one-page guide-map to which they can refer as they walk through the field, following arrows and informative markers to a number of important sites: A structure typical of the Cherokee homes of the early 1800s; the site of the home of Elias Boudinot, editor of the *Cherokee Phoenix*; a reconstruction of the building in which the *Cherokee Phoenix* was printed, with a printing press and printing implements similar to those used in the printing of this newspaper; the Vann Tavern, an original Cherokee structure built around 1800; the Worcester House, home of missionaries who figured so importantly in New Echota history, built in 1828 and restored in the 1950s; and a reconstruction of the 1829 Cherokee Supreme Court Building. An interesting item in the Vann Tavern is this sign: "Room and board 25 cents, clean sheets 10 cents, whiskey $1.60 a gallon, salt $4.00 a bushel, tobacco 50 cents a pound, coffee two pounds for $1.00."

The New Echota Historic Site is located just one mile east of I-75 Exit 131 on Highway 225. It is open year-round, Tuesday–Saturday, 9 a.m.- 5 p.m.; Sunday, 2 p.m.-5 p.m. Closed Monday, Thanksgiving and Christmas Day. 1211 Chatsworth Highway, N.E., Calhoun, Ga 30701; 706-629-8151.

Barnsley Gardens

In 1856, workmen put the finishing touches to the manor house at **Barnsley Gardens.** It had taken nearly 16 years to complete, but at the end, it fulfilled most of the original plans of its creator and owner, Godfrey Barnsley, an Englishman who had come to America in 1818 and made a fortune as a cotton merchant.

Unlike the classical antebellum mansions of the era with their Greek revival columns and porticos, this was a villa in the Italian style, with some Gothic touches added.

The sprawling, solid brick structure stood two stories high in the center, topped by a tower, and two stories high in the wings. Arched doorways and windows, framed out in Italian marble, were 12 and 14 feet tall; fireplace mantels and hearths were also of marble. Great doors and paneling had been imported from England.

The 26-room mansion contained elaborate dining and banquet rooms, a library, drawing rooms, numerous bedrooms, two kitchens, a billiards room, and a wine cellar stocked with the finest imported wines. A 300-gallon tank in the tower, filled from a spring by means of a hydraulic pumping device, supplied the house with running water. Water pipes built into the chimney wall provided the occupants with hot water. A unique

Barnsley Gardens circa 1857

stove built from plans drawn by Leonardo da Vinci featured a rotisserie and could cook for more than 100 people.

The manor was furnished with elegant pieces, rare and costly antiques and objets d'art imported from all over the world.

The grandeur of the interior was matched by near-marvels of the exterior: an oval-shaped boxwood parterre garden laid out in intricate, symmetrical design with a marble fountain at its center; two rock gardens; a rose garden including every known variety; an aquatic garden (bog garden) with 5,000 plants; an Oriental garden and fish pool stocked with Japanese carp; a pond in which black swans floated; a deer garden in the English style. Trees were imported from England, the Middle East, China, and Germany and planted on the grounds.

All this splendor had been accomplished, but the person for whom it was intended–Barnsley's wife, Julia–was no longer alive. Barnsley had met Julia Scarsborough in Savannah through his business associations in that city. In 1828 they were married and made their home there. In the 1830s, Julia became ill with tuberculosis, and Barnsley decided to move the family, on the advice of a friend, to the northwest Georgia mountains so his ailing wife could benefit from the cool and healthy climate.

In 1838, he purchased several thousand acres at the present location of Barnsley Gardens, and made plans to build there a beautiful mansion for his beloved Julia. (Originally–and for many years–the estate was named Woodlands. Later the name was changed to Barnsley Gardens.)

The family first moved into a log cabin while the initial section, the left wing, was being built, and then in 1842, into the right wing while the main house was being built. But Julia was not destined to enjoy the fulfillment of her husband's dream for her. In 1845, she died and was buried in Savannah.

However, the construction did not stop with Julia's death. From letters and other sources, it has been learned that Barnsley felt he had to fulfill a commitment to Julia to complete the manor. He claimed to have been in communication with her through a spiritualist and to have been guided by her in respect to various aspects of the construction.

Finally, in 1856, the main section of the structure was ready to be inhabited, and Barnsley and his five children moved in. In the next several years, the family prospered, and Barnsley Gardens became the center of social life in the region.

Then came the Civil War, and misfortune, in many forms, struck Barnsley Gardens.

The Union blockade of southern ports shattered Barnsley's business, based as it was on trade with England and northern American ports.

Union troops, under the command of General J. N. McPherson, occupied the manor and the estate. Except for some pilfering, they did little damage, but when McPherson and his troops left, vandals and looters ransacked and pillaged the home. However, the structure remained intact. Subsequently the family scattered and Barnsley moved to New Orleans.

After the war, the Barnsleys' daughter, Julia, moved back to Barnsley Gardens with her husband, Captain James Peter Baltzelle, and they began their nearly hopeless efforts to restore the estate. Shortly thereafter, Captain Baltzelle was killed in an accident, and Julia once more abandoned the manor and, with her infant daughter Adelaide, moved to New Orleans and joined Godfrey Barnsley, now an aged and ailing man. Godfrey died in 1873, virtually a pauper. By then Julia had remarried and she and her husband Charles Henry von Schwartz brought Godfrey back to Barnsley Gardens for burial. (His grave is still there together with those of 35 men, women, and children who had worked for the Barnsleys. It was Godfrey Barnsley's wish that they all be buried together, black and white, as "part of the family.")

Adelaide Baltzelle, now grown, married B. F. A. Saylor, and together they took up the task of trying to restore Barnsley Gardens, continuing the all-but-futile efforts of the von Schwartzes. But lacking funds, they could accomplish very little.

In 1906, a tornado tore off the roof of the central section of the manor, and the Saylors moved into the right wing. Despite pressures from many sources they refused to sell Barnsley Gardens. But when Adelaide Saylor died in 1942, the estate was liquidated. Subsequent owners did little to preserve the buildings, gardens, and grounds, letting them fall into disrepair and ruin.

In 1952, Medora Field Perkerson wrote about Barnsley Manor in a book titled *White Columns in Georgia*. There were some truly touching lines in that account:

> These gardens with their oval boxwood (terrace), great lawns, English and Japanese yews, and other fine old trees are still green after more than 100 years. Red Louis Phillipe roses bloomed there bravely on the day of our visit, and other flowers, too.

> But the big house facing these gardens is a roofless shell, a gaunt ruin on an acorn-shaped hill, surrounded by the green isolation of wooded mountains. Cottonwood trees, growing up through the rotted floors of the spacious rooms push their branches through empty window arches. The bare inner walls are covered with the pale green tapestry of flattened wisteria leaves on vines which have wandered far from the gnarled roots outside the house. Gone from the wide hall is the grand staircase under which a vault for valuables was built. There is no sign now of the huge tower tank from which pipes carried water to the many bedrooms, warmed by the heat of the chimney flues.

That was the situation in 1952. In 1988, Prince Hubertus Fuerst Fugger-Babenhausen of Augsburg, Germany, whose noble lineage goes back to the 1400s, bought the property and decided to restore it. At the time of the purchase, deterioration had gone even further, with walls and arches crumbling and kudzu threatening to engulf the property.

Prince Fugger considered restoring the house to its original state, working from drawings and plans left by Godfrey Barnsley together with several thousand other papers that had been stored in the archives of the University of Georgia, Emory University, Duke University, and the University of North Carolina. However, he decided against this, opting instead to stabilize the ruins of the main house, restore the gardens, plantings, and ponds as nearly as possible and convert the right wing into a museum. That building was still in very good shape. The left wing was gone.

The restoration was completed in October 1991.

The ruins of the main house have been stabilized, and one may walk through its spacious, roofless rooms, marvel at this European villa in its north Georgia mountain surroundings and observe the peacocks strutting about the grounds.

The parterre boxwood gardens, still hearty and thriving, but overgrown, have been "tamed," and a beautifully sculpted fountain graces its center.

Both rock gardens have been restored, and one has been planted with ferns and flowering bulbs.

Two parallel borders of old-fashioned roses and herbaceous plants have been replanted behind the manor.

The bog garden or sunken garden once again teems with exotic flowers and plants. In the Oriental pond, Japanese carp once again swim among the lotus plants. Black swans once more float gracefully in the Black Swan pond. The banks leading down to the ponds are covered with jasmine.

On "rhododendron hill" more than 400 rhododendron bushes have been planted and below this hall there is a natural fern bank with more than 100 ferns of different varieties.

A magnificent arbor has been installed on the south slope overlooking the bog garden, and, on the slope below the arbor more than 40,000 daffodil bulbs have been planted.

A wildflower meadow at the top of a hill has been seeded with poppies, bachelor buttons, daisies, phlox, and many other varieties to present an ever-flowering, ever-changing blanket of all of nature's colors throughout the spring and summer months.

Beyond the Oriental Pond, a nature area has been re-created in the woods, bringing back the plants that were there when the Barnsleys strode these grounds.

The museum in the restored right wing overflows with exciting memorabilia, documents, pictures, and artifacts. One section is devoted to the Barnsley family and other families that lived nearby in the 1800s. Another section is given over to the native Americans–the Indians who inhabited this area not only in the recent past, but thousands of years ago. The third section features events that took place on or near the estate during the Civil War, and important personages involved in those events.

More than $2,000,000 has been spent by Prince Fugger in the restoration. Whatever income will come from visitors will go toward maintenance of the Barnsley Gardens enterprise. Fugger shares credit for this splendid achievement with Carl H. Cofer, Bobby McElwee, who is in charge of building restoration and is also Barnsley Gardens manager, and with Gardens Manager Steve Wheaton, under whose direction the gardens and grounds were restored.

Barnsley Gardens is open as follows: March 1 to November 15, Tuesday through Saturday, 10 a.m. to 6 p.m.; Sunday Noon to 6 p.m. November 16 through February 28, Tuesday through Saturday, 10 a.m. to 4:30 p.m.; Sunday Noon to 4:40. Closed Mondays.

General admission is $6; age 11 and under free.

To get to Barnsley Gardens: via Highway I-75, Exit 128 at Adairsville, west on Highway 140 about 1.5 miles (across old Highway 41 and R.R. overpass) to Hall Station Road on the left. Go south on Hall Station Road about 5.5 miles to Barnsley Garden Road. West on Barnsley Garden Road about 2.5 miles to entrance on left. Barnsley Garden Road, Adairsville, Ga 30105; 706-773-7480.

James H. Floyd State Park

This state park is primarily a fishing park. There are two lakes, one 15 acres, the other 35, both stocked with bass, catfish, bream, crappy, and other species. Each lake has a boat ramp and boat dock. Fishermen (or fisherwomen) may bring their own boats with a trolling (electric) motor, or a rowboat or canoe (gasoline powered boats are not allowed). Or they may rent a fishing boat from the park. There are also pedal boats for rent. Swimming is not allowed.

This park has no cottages or lodge, but it does have 25 tent and trailer sites, each with water, electricity, a picnic table, and grill. These are nicely placed in a wooded area. There is also a playground and centrally located comfort station. Primitive camping is available for organized groups. Picnic areas, including two that are sheltered, are located throughout the park.

The setting is that of farmland with many wooded areas. The park's 289 acres are situated at the base of Taylor's Ridge, which is part of the Chattahoochee National Forest.

A large number of migratory Canadian geese and wild ducks have made this a stopping place, remaining a month or two and then traveling on. This park has also become a bluebird sanctuary, thanks to Daryl Rush ("Mr. Blue Bird"), state park manager. Starting several years ago, Rush set up bluebird boxes in different locations in the park, increasing the number every year. He estimates that more than 125 bluebirds are hatched here each year, and the number is expected to increase as Rush added additional boxes. At this writing there were 91. Rush also constructs and sells hundreds of bluebird boxes through the state park system.

The park is located 3 miles southeast of Summerville, off Highway 27. Route 1, Box 291, Summerville, Ga 30747; 706-857-5211.

Cloudland Canyon State Park

The stellar feature at **Cloudland Canyon State Park** is its spectacular canyon, a gorge cut into the mountain by Sitton Gulch Creek. The canyon is a quarter mile across from east rim to west rim and is 1,800 feet deep at its deepest. The sides of the canyon are covered with lush growth in the summertime except where there are massive clifflike outcroppings. From a fence-protected trail along the east rim you can look across to the west face of the canyon with views of two waterfalls, outpourings of Daniel Creek. Along both rims there are hiking trails with several overlooks providing breathtaking views.

The canyon is but one of the many outstanding attractions at this park. There are tennis courts and a swimming pool in settings more like that of country club than a state park–a grassy, wooded plateau surrounded by the mountains.

There are 75 tent and trailer sites, all with water and electricity. A walkin campsite enables you to get away from the vehicles. You park your car and walk to the site with your tent and camping gear. A 40-bed group camp is heated for winter use and fully supplied with kitchen equipment. All you have to do is bring your own bed linens.

Sixteen comfortable rental cottages, in nice wooded settings, have fireplaces, screened porches, outdoor grills, and picnic tables.

The park has 2,160 acres and deliberate efforts, it appears, have been made to keep the different elements–the swimming pool and tennis courts, the cottages, the camping sites etc.–spread out and away from each other in this vast mountain woodland. In addition, wherever you drive, there are picnic tables, picnic shelters, playgrounds, all in wooded groves, everything well-tended in immaculate, manicured condition. The atmosphere throughout is that of peacefulness, quiet, and serenity. In fact, as we drove up to the park office, about ten in the morning, a large deer bounded across the path, up a slope and into the woods. One may also sight hawks and eagles.

Cloudland Canyon State Park is located on Route 136, 8 miles east of Trenton and I-59 and 18 miles northwest of LaFayette on Highway 27. Route 2, Box 150, Rising Fawn, Ga 30738; 706-657-4050.

Chickamauga Battlefield
and Military Park

The Chickamauga Battlefield, situated in the northwest corner of
Georgia, was the site, in September of 1863, of one of the most bloody
and costly battles of the Civil War. In its aftermath, the South lost
Chattanooga, just a few miles to the north. This was the beginning of the
end for the Confederacy, since Chattanooga was the gateway to Georgia
and the Deep South and a vital rail link with the rest of the Confederacy.

This crucial campaign began late in August 1863. Some 97,000 rebels
under the command of General Braxton Bragg were in control of Chattanooga when a force of about 60,000 Federals, under the command of
General William S. Rosecrans began to outflank that city. The defenders
pulled back into northwest Georgia, spread out along a line of about 20
miles, north to south, and awaited reinforcements. (Their location was
on both sides of the LaFayette Road, following, approximately the route
of today's Highway 27.) Rosecrans and his troops took off in pursuit. After
a good deal of skirmishing in advance, the first crucial battles took place
on September 19, with neither side gaining decisive advantage.

In the meantime, some 15,000 Confederate troops under the command
of General James Longstreet, were on the way to reinforce General Bragg,
traveling over 900 miles of rail lines from Virginia, through North and
South Carolina and Georgia.

On the morning of September 20, Longstreet's forces broke through
Rosecrans's line, cutting his army in half, sending the Federal troops in
disorderly retreat northward to Chattanooga. A superb last-stand action
by Major General George H. Thomas prevented complete chaos and permitted Rosecrans's army to get back to Chattanooga and dig in. Because
of this stand, General Thomas became known as "The Rock of Chickamauga." In the bloody battle of Chickamauga some 4,000 men were killed,
and over 30,000 wounded.

Pursuing Rosecrans, Bragg laid siege to Chattanooga and by mid-October
the Union forces were near to starvation. But then, reinforcements began
to arrive. One force under "Fighting Joe" Hooker came from Virginia,
traveling 1,200 miles by rail in six days to get there. Another force under

Brotherton Farmhouse at the Chickamauga Battlefield

General William T. Sherman took off from Vicksburg by boat, train and foot, reaching Chattanooga on November 23.

Under the command of General Grant himself, the Union army attacked Bragg's forces on November 25, throwing them into a disastrous retreat into north Georgia. It was from that hard-won base in Chattanooga that Sherman, the following spring, began his fateful march through Georgia.

Today, this battlefield, not very much changed in terrain from the last days of fighting in 1863, is a national memorial. Its 8,000 acres have been preserved as nearly as possible, in their original state.

The visitor's center, your first stop after you enter the gates to the military park, is a handsome building, flanked by batteries of Civil War cannons. Inside, there is a museum, a bookstore with a splendid collection of books on the Civil War and other subjects of regional interest, and a theatre, where a half-hour multimedia presentation, "The Battle of Chickamauga," is given throughout the day. Visitors are supplied with maps of the battle-field and another map outlining a seven-mile tour through the battlefield which the visitor can make by automobile, following a route marked by arrows and informational tablets. There are also three guided tours daily, the visitors' cars following behind the guide's car, and stopping at each point of interest.

We made the tour on our own. It was a never-to-be-forgotten experience. At every turn, and throughout the battlefield, there were little stone memorials, like gravestones identifying the company, or battalion, or other army group—Confederate and Federal—that stood there and fought; large, beautiful sculptured memorials some depicting heroic stands, others identifying the state—Confederate and Union—whose soldiers had fought there.

Scattered throughout were solitary cannons and batteries of cannons which had fired their shots in the bloody battle. Two cabins are still there, the Brotherton farmhouse, where Longstreet's troops broke through the Union line, and the Snodgrass cabin on the hill, where General Thomas held back the Southern forces enabling Rosecrans's army to retreat to Chattanooga.

There is a stillness there, enabling your mind to travel into the past, to see the troops locked in battle at each marked site, hear the thunder of the cannons, the cries of the soldiers … in all an intensely moving experience.

The Chickamauga Battlefield is a few miles west of I-75, south of Rossville. Exit at Battlefield Parkway (Georgia Route 2) and follow the signs to the park entrance. It may also be reached by following Highway 27 north from LaFayette. Hours are 8 a.m.-5:45 p.m., Memorial Day to Labor Day; 8 a.m. to 4:45 p.m. the rest of the year. P. O. Box 2128; 706-866-9241.

Region Six

Highlands, North Carolina

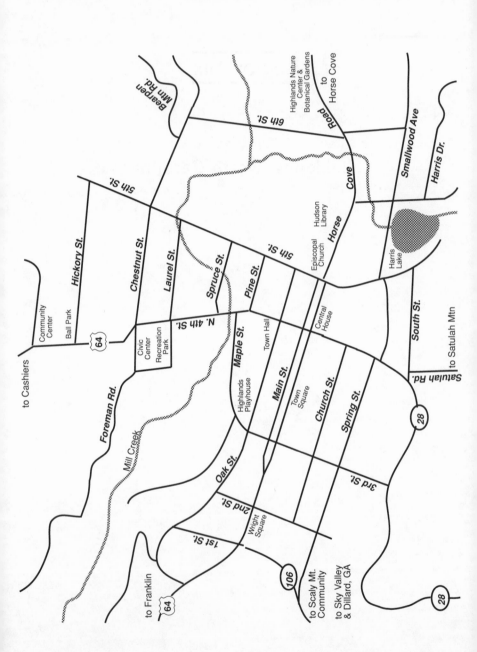

Highlands

Highlands, North Carolina, just 14 miles from Dillard, Georgia, is a pretty little resort town nestled in a beautiful natural setting. The village tends toward quiet sophistication, with its nice shops, galleries, auction houses, book stores, and fine restaurants. Every summer it hosts a chamber music ensemble of top professional caliber and a season of up-to-date plays and musicals, as well as classics.

In their book *Valley So Wild*, Alberta and Carson Brewer wrote,

> The town is an example of what can happen when mountains, money, planners, and architects of good taste get together. This is obvious in the landscaping, in the quiet good taste of shop-keepers' merchandise, and in the absence of the garish scenes which plague many resort towns.

Another writer heralding the beauty of Highlands and the surrounding area is Evangeline M. Davis. She says in her book *The Lure of Highlands*

> Consider an environment having a moderate temperate climate, a rich flora with a wealth of flowering herbs and shrubs, cascading mountain streams, and rugged high terrain offering unsurpassed vistas of distant peaks and valleys. The image readily serves to describe the Highlands Plateau – a remarkable and unique mountain region near the southeastern terminus of the Appalachians.

At an altitude of 4,118 feet, Highlands is the highest incorporated town east of the Mississippi River. The Highlands area is bathed by cool, fresh breezes even in the height of the summer. It was this feature which motivated the town's founders, Clinton Hutchinson and Samuel Kelsey, in the middle 1880s, to promote Highlands as a health resort, emphasizing the clean air and cool, comfortable summers. They claimed in their pamphlets that the altitude of Highlands was a cure for such illnesses as yellow fever and consumption, asserting, "There is no better climate in the world for health, comfort, and enjoyment."

Attesting to this, a Mr. Eldredge H. Blood from Lynn, Massachusetts, wrote in a letter to a relative, "I can heartily recommend the town of Highlands, N.C. as a health resort. I arrived there in the spring of 1886, very much broken in health from chronic bronchitis. After a stay of seven months, I was so far recovered as to be able to attend to my business. I ascribe this result to the wonderfully pure air and water and the remarkable evenness of the temperature during the summer months."

By 1927, some 400 people, attracted by these features and by good farming and business opportunities, were living in Highlands. In summer, entire families would come to vacation homes from Georgia, North Carolina, South Carolina, Louisiana, and other states. It is reported that Robert W. Woodruff, who developed the Coca-Cola Company, once traveled to Highlands with his wife, taking a week on horseback to get there.

Among other prominent summer people who came here many years ago was the Benet family including brothers Stephen Vincent Benet and William Rose Benet, then children. Both later became poets of national importance.

Golf came to Highlands in a big way in 1929 when the Highlands Country Club was built on 250 acres by Atlanta businessmen. Renowned golfer Robert Tyre (Bobby) Jones, a frequent visitor for many years, officially opened the club upon its completion. Today, golf and country clubs abound in Highlands and nearby Cashiers (Cash-ers), most all of them private.

Highlands' year-round population is only about 1,000, but it swells to many times that number when, in the spring and summer, folks from surrounding states (and many from distant states) come to occupy their vacation homes scattered throughout the surrounding mountains and valleys.

Summer and fall are primary tourist seasons in Highlands. Winter is quiet with little activity in the village. Some shops close as early as October when many owners return to their Florida winter abodes. By early January, a significant number of businesses are closed until spring. The hours for those that remain open through winter are often determined by the whims of the owners.

Highlands shops offer everything from fine imports to items handmade by area artists and craftsmen. Expect to see quality labels, wide selections of some items, and prices comparable to boutiques, galleries, and fine stores in large cities.

The town's restaurants offer a wide variety of choices – from simple sandwiches and home cooking to elegant gourmet.

The surroundings offer beautiful scenery, waterfalls, forests with multitudinous flowering shurbs and wildflowers and numerous opportunities for hiking, fishing, hunting, and other activities.

On the following pages, we will guide you to each of these attractions.

Antiques

C. K. Swan /Antiques and Folk Art carries antique silver and ornate silver trays and other silver pieces; old instruments such as mandolins; antique furniture – chairs, couches, etc.; hand-carved toys and animals; and an interesting selection of lamps. The shop is in the Mountain Brook Center on Fourth Street, just a block downhill from the red light at Fourth and Main streets. 704-526-2083.

Fletcher & Lee, also in the Mountain Brook Center, specializes in French and English antiques, reproductions, art, gifts, and accessories. The shop offers Portuguese, Spanish, and Italian porcelain, original etchings and oil paintings, hand-tooled brass horn candlesticks, hand-painted and engraved plates from Greece, and brass checkerboards. Open all year, except late December and early January. Prices range from a few dollars to a several thousand dollars. From Main and Fourth, proceed down the hill on Fourth for one block. Mountain Brook Center is on the right, and the shop is on the left side. 704-526-9624.

Juliana's is filled with interesting items, including antique quilts, majolica, and bric-a-brac. The shop also carries dollhouse furniture and a variety of gift items. Open till Christmas, but weekends only after Thanksgiving until spring. To reach Juliana's, drive down Main Street from the intersection of Main and Highway 106. Proceed into the village. Soon after passing Third Street and Oak Square on the left, begin looking for the shop, also on the left side of the street. 704-526-4306.

Mirror Lake Antiques carries American and European antiques. Items on display include antique furniture, clocks, and lamps as well as estate jewelry and antique glassware. The shop carries many antique silver pieces and offers a complete silver matching service. Located on Fourth Street at the top of the hill, less than a block from Main Street. 704-526-2080.

Clothing Shops

House of Wong, on the corner of Main and Fourth streets, caters to women of all ages. Specialties include silk blouses and hand-embroidered blouses from the Orient ($40 to $200). You'll find casual clothes as well as dresses for church, dinner ,and cocktail parties, and other occasions. Prices for dresses and other outfits range from under $100 to about $600. The shop also carries accessories including evening bags, leather bags, and costume jewelry. Open Monday through Saturday, 10:00 a.m. to 5:00 p.m. 704-526-3865.

Le Pavillon features casual and designer clothes and accessories for women, including lines of colorful dresses and pant suits. There are plenty of accessories to choose from for casual as well as dressy occasions. The merchandise is medium to high in price. Located at the top of the hill on Fourth Street, a block from Main Street (near Mirror Lake Antiques). 704-526-3196.

McCulley's is an importer of fine cashmere, wool, and cotton apparel. You'll find an extensive and colorful line of sweaters, suits, belts, scarves, hats, slacks, and shirts for both men and women. Also, there is a nice line of women's shoes. Owners Mary Alice and Robin Wheaton work with designers in Scotland to produce original designs for cashmere sweaters. Prices are from a few hundred dollars to much more. Located on Church Street, next to the Condiment Shop, just off Fourth Street on the Hill. From Main Street, go up the hill one-half block and turn left. The shop is on the left. Open year-round. 704-526-4407.

Spoiled Rotten. Shopping is an experience in this unique ladies' boutique. The merchandise is mostly very expensive, but the dresses and party clothes are extremely colorful–even glitzy–and are imported from all over the world. Dresses, pantsuits, and party clothes range from pieces designed in Israel to Western clothes with glitter and sequins. There is also a wide selection of accessories and costume jewelry. Located in Town Square on Main Street. Traveling down Main from the light at Highway 106, continue just past Third Street. Town Square is on the right. 704-526-3608.

T.J. Bailey For Men is one of the finest men's shops in the area. There are beautiful and colorful lines of shirts, slacks, scarves, ties, sweaters, jackets, hats and more. Fine brands such as Nautica fill the store. Very helpful and friendly staff. In Town Square on Main Street, just around the boardwalk from Spoiled Rotten. 704-526-2262.

Galleries, Museums, Art, Crafts, and Gems

Ann Jacob Gallery. The artwork here ranges from folk art and wood carvings by regional artists to traditional and contemporary oil paintings, watercolors, and sculpture by noted artists. Items on display may include hand-carved, wooden signs and sculptures with fish, owls, and other animals as the subjects. Many of the folk art pieces, including primitive houses, barns, cats, dogs, and cows are designed with a humorous touch. Open late in the season; then closed until late spring. Located on Main Street one building from the intersection with Fourth Street. 704-526-4640.

Bascom-Louise Gallery. This tiny gallery displays, art, crafts, and sculpture pertaining to Highlands. Everything here is by artists resident to the area. Located inside the Hudson Library on Main Street. From the light in the middle of town at Main and Fourth streets, proceed on Main past the Highlands Inn and the Episcopal Church. The library and gallery are on the left. 704-526-4949.

Basket Works of Cashiers has opened an adjoining shop to the Summer House. Well known for a wonderful selection of local basket designs and collections from all over the world, the shop will offer all the special gift items found in Cashiers. 704-743-5052.

The Christmas Cottage. At the entrance to this shop, Christmas bells are always ringing. In the front window are several different types of electric trains, all moving at a different pace. Outstanding items include hand-crafted, life-like doll sculptures that look like antiques by Avigail Brahms and other sculptors. Some of these are priced at a thousand dollars or more. A variety of life-like Santas are carved in wood and dressed in fabric by Norma Lizabeth DeCamp. Good selection of Christmas decorations, manager scenes, and special gift items. Closed January until April. Located in Oak Square on Main Street. 704-526-4129.

The Christmas Tree carries hand-carved Santas, hand-painted eggs and other hand-painted items, and a wide variety of Christmas decorations including some made of stained glass. The store also has interesting picture frames and other gift items. From Main Street, proceed up the Fourth Street hill. The Christmas Tree is on your left. 704-526-3687 or 1-800-523-6558.

Cypress Potters located next to the Ski Scaly offers a full range of hand made pottery which is created on the premise by local artisians. Charlie Frankowski, the popular roving "chainsaw sculptor", creates beautiful one of a kind animals and birds on the front lawn of the pottery shop. 704-526-2064.

Highlands Art Gallery. In summer, most every night at 8:00 p.m., there's an auction crowded with Highlands summer folk at Highlands Art Gallery on Main Street. You'll find everything under the sun including American and imported furniture, bronze and porcelain statues and clocks, original oil paintings as well as reproductions, Chinese urns, and Oriental rugs. The seating is ample, and people tend to come and go throughout the evening. This is a major pastime in Highlands. Auctions begin in mid-May and continue throughout the summer. Located in the heart of town on Main Street, between Town Square and The Stone Lantern. From the light at Main Street and Highway 106, drive down Main Street till you see the gallery on your right. 704-526-4640.

The Highlands Gem Shop offers a large variety of precious and semi-precious gems, many of them found in the mountains of western North Carolina. The experts here will create custom-designed fine jewelry using gold and an array of gems such as amethyst, diamond. garnet, ruby, sapphire, and topaz. Located midway up the Fourth Street hill, just half a block from Main. 704-526-2767.

Kandle Korner. The mainstay of this store is handcrafted candles in every imaginable shape, size, and color. You'll also find handmade towels, wreaths, and hand-painted pots and pans. Many items are created by regional artists. Closed in winter, except weekends. Driving from the light at Highway 106 and Main Street, proceed toward the middle of town and look for Town Square on your right. Kandle Korner is located at the rear of the square. 704-526-5556.

Lick Log Mill Store is partially housed in the front of an old church built in 1851. The quaint old building is very close to the road. Owners Karen and Chris Waldron have expanded the floor space considerably to accommodate a wide selection of interesting, handcrafted pieces from all over America and Europe. This shop is really a gallery of designer accessories. You'll find baskets by some of the country's finest basketmakers including Martha Weatherby and Stephen Zeh. Handwoven Afghans are made in the area. Some of the quilts are custom-designed and then made by Mennonite ladies in Indiana. Kaleidoscopes, many handmade in Guatemala, are constructed of rosewood, eastern walnut, feathers, flowers, and stained glass. Moving kinetic sculptures are built by a physicist from Connecticut. There are hand-carved wooden birds, handmade Santas, animals, and other folk art. Lick Log also carries porcelain pieces from Spain and original art. Prices range from less than a dollar to thousands of dollars. Traveling west on Highway 106 toward Scaly Community, drive 2.6 miles. You'll see Lick Log on your right. Open year-round; mostly on weekends in winter. 704-526-3934.

MasterWorks of Highlands is a gallery dedicated to the American craftsman and contemporary American crafts. On display are works by about 150 craftsmen from 32 states. New artists are often added. You'll find clay sculptures, stained glass, hand-blown glass, and artwork ranging from abstract to realistic. The jewelry selection includes pieces made of anodized aluminum. Owner Paul Pinault says his wife and members of the staff make some of the jewelry themselves. Open every day from April to year-end and on weekends throughout the winter. From the light at Highway 106 and Main Street, continue toward town for only a few yards. Turn right into Wright Square. MasterWorks will be on the right end of the square. 704-526-2633.

Lick Log Mill Store

Middle Creek Barn. This shop has a variety of antiques and collectibles including an old gas pump, primitive tools, old signs, books, and magazines, and "Coca-Cola art" from earlier in this century. Browse here a while, because you just might miss something. From Dillard, turn onto the Highlands road (Highway 246) and proceed for 5 miles. The store is on the right. From Highlands, follow Hwy. 106 about nine miles and look for the store on the left. Usually closed in winter. 704-526-4587.

Re/Collections is a small boutique which features antiques from estates in the northeast. Samples of womens designer clothes, unique prints and glassware are featured. Bill and Frann Hohns' shop is located one quarter of a mile below the Scaly Post Office. 704-526-9819.

Scottish Tartans Museum is of particular interest to those of Scottish descent. Everyone can appreciate the collection of kilts, plaids, and tartans. The museum is the American extension of the Scottish Tartans Museum in Comrie, Scotland. Located in the center of town on the corner of Main and Fourth Streets, inside the Highlands Inn building. 704-526-5413.

Scudder's Galleries. Like Highlands Art Galleries, almost directly across Main Street, Scudder's Galleries has auctions nightly during the summer. Probably the most outstanding items here are the fine Oriental rugs and Oriental furniture. You'll see ivory carvings, brass reproductions of western art by Remington, European antiques, reproductions of Georgian furniture, porcelain, and jewelry. Many of the bids during the auction reach hundreds or thousands of dollars. Auctions nightly, usually at 7:30 p.m. From the light at Highway 106 and Main Street, drive into town just past Third Street. Scudder's is on the left in the middle of the block. 704-526-4111.

Southern Hands. Everything in this shop is handmade in the southern states, according to owners Nancy Gould-Aaron and Bill Aaron. The Aarons take an intensely personal interest in every artist Southern Hands represents. They travel and meet each artist to see where and how he or she works. You'll find fine pottery from many states including Alabama, Georgia, Kentucky, and North Carolina. Other items include hand-carved wood furniture, blown glass, textiles, handcrafted copper and brass, iron and tin sculptures, folk art carvings, and furniture accent pieces. You'll also find some original and limited edition art. Some of the more renowned artisans represented are Glenn Harbin, Goodwin Weavers, Jane Peiser, and Dorothy Basista. Open year-round. From the light at Highway 106 and Main, proceed toward town on Main for a few yards. Turn right into Wright Square. The shop is on your right. 704-526-4807.

The Stone Lantern. Without question, this is Highlands' most intriguing shop. This fine store offers imported goods including oriental antiques, jewelry, cloisson'e, garden statues and accessories, rosewood and teak pieces, and Japanese and Chinese screens. You'll also find gift items such as candlesticks, serving trays, and note cards. At the rear of the shop is a Japanese garden. The owner travels many areas of the world to make his purchases. Prices may range from as little as $10 for a small figurine or candlestick to thousands of dollars for an Oriental screen or antique urn. Open year-round, though hours are shorter in winter. Located at the center of town at Main and Fourth streets. Closed on Sunday except during the fall season. 704-526-2769.

Summer House at Scaly Mountain provides a special opportunity to see the showcase of beautiful handcrafted lamps, mirrors, and wide ranging furniture pieces that has given Tiger Mountain Woodworks a significant reputation in unique designs. Everything for your summer home in the mountain including a wide range of garden artifacts from around the world and antiques from Lady B. Goode of Winston Salem, North Carolina. Appointments with owners Paula and Barry Jones for funiture designs can be arranged through the shop. Located in the Scaly Community on Highway 106 next to the Post Office. Hours are Thursday-Saturday 10-6 pm, Sunday 12- 5 pm. 704-526-5577.

Book Stores

Cyrano's. A small but interesting book shop. You'll find quite a variety of books about the South, particularly North Carolina and Georgia. An extensive nature section includes books on the Bartram and Appalachian trails as well as forests, birds, and wildflowers. The Foxfire series of books is on sale here. And there is a children's section. Cyrano's carries most of the current best sellers as well as classics. Many books are available in paperback. You'll also find a selection of classical tapes. In summer, the shops hosts book signings for regional authors. Open all year; however not open every day in winter. Cyano's is located near the center of town on Main Street, just a few stores away from Fourth Street and across Main from the Stone Lantern. 704-526-5488.

Fireside Books. This shop has a large selection of books about nature and the outdoors, including books on fly fishing, camping, backpacking, rock climbing, canoeing, golf, horseback riding, and other activities. Many books are of interest to those in North Carolina and the surrounding region. You'll find a number of folk books pertaining to the Southern Highlands. The store also carries best sellers and classics and books on gardening, psychology, art, and other subjects, many in paperback. Also on display are cards, calendars, and other items. Open year-round. To reach Fireside Books, proceed into town on Main Street from the light at Main and Highway 106. Look for Fireside on the right, soon after you pass Town Square. 704-526-5454.

Shops for the Outdoorsman and Nature Lover

The Bird Barn has everything to do with birds and other wildlife. The store offers a wide selection of bird feeders, brass animal faucets, wood-carved ducks, and ceramic birds and animals. You'll also find cassette tapes of New Age music, cards, and gift items. Closed from early in the year till spring. From the light in the center of town, proceed on Main Street past the Old Edwards Inn on your right. The Bird Barn is on the right. 704-526-3910.

Mainstream Outfitters has an interesting variety of clothing for the fly fisherman, the hiker, the hunter, and others who love outdoor activities. You'll find a colorful variety of quality all-weather coats and hats, as well as socks, gloves, belts, and scarves. The shop also carries note cards and gift items appropriate for your fisherman friends. Owner Jack Cabe offers personalized fly fishing lessons in many of the trout streams in western North Carolina and northeast Georgia. From the light at Main and Highway 106, continue a few yards toward town and turn right into Wright Square. The shop is on the left side of the square. 704-526-5649.

Wilderness Taxidermy and Outfitters. Owners Bill and Linda Fuchs specialize in custom museum quality mounts and personal hunting and fishing adventures. Inside their studio is a fascinating museum and wildlife art gallery where hundreds of specimens of animals and birds from around the world are on display. Open year-round from 9:00 a.m. to 5:00 p.m. Closed Wednesday, Sunday and after noon on Saturday. Located four miles east of Franklin on Highway 64 (the scenic road between Highlands and Franklin). 704-524-3677.

Dining In and Around Highlands

In Highlands, you'll find the finest in German, Italian, and Continental and American cuisine as well as delicious barbecue and southern home cooking. Many restaurants post their menus outside. Reservations are usually needed for dinner.

You may want to inquire about a particular establishment's policy on alcoholic beverages. A number of restaurants serve wine, and some have
brown bag licenses. But some do not. If you wish to brown bag, go to the
ABC Store on Oak Street, next to the Highlands Playhouse.

Expect premium prices at some restaurants. In return, you're likely to
experience attentive service and a meal that is good to delightful.

Central House Restaurant, located in the middle of town on Main Street
inside the Old Edwards Inn. The decor has been restored to the country
manner in which the building was constructed well over a century ago.
The atmosphere here often seems busy, even bustling. For lunch, leave
your name and expect a wait. Call in your reservation for dinner. Lunch
items always include a soup of the day and a soup and salad combination
as well as shrimp dishes. On the dinner menu, specialties may include
Cajun shrimp, oyster dishes, stuffed flounder, grouper, halibut, snapper,
and mountain trout. Open for lunch and dinner. Moderately priced.
Closed after Thanksgiving until spring. Located in the center of town at
Main and Fourth streets, inside the Old Edwards Inn and across Main
Street from Highlands Inn. 704-526-9319.

Fireside Inn, a large, unpretentious place, is the only restaurant in
Highlands that seems to be open for three meals a day, seven days a
week. Menu selections include a little of everything – burgers, fries,
chicken, soups, salads. Breakfast is served all day and includes eggs, biscuits and gravy, bacon, sausage, and hash browns. Lunches and dinners
(many including vegetables and bread) are inexpensive. Open 7:30 a.m.
to 9:30 p.m. year-round. From the light at Main and Highway 106, proceed for a few yards toward town. Turn right into Wright Square. The
restaurant is approximately in the center of the square. 704-526-5242.

The Highlander Restaurant on Main Street is a popular, casual place for
family dining. It is open for breakfast, lunch, and dinner most days of the
year. The atmosphere is friendly and the food tasty ... all for a reasonable
price. A breakfast is served until about 11:00 a.m. Included are eggs,
sausage, bacon, biscuits, and other items. The lunch and dinner menu
includes a little of everything – beef, pork, chicken, vegetables, desserts.
Open year-round. From the corner of Main and Third streets, continue
toward the center of town on Main. The Highlander is on your left in the
middle of the block. 704-526-3169.

Central House Restaurant

Highlands Inn Restaurant is located inside the historic Highlands Inn, operated by the management and chef of Central House Restaurant. Open for dinner Wednesday through Saturday, 5:30 to 9:00 p.m. and also for Sunday brunch, 11:30 a.m. till 2:30 p.m. Each dinner entree is accompanied by a cup of soup, salad and desert.. Main course dishes include Mississippi farm-bred catfish pan sauteed with English walnuts, roast loin of pork with apple butter sauce, fried chicken, and shrimp with garlic buttter and wine. A variety of delicious "country style" vegetables are served. In addition, nightly specials are offered. Sunday brunch menu includes fried chicken, pot roast, catfish, blueberry pancakes, steak and eggs, and baked Swiss eggs. Moderately priced menu. Choose a wine from the wine list. Brown bagging of liquor and beer is acceptable. The Highlands Inn is located at the corner of Main and Fourth streets. 704-526-9380.

Highlands Seafood & Smokehouse Restaurant, on Highway 64 west of town, is a very casual place specializing in smoked barbecued beef, pork, ribs, and chicken. Also on the menu are shrimp, scallop, and seafood dinners, smoked mountain trout, and smoked turkey dinners. Moderately priced. The Tuesday feature at the Smokehouse is all-you-can-eat beef ribs; the Thursday feature is all-you-can-eat chicken. Open May through

November. From Highlands, follow Highway 64 west for about a mile. You'll see the restaurant on your right. 704-526-4799.

Hildegard's, housed inside a quaint old two-story house, specializes in German-American cuisine. A variety of German dishes, are on the menu, including sauerbraten and schnitzel. Also several American dishes, including rack of lamb. German wines also are available. You can dine in one of the small, cozy rooms, on the porch, or in a very large room where, on special occasions, live entertainment is featured. Open for lunch and dinner, Monday through Saturday. Moderately priced menu. Reservations for dinner. Closed from New Year's Day until spring. Hildegard's is set back from Main Street near the intersection of Fifth and Main. Proceed into town on Main from the light at Highway 106. After crossing the intersection at Main and Fourth, go almost another block and look for Hildegard's on your left. 704-526-3807.

Lakeside Restaurant, on Harris Lake on the edge of town, is a cozy, friendly gourmet restaurant with a diversified menu. During summer, lunch is served Monday through Saturday, 11:30 a.m. to 2:30 p.m., and dinner is seven nights a week, beginning at 5:30 p.m. Lunch may include soup, salad, and seafood or chicken dishes. Dinner entrees often include fresh trout, steak, chicken, and a variety of seafood creations served with a vegetable dish and fresh-cooked breads. Salads are extremely tasty and fresh. Nice wine selection. A variety of freshly made desserts are prepared in the kitchen. Lunch and dinner prices are moderate. Sometimes open for dinner in winter, but call ahead for days of operation. During the season, reservations are always recommended. From the light at Main and Fourth streets, continue on Main past the Highlands Inn to the light at Main and Fifth. Turn right and and then make a quick left onto Smallwood Avenue. The restaurant is on the right. 704-526-9419.

Louie Michaud's, upstairs in Mountain Brook Center, is open for lunch every day, for dinner Monday through Saturday, and for Sunday brunch. This is an elegant yet comfortable restaurant which has a nice, soft ambience in the evening. There is comfortable spacing between tables, many of which are positioned around a gazebo in the middle of the main room. The wine bar is open nightly and on some evenings. At Sunday brunch and on some evenings, the restaurant offers live entertainment such as a singer/guitar player or pianist. For lunch, sandwiches, soups, and hot salads. Dinner entrees include trout, catfish, and shrimp and other seafood dishes. Other main dishes are turkey piccata, grilled chicken, pork medal-lions with bleu cheese, rack of lamb, and several cuts of steaks including chateaubriand for two. Menu is moderately priced. At Sunday brunch, you will choose from meats at the carving station, omelettes, pasta salads, veg-etable souffles, fresh fruit, vegetables, and fresh baked breads. The dessert tray here is always quite tempting. Reservations requested. Private parties welcome. From the light at Main and Fourth streets, drive down the hill on Fourth Street one block. Mountain Brook Center is on the right. You can enter the restaurant from either side of the center. 704-526-3573.

Mimi's, which offers fine gourmet dining from May to October, is a small but elegant place and a favorite of theatergoers. Among the items on the menu are fresh fish and filet mignon. Tableside salads are served. Reserva-tions required. Open for dinner only from June through September. Din-ner entrees are moderately priced. From the light at Main and Fourth streets, turn down the hill on Fourth and then make an immediate left on Oak Street. Mimi's is on the left, across from the Highlands Theatre. 704-526-3169.

Mountaineer Restaurant, a casual little place on Main Street, is usually open throughout the year (though days of operation vary in winter) and offers home-cooked meat dishes, vegetables, burgers, and more. Prices are very moderate and servings ample. Breakfast, beginning at 7:00 a.m., may include egg dishes, ham, sausage, gravy, and homemade biscuits. From late morning until 7:00 p.m., seafood, ham, and chicken dishes are served along with vegetables and bread. Inexpensive menu. Driving down Main Street from Hwy. 106, look for the restaurant on the left, between Third and Fourth streets. 704-526-3368.

Nick's, which serves lunch, dinner, and Sunday brunch, offers a wide-ranging menu including French and Italian cuisine. The menu features fresh pastas and veal and steak dishes. Veal and steaks are cut on the premises. Locals often praise the prime rib. Dinners, which include soup, salad, vegetable of the day, and a choice of spaghetti, potato, or rice pilaf, range. Serving brunch and lunch daily from 11:30 a.m. Dinner begins at 5:30 p.m. Moderately priced menu. Reservations requested. Located two blocks from Main at the corner of Highway 28 and Satulah Road. From Fourth and Main, drive up the hill on Fourth past all the shops. Continue & look for Nick's on the right, across from the King's Inn. 704-526-2706.

On the Verandah, which claims to offer Highlands' "most scenic dining setting," overlooks Lake Sequoyah on Highway 64, a short distance from the village. In the comfortable wine bar, you may be entertained by a talented pianist. A special treat is to dine here in early evening and watch the sunset over the lake. Menu features at this gourmet establishment may include grilled trout, frog legs, Carolina quail, Long Island duck, medallions of veal, pasta dishes, and special soups. Open for lunch and dinner most days beginning in late spring and also for Sunday brunch. Moderately priced. Closed in winter and early spring. Reservations are usually necessary. From the light at Main (Highway 64) and Hwy. 106, proceed away from Highlands on Hwy. 64 toward Franklin for just over 1 mile. The restaurant is on the left. 704-526-2338.

Paoletti's is hailed by many locals to have the best classic Italian cuisine in the mountains. Naturally, homemade pastas are the specialty. Dinner is served from late spring to October. A variety of Italian wines are offered. You can choose from a beautiful selection of antipasti dishes from the buffet, or you can select an antipasti from the menu, including escargot a la Bourguignonne and eggplant with ricotta, mozzarella, Fontina and parmagiano cheeses. Pasta entrees include canneloni all Emilian and crepes filled with veal, spinach and ricotta, baked with Bolognese and Bechamel. Other entrees include scalappine di vitello, roast rack of lamb with garlic and fine herbs, and stuffed chicken breast with prosciutto, mozzarella, and herbs.

Including appetizer, entree, salad, and wine, this is a pricey establishment, but worth it. Paoletti's is located on Main Street. From the intersection of Main and Fourth, continue on Main past the Highlands Inn. The restaurant is on the left. Open for dinner from 6:00 p.m. Tuesday through Sunday. Call 704-526-4906 for reservations.

Gourmet Coffees, Ice Cream, Yogurt

Cocky Cardinal Ice Cream Parlor. Many unusual as well as typical ice cream flavors are available for cones, cups, shakes, malts, banana splits, old-fashioned sodas, and sundaes. Espresso and cappuccino coffees, hot dogs, chili, and soft drinks are served. Open all year. Located in Town Square on Main Street. From the light at Highway 106 and Main, proceed into town on Main. Right after you pass Third Street, look for Town Square on your right.

Highlands House of Coffee is a popular, comfortable little place literally suffused with the aroma of gourmet coffees. There are several tables available, and people tend to flock here, particularly on a cool day, to chat and enjoy specialty coffees and hot cider drinks. Cappuccino, espresso, and other coffee drinks are favorites. Open most days during the season and until Christmas. Open Saturdays only from January through March. Located inside Oak Square on the lower level. The square is at the corner of Third and Main. 704-526-5578.

SweeTreats is an ice cream and yogurt shop where each cone is custom blended to your specifications. Choose from ice cream or yogurt and your favorite candy, fruit, or nuts. The yogurt is 99.5 percent fat free. The shop also sells fine chocolates, hard candies, nuts, and soft drinks. Open daily from noon to 5:00 p.m., and Friday and Saturday evenings from 7:00 to 9:00 p.m. Located in Mountain Brook Center. From the intersection at Main and Fourth streets, proceed one block down the hill on Fourth. You'll see Mountain Brook Center on the right. SweeTreats is on the left corner of the center. 704-526-9822.

Theatre

The Highlands Playhouse has presented successful summer theatre since 1969. There are four productions each summer. Evening performances are Tuesdays through Saturdays, and there is a Sunday matinee.

The playhouse is located on the hill on Oak Street, behind Town Hall. From the intersection of Main and Fourth streets, follow Fourth down the hill and take the first left onto Oak Street. The playhouse is on the right. For schedules and ticket information, call the box office at 704-526-2695 or the business office at 704-526-9443.

Nature Center and Botanical Garden

Highlands Biological Station, Nature Center, and Botanical Garden are all located on Horse Cove Road on the outskirts of town. Colleges and universities have contributed to the biological station, and their biologists and others have conducted research here on endangered species, clear cutting, and other topics. Inside a small museum are displayed various natural history collections from early settlers as well as Indian artifacts, mineral specimens, and mounted animals.

The Nature Center offers a variety of educational programs. Information about these and other area activities can be obtained from the Highlands Chamber of Commerce: 704-526-2112 or from the Nature Center: 704-526-2623.

Behind the museum is an outdoor amphitheater where special programs on natural history are presented. Adjacent to this is an extensive botanical garden where at least 450 species of fungi, moss, lichen, trees, ferns, and flowers grow in a natural area of woods, boggy marshes, and open areas. The garden is a pleasant place to walk and offers a refreshing change of pace for those have spent most of the day shopping. The museum is open to the public June 1 to September 1, and the botanical garden is open all year.

From the center of town, follow Main Street past the Highlands Inn, the Episcopal Church, and the Hudson Library. Continue on Main, for less than a mile past the last of the shops and businesses. Main becomes Horse Cove Road just before you reach the Nature Center, on the left. 704-526-2623.

Scenic Beauty, Flora, and Fauna

About half the land around Highlands is privately owned. The rest is part of the Nantahala National Forest. The Highlands Ranger District alone manages more than 67,000 acres. The National Forest lands have many miles of well-maintained scenic hiking trails through lush, dense woodlands. Many trails pass by scenic overlooks and thunderous, cascading waterfalls. Nonhikers, never despair! Scenic views from the highways are no less than breathtaking.

Episcopal Church of the Incarnation

Rhododendron and laurels grow in the deep shade of towering hemlocks and in dense thickets alongside mossy brooks. Several species of pine and mountain magnolia and a variety of oak, hickory, maple, and birch are scattered throughout the forest. Also present are tulip poplar and mountain ash trees.

In winter, the leaves of the rhododendron remain green but curl under or hang limp in the chilly air. Giant stalactites of ice hang from rocks in the forest and along the roadsides. Waterfalls gush from caverns of ice.

Winter is a wonderful time to hike in the National Forest, or simply to take a drive through the Highlands area. Providing there is no fog (and there often is!), the views are more distant than in summer. On a clear day, the starkness of rock-faced mountains and the views of blue valleys and mountaintops is a sight to behold. Perhaps most exciting of all is a drive through the area after a light snow is truely a "winter wonderland."

The western North Carolina mountains are a botanical treasure house. Particularly in spring, but also in summer and fall, a wide variety of wild-flowers bloom in the forest. Travelers can enjoy much of the beauty from the comfort of their cars. According to local author, Gert McIntosh 750 species of wildflowers have been found here, including 24 types of violets.

In the forest are many species of trillium, named after the Latin word for "three." All the trillium's parts are in threes and flower colors range from pale pink to purple. Other beautiful wildflowers here are lady slippers, deep blue geraniums, and rare orchids. In the fall, asters, goldenrod, and sunflowers predominate. For the wildflower enthusiast, a guidebook is a must. Please enjoy the show of wildflowers, but leave them for others who come after you.

Observant hikers in the forest will notice that many rocks and trees are covered in lichens, plant organisms composed of fungus and algae. The lichens are said to be a sign of very pure air, unspoiled by pollution. Hikers may also encounter a wide variey of wildlife. Rabbits, grey squirrels, chip-munks, raccoons, possums, groundhogs, owls, grouse, and quail are all prevalent.

One of the earliest explorers to walk much of this land was William Bartram, a botanist, naturalist, writer, and traveler. Soon after the American Revolution, Bartram journeyed on horseback, mostly alone, through much of the Carolinas, Georgia, Florida and other states. He wrote vibrant descriptions of unspoiled, original America. The book Bartram wrote as as result of his travels, *The Travels of William Bartram*, is considered a travel literature classic.

While in the southern Appalachian area, Bartram discovered and named the magnificent flame azalea (Rhododendron calendulaceum). This beau-tiful native shrub blooms fiery orange to red in spring, proclaiming from the hillsides the botanical glory of the southern Blue Ridge.

In April and May, dogwoods bloom in the Highlands Plateau. The purple, or Catawba, rhododendron blooms in May and early June, and the great white rhododendron flowers in June and early July. These blooming times vary somewhat, depending on weather.

Once these woods were thick with chestnut trees. One old-timer, interviewed for the Foxfire books, recalled, " This country was literally covered in chestnuts. You'd cut one down and two'd jump in front of you." Many of the trees were said to be 16 feet in diameter and 200 feet high.

But then the chestnut blight struck, moving down from New England into North Carolina, destroying the magnificent trees that had not yet been cut by the lumbering industry.

Today, the remains of giant chestnut trees can be found decaying in the forests. You'll see them on many of Highlands' hiking trails, some with laurels and other plants growing from their giant, deteriorating trunks.

Hiking Trails

The U.S. Forest Service maintains many hiking trails in the Highlands area. Some lead to waterfalls, and others to cliff tops. The trails range from easy 10 minute walks near the highway to difficult hikes up steep mountainsides requiring several hours. Following are few of the more accessible trails around Highlands.

Bartram Trail. In North Carolina, more then 100 miles of trails are designated as the Bartram Trail. Excellent access to the Blue Valley section of the trail can be found on NC 106 at the Osage Mountain Vista. Below the lookout site, the trail descends and winds for 3.7 miles through dense green forests. Wooden foot bridges traverse several brooks along the way. The trail meanders along side Rocky Knob and Osage Mountain, ending on Hale Ridge Road, about three miles from the U.S. Post Office in Scaly, North Caralina. Hiking time (one way) is two to three hours. The trail is moderately difficult.

On the opposite side of NC 106 at Osage Mountain Vista is the Scaly Mountain section of Bartram Trail. The trail ascends sharply up a steep bank and continues upward through the forest for most of two miles where it connects with **Scaly Mountain Trail.** Though the Bartram Trail is supposedly marked with yellow paint, this intersection is poorly marked.

The route to the left leads to the summit of Scaly Mounatin while the trail straight ahead leads to Hickory Gap Road. Hiking time (one way) may range from one-and-a half to three hours. This hike is moderately difficult.

To reach the Osage Mountain Vista, drive north on Highway 106 from Dillard and continue past Scaly. The overlook and the trail, which are about eight miles from Dillard, are marked by U.S.F.S. signs.

Glen Falls Trail. Of the 44 miles of trails maintained by the Forest Service in the Highlands area, many lead to waterfalls. Some falls are spectacular as well accessible. Glen Falls, a prime example, is a series of three large falls along the east fork of Overflow Creek. The hike along the 1.4-mile foot trail is manageable for most folks. The trail, which meanders downhill through a rhododendron thicket, is steep, but beautiful. The falls are magnificent, particularly after a heavy rain. Views from this trail include Rabun Bald, Georgia's second highest peak. The trek back up is strenuous; however, the Forest Service does an outstanding job of keeping the trail in shape. Wooden steps and hand rails have been placed where necessary. Hiking time is one to two hours. The walk to the first falls (one way) is about 15 minutes.

To reach the head of Glen Falls Trail from Highlands, follow the Dillard Road (Highway 106) about 3 miles and look for the U.S.F.S. sign on your left. Turn here and follow the dirt road for a mile or more. The road dead-ends at the trail parking lot.

Sunset Rock. For a more leisurely, short walk, try the 20-minute moderate hike to Sunset Rocks which overlooks the town of Highlands. The trail begins just across from the Highlands Nature Center on Horse Cove Road. Looking east from Sunset Rocks, you can view all of Horse Cove. Also near here is the second largest poplar tree in the eastern U.S. This magnificent tree is marked by the U.S. Forest Service. From the center of town, drive down Main from Fourth Street past Fifth Street and all the shops. Continue for less than a mile, and look for the Nature Center on the left. Parking and the trail to Sunsets Rock are on the right.

Nantahala Hiking Club. If you're really a hiking enthusiast, it's a good idea to check the weekly Highlander newspaper for activities of the Nantahala Hiking Club, which always welcomes nonmembers. This club, which takes hikes almost every Saturday of the year, will guide you to pristine areas you would probably never find on your own. The club also does an outstanding job of helping the Forest Service to maintain hiking trails in the vicinity.

Scenic Drive: Franklin to Highlands

The road from Franklin to Highlands presents one of the most spectacular series of falls, cascades, and pools anywhere in North Carolina. The road borders the Cullasaja River and Cullasaja Gorge most of the way. At several places along this 17-mile drive from Franklin, you can view beautiful falls and rushing cascades as well as calm pools of water.

The construction of the road itself, which took place in the late 1920s, was one of the most difficult jobs imaginable at the time, largely because the equipment needed to move massive amounts of granite was not even invented until a few years earlier. Today, this drive is one that Highlanders often recommend to their guests.

From Dillard, drive north for about 13 miles on Highways 23/441 toward Franklin. Turn right onto Highway 64 East and follow the signs to Highlands.

With every mile, the scenic beauty builds. The first part of the road carries you through pastureland, with frequent glimpses of the Cullasaja River, which is calm here in the lush green valley. Mountains, in shades of blue and purple, form the backdrop for this colorful scene. About seven miles from the turn onto Highway 64, the road narrows and begins climbing rapidly. White water rushes over giant rocks in the river below, muffling the sounds of any traffic. On the left side of the road, opposite the river, massive rock which appears to be a 50 feet high – and higher – line the highway. All this rock is extremely close to the narrow, winding road. Drive slowly and carefully.

After about the seventh mile on Highway 64, look for a National Forest Service sign that reads: **Cullasaja River Gorge** – Next 7.1 Mi. And a dramatic 7 miles it is. The road seems to narrow even more. The rock bordering the road is dripping wet and covered with moss and ferns. On the gorge side, a low rock ledge is all that lies between you and edge of the gorge. One cascade after another crashes through magnificent Cullasaja Gorge. On much of the opposite side of the gorge are imposing masses of steep, bare boulders, topped by many types of trees.

Be sure to stop at one or more of the dirt or graveled pull-off areas on the right. These are often only a few feet from the gorge edge, and none can accommodate more than three or four cars. In fall, with all the "leaf traffic," it is often difficult to find a stopping place. Depending on the time of year, you may see a full view of the series of tremendous falls and cascades, or you may have to glimpse them through the trees.

Shortly after passing the U.S.F.S. sign, there is one pull-off where you can almost always get a clear view of **Cullasaja Falls** storming through the gorge as it cascades some 250 feet. The water descends over a series of wide, broken ledges before falling into the gorge below. Ask fellow passengers to keep an eye out for this place. Standing a safe distance from the gorge edge, take in the sounds and beauty of this gorgeous spot.

By the ninth mile into your climb up Highway 64, the river calms, and a quiet beauty prevails. The water meanders around rocks and boulders of every size. On the riverbank, in May, mountain laurel blooms profusely.

Soon, the river is calm enough for wading. But, more waterfalls await you. About 14 miles into your drive, you'll see another U.S.F.S. sign: **Dry Falls Scenic Area.** The pleasant, five-minute walk to this 75-foot falls is a must. You can even walk under the falls without getting (very) wet!

A half mile further up the road is **Bridal Veil Falls,** where the water drops 120 feet. The old highway went under the falls, and even today, you can drive underneath them.

The next scenic view is beautiful **Lake Sequoyah,** a small lake bordered by forests and a few homes. At the dam is another falls which are visible from the highway. From here, the village of Highlands lies just one-and-a-half miles away.

Scenic Drive: Dillard to Highlands

Another scenic route is the drive from Dillard to Highlands. From Georgia Hwy 23/441 north of Dillard, turn right on Georgia 246. When you cross the North Carolina line, this road becomes N.C. Highway 106. Just 1.3 miles after your turn onto Hwy 246, look up and to the right for a beautiful waterfall. **Estatoah Falls,** which is located on private land, can be viewed only from the highway. Next, watch for the first paved overlook on the right which is marked by a U.S. Forest Service sign. This overlook offers a serene view of the Georgia communities of Dillard and Rabun Gap, both nestled in valleys surrounded by farmland and situated beneath the Blue Ridge mountains. The overlook is three miles from the turn onto Highway 246 from Highway 441.

Seven miles after making the turn off Hwy. 441 and after crossing the North Carolina state line, you'll pass through the little community of Scaly. The most interesting aspect of Scaly is its tiny ski area, **Ski Scaly,** which is open whenever the temperature is below 29 degrees F. long enough to make snow. Recommended for beginning or intermediate skiers, Ski Scaly has a double chair lift and a 300-foot tow for novices. For further information, call 704-526-3737 or 1-800-342-1387.

Scaly, like Dillard and Mountain City, Georgia, is cabbage farming country. In the fall, all along the rolling hills of Hale Ridge Road (which intersects Hwy. 106 at Ski Scaly), farmers gather cabbages from the fields, load them into old-fashioned wooden wagons, and haul them off to market.

As you proceed toward Highlands, prepare to stop at two outstanding scenic overlooks – **Osage Mountain** and **Blue Valley.** The ever-changing blue and green hues of the mountains from these two vantage points make for different views every time you stop. Sunsets are often spectacular.

Two miles before you reach Highlands, look for the U.S.F.S. sign to **Glen Falls Scenic Area** on your right. (See the section on hiking trails for information about reaching this beautiful falls.)

After you pass the Highlands city limit, the surroundings become noticeably more sophisticated. Of particular note is the Highlands Country Club with its beautifully manicured golf course, lake, and winding roads through beautiful, long-established residential areas.

The drive from Dillard to Highlands is just 14 miles. But with all the twists and turns in this narrow road, and with all there is to see along the way, the drive seems quite a bit longer.

Other Outdoor Activities

One the most interesting activities anyone can enjoy in Highlands is bird watching. Ornithologists are delighted by their findings on the Highlands Plateau – more than 180 species of birds! As many as 79 of these are known to breed here. In addition, the western North Carolina mountains are the flyway for birds migrating north.

Among the birds around Highlands is the Peregrine falcon. Restoration of this endangered species began in Highlands and surrounding areas several years ago when the North Carolina Wildlife Resources Commission began releasing young birds from atop mountains in the western part of the state. One of the places where the falcons have been sited recently is Whiteside Mountain, an awesome bald-faced peak said to be the world's oldest mountain, between Highlands and the town of Cashiers.

More typical bird species are the brown thrasher, cardinal, chickadee, gold finch, rose-breasted and evening grosbeak, hummingbird, white-breasted and red-breasted nuthatch, pine sisken, titmouse, and many species of warbler. In summer, huge pileated woodpeckers are often heard, but seldom seen. Whip-poor-wills sing at dusk, and owls hoot.

For hunting enthusiasts, the area has white-tailed deer, black bear, gray squirrel, ruffed grouse and wild turkey. Contact the N.C. Wildlife Resources Commission. 1-800-662-7137 for specific information on hunting, (For those who prefer to visit the area when there is no hunting, the best time is between May 1 and October 1.)

Fishermen who like stream fishing will enjoy coming to Macon County where there are 534 miles of clear trout streams, many with cascades and water falls. These streams support large populations of brook, rainbow, and brown trout. Area lakes have populations of black bass, walleyed pike, crappie, and other species. A North Carolina state fishing license and trout stamp are required for anyone over age 16 who wants to fish. These are available in local hardware stores and some pharmacies.

While Highlands' few lakes are great for canoeing, they are all too small for water skiing or sailing. Canoe and rowboat rentals are available for $8.00/hr. on Mirror Lake, on Hwy. 64 a short distance from town. Call 704-526-5947.

Still another outdoor activity in Highlands is miniature golf. At Satulah Park on Hwy. 28 is the picturesque, 18-hole Miniature Golf Course. During the season, the course is open daily. From the center of town, proceed up the hill on Fourth Street, past all the shops. Bear right on Hwy. 28 and you'll see the golf course on your left, next to Nick's Restaurant. Open 11:00 a.m. to 11:00 p.m. Monday through Thursday and 11:00 a.m. to 12:00 p.m. Friday and Saturday. Sunday hours are 2:00 p.m. until 9:00 p.m. The price per person is about $3.00.

Camping

There are two developed campgrounds near the village and one recreational vehicle (RV) park. Signs to both campgrounds are about 4.5 miles west of town on Hwy. 64.

Vanhook Glade Campground, which is usually open from mid-May until late October, offers 21 family camping units, each with a parking spur, grill/fireplace, table and tent pad. The parking spurs will accomodate small to medium sized trailers. There are five water spigots and a flush toilet; however there are no electrical or sewer hookups. Use is limited to 14 days per season.

Cliffside Lake Recreation Area has 11 units near the lake that may be used for overnight camping. Seven individual picnic tables are reserved for day picnicking. Other facilities here are shelters, a bathhouse with cold water showers and flush toilets, a lake for fishing and swimming, and hiking trails. There are no facilities to handle trailers. Stays at the campground are limited to 14 days. Cliffside is open year-round; however, no water is available from late October to mid-May.

Within Cliffside Lake Recreation Area is Cliffside Vista Trail which begins at a small hiking trail sign on the left side of the road leading to the recreation area. This is a pleasant one-and-a-half-hour hike through the forest. Mountain vistas are spectacular. From a wooden gazebo, built beside the trail in the 1930s, is a view of the lake below.

Highlands Recreational Vehicle Park, the town's only R.V. park, is located at the corner of 5th and Chestnut streets. This small facility, can accommodate only five vehicles. Among the amenities are a barbecue pavilion, sewer, water, and electric connections, cable TV, and washer and dryer. A phone also is available. Reservations are recommended. From the center of town, at Main and Fourth streets, proceed down the hill on Fourth. Chestnut Street is the fourth street on the right. Turn here, drive a short distance, and look for the R.V. park on the right. 704-526-5985

A Word About Weather

In Highlands, the weather is ever-changing. Precipitation averages 90 inches a year, among the highest in the East. During various times of year, the mountains are shrouded in fog, making driving difficult, particularly at night. The temperature is usually at least 10 degrees cooler than in north Georgia. The average maximum summer temperature is 76 degrees F. In winter, the average is 35 degrees. Keep these cooler temperatures in mind when planning your trip here. Gloves, scarf, hat, and coat are often a must.

Appendices

Georgia State Parks Accommodations
The Chattahoochee National Forest
Georgia Visitor Information
and Welcome Centers
Chambers of Commerce

Georgia State Parks Accommodations

Cottages	Daily Sun–Thurs	Daily Fri–Sat
One Bedroom	$40.00	$50.00
Two Bedroom	50.00.00	60.00
Three Bedroom	60	70.00

Amicalola Falls	Dec 1–Mar 31	Apr 1–Nov 30
Double/King Room	$45.00	$55.00
Junior Suite/King Loft	65.00	75.00
Executive Suite	90.00	100.00

Unicoi Lodge	Dec 1–Mar 31	Apr 1–Nov 30
Double Room/Loft Weekdays	$30.00	$50.00
Double Room/Loft Weekends	40.00	50.00

Lodge rates based on single occupancy. Each additional adult $6. Children 12 and under free when accompanied by adult in same room.

Campsites	Fees
Tent/Pop-up/RV Campsites	$10.00
Reservation fee	5.00
Walk-in Campsites & Squirrel's Nest	6.00
Pioneer Campsites per person	1.00
(Supervised groups only–$15 minimum)	
Primitive Camping per person	3.00
Senior Citizens (65 & over)	8.00

Rate applies only when vehicle registered to senior citizen. Limited to one site per registration.

Group Camps	Fees
Group Camps per person/per day	$3.00

Each camp has a minimum occupancy and a one week minimum stay during June, July and August. $10 handling fee for cancellations and a cleanup/damage deposit required. Camp facilities vary, but typically include dormitory sleeping quarters, restrooms/showers, kitchen, and dining area. Call individual park for details.

Group Lodges	Daily Rates
Cloudland	
June 1–Labor Day	$100.00
After Labor Day–May 31	80.00

Group Shelters	Daily Rates
50–75 Capacity	$30 to 70.00
75–100 Capacity	50 to 90.00
125–175 Capacity	85 to 125.00
Damage/Cleanup Deposit	$100.00

Group shelters are available at many of the parks. Call for more information.

Picnic Shelters	Fee
Reservation Fee	$25.00

Picnic shelters may be reserved in advance. Shelters not reserved are available at no charge on a first-come/first-served basis. (Does not include Group Shelters.)

Swimming Pools and Beaches	Fees
Pools (all ages per day)	$1.25
Beaches (all ages per day)	1.00
Two years and under	Free
Lodge and cottage guests	Free

Season Pass (use limited to single park)

	Fees
Adults	$20.00
Senior Citizens (65 & over)	15.00
Children (12 & under)	15.00
Family (up to 6 people)	40.00

Miniature Golf	Fee
All ages–per round	$1.25

Fishing Boats or Canoes	Fees
One hour	$3.00
Four hours	8.00
Eight hours	12.00

Pedal Boats	Fee
Half-hour (per person)	$1.50

COTTAGES

All cottages are fully equipped with stoves and refrigerators, all necessary cooking and serving utensils, towels, bed linens and blankets. All cottages have heat and most have air conditioning. Many cottages have porches/decks and woodburning fireplaces/stoves (firewood not provided).

Reservations. All reservations are taken by the individual parks and are accepted up to 11 months in advance. For example, a person may at any time during the month of June, make a reservation for a cottage to begin at any time within the next 11 months or up to and including the entire month of May the following year.

A deposit of one night's lodging is due within five days of receipt of the reservation notice. A reservation will not be confirmed until a deposit is received and accepted by the Park Office. Deposits not received within the allotted time result in automatic cancellation.

One night occupancy is allowed with an additional surcharge, but reservations will not be taken for less than two days. From June 1 to Labor Day a reservation for less than one week is not allowed unless the reservation is made less than 30 days in advance.

Reservation Preference. Preference is given to reservations made: 1) In person; 2) By telephone; and, 3) By mail. Priority is given to the longest stay requested.

Deposit. Equivalent to one night's lodging. Park office will accept no more than one night's deposit.

Registration. Register at Park Office or Check-in Station upon arrival.

Check-In Time. 4 p.m.-10 p.m. Yellow reservation deposit slip and balance of payment must be presented when checking in.

Check-Out Time. 11 a.m. A late check-out fee will be charged after this time unless extension is permitted by the Park Office. Extension can be granted only when others are not waiting for cottage.

Late Arrivals. Park must be notified of late arrival. After 10 p.m., late arrivals will only be allowed to register under emergency conditions. Reservations will not be held after 11 a.m. of second day, and both reservations and deposit are forfeited unless Park Office has been notified of late arrival.

Refund. Deposit will be refunded if a minimum of 72 hours notice is given to the park, however, a $10.00 per unit cancellation fee will be deducted from the deposit. Deposit receipt must be returned to the park for refund. Any unused portion of a reservation period can be refunded if minimum occupancy has been satisfied (minimum occupancy from June 1 through Labor Day weekend is one week; at other time of the year it is two days.)

Occupancy Limitation. Occupancy of a cottage is limited to 14 nights. Cottage may not be used overnight to accommodate more than normal bed capacity. Maximum occupancy of cottages may vary from park to park.

Eligibility. Cottages are not available to organized groups such as church or civic groups, fraternities, sororities, school groups, family reunions, scouts, etc. An adult must accompany all unmarried cottage guests under 18 years of age.

Pets. Pets are not allowed in cottages or cottage areas. Kennels are not available on parks.

Firewood. Firewood is not provided, however, in some parks, firewood may be purchased.

Checking Out. Cottages should be left in good condition. Dishes and cookware should be washed and put away. Beds should be left unmade. Equipment, furnishing, or bed linens may not be carried outside the cottages. Occupants may be charged for damage or missing items.

REGULATIONS

Intoxicants. It is unlawful for any person to consume or use alcoholic beverages or intoxicants in any public use area of a park, lodge, historic site, or recreational area.

Weapons. Firearms, bows and arrows, explosives, fireworks, slingshots, fishing spears, or any device that discharges projectiles by any means are prohibited in state parks.

Collecting. All wildlife, plantlife, artifacts, driftwood, or any other natural or manmade features are protected at all state parks and historic sites. Please leave them undisturbed so other visitors may enjoy them too. Use of electronic devices for "treasure hunting" is prohibited.

Motor vehicles. Park roads are public roads. All vehicles are subject to license safety requirements and regulations of the Georgia Department of Public Safety. Motorized bikes are restricted to park roads.

Noise levels. Consideration of others is a must at all times. Musical instruments, radios, televisions, or other noise making devices are not to be used between 10 p.m. and 7 a.m., and in moderation at all other times.

Visitors. Visitors to cottages, campsites, and lodge rooms are welcome; however, the number of visitors and registered guests must not exceed the stated capacity at any time. Visitors are required to leave prior to park closing time of 10 p.m.

Group activities. All parties or group gatherings in park facilities must conclude by 10 p.m.

Credit cards. MasterCard and Visa are honored for camping at most parks and for all cottges and lodge rooms and, in addition, American Express and Diners Club are accepted at the lodges.

Returned checks. Fee for returned checks.

These rates and guidelines are subject to change without notice.

Georgia State Parks and Historic Sites are operated by the Georgia Department of Natural Resources. For more information call Monday through Friday, 8:30 a.m. to 4:30 p.m. Toll-free inside Georgia 1-800-342-7275; Toll-free outside Georgia 1-800-542-7275; in Metro Atlanta 656-3530.

The Chattahoochee National Forest

The Chattahoochee National Forest accounts for about 750,000 acres of undeveloped land across the Georgia mountains, from the "Wild and Scenic" Chattooga River in the east to the Cohutta Wilderness near the Alabama border in the west. Its name–another of the region's Indian words–comes from "chatta," for "stone," and "ho chee," for "marked" or "flowered," and was taken from the Chattahoochee River, whose headwaters begin in the mountains near Brasstown Bald.

The National Forest System itself began in 1891, under President Benjamin Harrison. Forty-five years later, in 1936, President Franklin D. Roosevelt signed a proclamation separating the Chattahoochee National Forest from the Nantahala and Cherokee National Forests in North Carolina and Tennessee. Shortly thereafter, a Forest Supervisor's office was opened, and two separate Ranger Districts, the Blue Ridge and the Tallulah, were created. More district offices were added over the years, until there were eight.

Most of the land in the Tallulah Ranger District, headquartered in Clayton, was purchased through the negotiations of Roscoe Nicholson, Georgia's first forest ranger. "Ranger Nick," as he was called, was responsible for many advancements, such as getting telephone lines strung between Clayton and the Pine Mountain community about 10 miles to the east; purchasing bloodhounds to track arsonists; and building the first firetower on Rabun Bald, Georgia's second-highest mountain. In recognition of his efforts, the Coleman River Scenic Area, off U.S. 76 West of Clayton, was dedicated to him.

Another early Georgia Ranger, Arthur Woody, promoted wildlife conservation by carrying trout back into remote areas and releasing them into the streams, and by buying fawns with his own money, raising them, then releasing them in the forest. The "Barefoot Ranger," as he was called, is credited with having restored the deer population in North Georgia. The

Sosebee Cove Scenic Area, a 175-acre tract of prize hardwood timber located south of Blairsville, was dedicated to him.

Prior to World War II, the Civilian Conservation Corps (CCC) did extensive work in the Chattahoochee Forest, planting trees; checking for and controlling erosion, disease and insect infestations; laying communications lines; and building firetowers, roads, ranger stations and recreation areas. The CCC's style of architecture, distinctive for its use of whole logs and other native building materials, is still evident today in such recreation areas as Warwoman Dell, three miles east of Clayton on Warwoman Road.

When World War II began, the CCC workers joined the armed forces, and the Chattahoochee National Forest contributed to the war effort by providing red oak for gun mounts and bridges, basswood for dough boards and drawing boards, and poplar for airplane construction.

The USDA Forest Service, which maintains the National Forest for outdoor recreation–hiking, fishing, picnicking, camping, sightseeing, swimming and boating–also manages the forest for its natural resources of water, timber, range, wildlife, and fish. In the years following World War II, the Forest Service has focused on environmental conservation and the creation of recreation areas within a 50-mile radius of every major town.

Most of the developed recreation areas–such as the seven listed below–are open from late spring to early fall, and some selected areas are open year-round to accommodate winter campers. Primitive camping is allowed anywhere, without charge or permit. General rules for trail and campground use follow. For a list of sites offering RV hookups, maps or more information, contact the U.S. Forest Service. Tallulah District, P. O. Box 438, Clayton, Ga 30525; 706-782-3320; or Forest Supervisor, U.S. Forest Service, P. O. Box 1437, Gainesville, Ga 30501; 706-536-0541.

Scenic Areas

Anna Ruby Falls Scenic Area, which adjoins Unicoi State Park, has a 0.4 mile, easy-to-moderate trail which passes through a hardwood forest and follows Smith Creek to the falls. Take Georgia 75 North from Helen to Robertstown Community and turn right on Georgia 356. After 1.3 miles, turn left at sign for Anna Ruby Falls, just before Unicoi Information Office.

Coleman River Wildlife Management Area has 330 acres of large, old growth timber along a river and was dedicated to Ranger Nick. The trail is nearly a mile long and easy to walk. Take U.S. 76 west from Clayton 8 miles. Turn right on unnumbered, paved road (at Persimmon Fire Department) for 4 miles, then turn left on F.S. 70 and go 1 mile.

DeSoto Falls Scenic Area is 650 acres, with several trails and waterfalls. Local lore has it that the area was named by early settlers who found a piece of Spanish armor near the falls and believed it had belonged to Hernando deSoto or one of his men. Take U.S. 19 North from Dahlonega toward Vogel State Park. Go 4.2 miles past joining with Highway 129 and look for sign on left.

High Shoals has five waterfalls and numerous rhododendron thickets on 170 scenic acres. Take Georgia 75 north from Helen for 12 miles. Just past intersection with Appalachian Trail, turn right on F.S. 283 for 1.5 miles to start of trail at Blue Hole Falls.

Keown Falls Scenic Area is the only scenic area in the western section of the Chattahoochee National Forest. Its looped 1.2-mile trail is easy to moderate and leads to falls. Take Georgia 136 Connector toward LaFayette from Calhoun. Seventeen miles past where highway crosses Oostanaula River, turn left onto F.S. 203 (at mile marker 30). After 2.2 miles, take fork to right, go another 2.8 miles and turn right on F.S. 702.

Raven Cliffs Scenic Area has a number of trails with streams, waterfalls, mountaintops, rock outcrops, and scenic vistas. Take Georgia 75 North from Helen to Robertstown Community, turning left onto Georgia 356. Go 2.3 miles then turn right onto Richard B. Russell Scenic Highway (Georgia 348). After 3 miles, the highway crosses Dukes Creek and the parking area is immediately to left.

Sosebee Cove Scenic Area has several short, interconnected trails leading through the 175-acre tract of prize hardwoods and rare wildflowers dedicated to Ranger Arthur Woody. Take U.S. 129 north from Dahlonega toward Vogel State Park. Turn left on Georgia 180 and continue 3.1 miles to parking area.

Trail Information

Permits. No permits are required to use most trails on the Chattahoochee or Oconee National Forests. Only Coosa Backcountry Trail, which begins at Vogel State Park and meanders onto the National Forest, requires a permit. Get a free permit at the Vogel State Park Visitor Center.

Camping. Camping is permitted anywhere, unless posted otherwise. All campsites are available on a first-come, first-served basis. A fee is charged for camping in developed recreation areas. Dispersed, primitive camping is free. Hikers are encouraged to camp away from trails and at least 100 feet from stream banks to reduce environmental damage.

Vehicles. The forests are closed to off-road vehicle use except in designated areas or on designated trails specifically marked for ORV use. Many of these areas and ORV trails are listed in Trail Guide to the Chatta-hoochee-Oconee National Forests (free at any Ranger District office). Check with the district ranger before you travel to these areas. From time to time, ORV trails and roads may be closed to allow recovery from overuse. See the safety tips and regulations in the trail guide.

Horses. Several horse trails are available. For your safety, horse use is prohibited on the Appalachian Trail and on many hiking trails, including several within the Cohutta Wilderness. Be sure to check with the local Forest Service office before taking horses on any trail. Caution is urged on all trails because narrow clearing widths and steep grades often make horseback riding dangerous.

Fires. You do not need a permit for a campfire. However, you are legally responsible for any damage caused by your fire. Only dead or down wood may be used to build campfires. Make sure your fire is dead-out before you leave!

Hunting and Fishing. Hunting and fishing are allowed only under state regulations. Many trails are within wildlife management areas where firearms are prohibited except during hunting season. For licenses, regulations, and season dates, check with the Georgia Department of Natural Resources, Game and Fish Division, Floyd Towers East, 205 Butler Street, S.E., Atlanta, Ga 30334. Telephone 404-656-3522.

Fords. During periods of wet weather or immediately after a heavy rain, avoid trails with fords such as the Jacks and Conasauga River Trails in the Cohutta Wilderness. Even short rains can raise river levels enough to make fording dangerous.

Appalachian Trail. The Appalachian Trail in Georgia stretches 79 miles from Springer Mountain to Bly Gap on the North Carolina State line. A detailed map of it is available for a fee from the Forest Service.

Cohutta Wilderness. A network of trails winds through this 37,000-acre wilderness. These trails are described on the Cohutta Wilderness Map, which is also available for a fee from the Forest Service.

Duncan Ridge Trail. This challenging trail follows ridges for 30.5 miles–most of its length. The trail begins on Long Creek near Three Forks, goes north, and crosses the Toccoa River on a 250-foot swinging bridge. The trail then leads north and east through Mulky Gap on to Slaughter Gap. Blue blazes on trees mark this trail. For more details, get a leaflet about this trail from the Forest Service.

The No-Trace Ethic and General Rules

Many people use Forest Service trails to access their favorite fishing, camping, or picnicking spot. Please use the "no trace ethic," along with these general guidelines so that the next person can enjoy a natural scene, and so that nature can replenish and endure.

- Select a site invisible from the trail and any other camping parties; don't camp in day-use areas such as picnicking, swimming, or scenic sites.

- Camp at least 100 feet from water sources and away from beauty spots; put tents and trailers only in places provided.

- Avoid using existing campsites that are obviously over-camped.

- Never cut standing trees and vegetation or pull up plants.

- Never dig hipholes or trenches.

- Wear lightweight, soft-sole shoes around camp.

- Avoid building campfires, or make only small fires in safe places such as stoves, grills, fireplaces, and firerings.

- Occupy your campsite the first night you arrive, then don't leave it unoccupied for more than 24 hours at a time.

- Only campers permitted inside campgrounds during established night hours, which are usually posted.

- Stay no more than 14 consecutive days, or as posted.

- Never wash dirty dishes, clothes, or yourself directly in a stream or spring.

- Use biodegradable soap and dispose of waste water at least 100 feet away from a water supply.

- Bury human waste 6 inches deep, at least 100 feet away from water.

- Leave your dog at home.

To leave a no-trace campsite:

- Pick up every trace of litter.

- Drown your campfire and erase all evidence of it.

- Replace and scatter twigs and leaves cleared for sleeping areas.

- Pack out all garbage.

- Check for any evidence of your stay–and eliminate it.

Chattahoochee National Forest District Offices

Forest Supervisor
U.S. Forest Service
508 Oak St. NW
Gainesville, Ga 30501
706-536-0541

Armuchee Ranger District
706 Foster Blvd.
LaFayette, Ga 30728
706-638-1085

Brasstown Ranger District
Hwy. 19/129 S., Box 216
Blairsville, Ga 30512
706-745-6928

Chattooga Ranger District
P. O. Box 196, Burton Road
Clarkesville, Ga 30523
706-754-6221

Chestatee Ranger District
200 W. Main, P. O. Box 2080
Dahlonega, Ga 30523
706-864-6173

Cohutta Ranger District
401 Old Ellijay Rd.
Chatsworth, Ga 30705
706-695-6736

Tallulah Ranger District
Chechero/Savannah Street
P. O. Box 438
Clayton, Ga 30525
706-782-3320

Toccoa Ranger District
E. Main Street, Box 1839
Blue Ridge, Ga 30513
706-632-3031

Visitor Information and Welcome Centers and Chambers of Commerce

NORTHEAST GEORGIA MOUNTAIN REGION

Visitor Information and Welcome Centers

Dahlonega-Lumpkin County Local Welcome Center
Public Square
Dahlonega, Ga 30533
706-864-3711

Greater Helen Local Welcome Center
Chattahoochee Street
(P. O. Box 730)
Helen, Ga 30545
706-878-2181

Lavonia Visitor Welcome Center
Interstate I-85
Lavonia, Ga 30553
706-356-4019

Rabun County Local Welcome Center
Highway 441
(P. O. Box 761)
Clayton, Ga 30525
706-782-5113

Toccoa–Stephens County Local Welcome Center
907 E. Currahee St.
Toccoa, Ga 30571
706-886-2132

State Patrol Numbers
Gainesville: 706-532-5305
Toccoa: 706-886-4949
For Georgia road conditions, call:
Weekdays, 8:15-4:45:
    404-656-5882;
Nights & Weekends:
    404-656-5267

NORTHWEST GEORGIA MOUNTAIN REGION

**Visitor Information and
Welcome Centers**

**Blue Ridge
Visitor Center**
Historic Depot
Blue Ridge, Ga 30513
706-632-5680

**Calhoun
Local Welcome Center**
300 S. Wall St.
Calhoun, Ga 30701
706-625-3200

**Chatsworth
Local Welcome Center**
Highway 52
Chatsworth, Ga 30705
706-695-6060

State Patrol Numbers:
Blue Ridge: 706-632-2215
Calhoun: 706-629-8694
Dalton: 706-272-2200
LaFayette: 706-638-1400
For Georgia road conditions, call:
Weekdays, 8:15-4:45:
    404-656-5882
Nights & Weekends:
    404-656-5267

CHAMBERS OF COMMERCE

Blairsville-Union County
P. O. Box 727, Blue Ridge Street
Blairsville, Ga 30512
706-745-5789

Chattsworth-Murray County
P. O. Box 327, Room 104,
Federal Building
Chatsworth, Ga 30705
706-695-6060

Copper Basin-Fannin
P. O. Box 875
Blue Ridge, Ga 30513
706-632-5680

Dahlonega-Lumpkin County
P. O. Box 2037
Dahlonega, Ga 30533
706-864-3711

Gilmer County
P. O. Box 818, Broad Street
Ellijay, Ga 30540
706-635-7400

Greater Helen Area
Festhalle Building
Edelweiss Drive
(P. O. Box 192)
Helen, Ga 30545
706-878-3677

Habersham County
P. O. Box 366
Cornelia, Ga 30531
706-778-4654

Lavonia
Old Depot, 30 Bowman Street
Lavonia, Ga 30553
706-356-8202

Rabun County
P. O. Box 761
Clayton, Ga 30525
706-782-4812

Toccoa-Stephens County
P. O. Box 577,
901 East Currahee Street
Toccoa, Ga 30577
706-886-2132

Towns County
P. O. Box 290
Hiawassee, Ga 30546
706-896-4966

White County
P. O. Box 1574, Hwy. 129 North
Cleveland, Ga 30528
706-865-5356

About the Authors and Artist

Harry Milt is the senior author of this book. It was written under his editorial direction. Mr. Milt was inspired to undertake this project when he moved south and fell in love with the mountains, their people and their folkways–an empathy reflected in the opening chapter and the others he wrote. Mr. Milt is the author of seven books in the field of mental health and psychiatry. His publishers include Warner Books, Scribners Sons, Prentice-Hall, and the American Psychiatric Press. His articles have appeared in *Readers Digest*, *Parade*, *Parents Magazine* and *United Press Features*. He is a member of the American Society of Journalists and Authors and the Authors Guild. He holds a B. S. from New York University and an M.A. in psychology from Columbia University. He was formerly news editor of the *Washington Times Herald*, Director of Public Information of the National Association for Mental Health and coordinator of the antismoking program of the American Cancer Society.

Karen S. Bentley is a free-lance writer and business communications consultant who lives in Clayton, Georgia. In addition to writing and consulting on the production of newsletters, brochures, and public relations and marketing materials, she has published numerous articles in magazines, newspapers and trade publications. Ms. Bentley also develops and teaches business writing and creative writing courses. She holds a B. A. from SUNY at Buffalo and an M. A. from The George Washington University, and is a member of the Georgia Freelance Writers Association and the International Association of Business Communicators.

David C. Jowers (1948–1991), a native of Clayton, Georgia, was a lifelong resident of north Georgia. He graduated from the University of Georgia with a Bachelor of Arts in Journalism. Mr. Jowers began his career with the Southern Company in 1971 where he held several executive positions in public relations over 17 years. His writings on the subject of the environment included works for Paul Harvey, Arthur Hailey, TVA, Electric Power Research Institute, *Grass Roots*, and a number of southeast newspapers and magazines. Mr. Jowers was Senior Editor of *Southern Highlights Management Magazine* and the Southern Company Annual Report. Most recently Mr. Jowers was President of Composium, Inc., a public relations firm in Atlanta.

Barbie White is an artist and illustrator who lives in Tiger, Georgia.

A

B

H

K

L

M

S

T

U